Hitchcock Lost and Found

Hitchcock
Lost and Found

The Forgotten Films

ALAIN KERZONCUF
and
CHARLES BARR

Foreword by
PHILIP FRENCH

 UNIVERSITY PRESS OF KENTUCKY

Scholarly publisher for the Commonwealth,
serving Bellarmine University, Berea College, Centre College of
Kentucky, Eastern Kentucky University, The Filson Historical
Society, Georgetown College, Kentucky Historical Society,
Kentucky State University, Morehead State University, Murray State
University, Northern Kentucky University, Transylvania University,
University of Kentucky, University of Louisville, and Western
Kentucky University.
All rights reserved.

Editorial and Sales Offices: The University Press of Kentucky
663 South Limestone Street, Lexington, Kentucky 40508-4008
www.kentuckypress.com

Library of Congress Cataloging-in-Publication Data

Kerzoncuf, Alain.
  Hitchcock lost and found : the forgotten films / Alain Kerzoncuf
and Charles Barr ; foreword by Philip French.
      pages cm. — (Screen classics)
  Includes bibliographical references and index.
  ISBN 978-0-8131-6082-5 (hardcover : alk. paper) —
  ISBN 978-0-8131-6084-9 (pdf) — ISBN 978-0-8131-6083-2 (epub)
  1. Hitchcock, Alfred, 1899-1980—Criticism and interpretation.
I. Barr, Charles. II. Title.
  PN1998.3.H58K48 2015
  791.4302'33092—dc23   2014044816

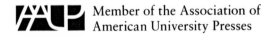

To my wife, Valérie
A. K.

To my daughter, Stella
C. B.

Contents

Foreword

In this valuable contribution to Hitchcock studies, a book of equal interest to the academic world and movie enthusiasts, Charles Barr and Alain Kerzoncuf quote Paula Cohen's confident claim that "to study him is to find an economical way of studying the entire history of cinema." Hitchcock has been part of my own experience of the cinema since 1939, the year I turned six, saw *Jamaica Inn* on its initial release, noted the name of the director, and began to develop the instincts of a discerning moviegoer. But not so discerning that good taste prevented me from enjoying its stirring tale of wreckers and revenue men on the Cornish coast (where the previous summer I'd spent my holidays) or saved me from being shocked like everyone else in the audience when Charles Laughton's Sir Humphrey Pengallan throws himself to his death from the riggings of the sailing ship. This would have been my first experience of the recurrent Hitchcockian motif of people falling from high places.

That year I committed to memory all fifty cards of movie stars given away with packets of Wills cigarettes, but Alfred Hitchcock was one of the only two directors I could name or recognize (the other of course being his fellow Londoner Charlie Chaplin). By the time I was ten or eleven I had learned a great deal about him—from listening to adult conversations or being told about him by my parents (both of them habitual but uninquisitive moviegoers), reading advertisements, and seeing his films, and by general osmosis—and I knew him to be someone of importance. He made signature appearances in all his movies, was a tubby cockney, had earned (or bestowed on himself) the sobriquet "master of suspense," had been accused of dodging the war by leaving the country for Hollywood just before it broke out, and was the director of the first British talkie. I could describe characteristic touches (a truncated finger that identified a villain, a windmill's sails turning in the wrong direction, a woman suddenly disappearing from a moving train) and came to see him as a man who liked peculiar challenges like setting a whole film on a lifeboat in the mid-Atlantic. The first two books on film I bought, both second-hand in 1949, were Roger Manvell's seminal Pelican paperback *Film* (1944) and Charles Davy's excellent anthology *Footnotes to the Film* (1938). The former contained the first filmography I ever read (actually called "Some Directors and Their Films"), listing seven Hitchcock films, starting with *Blackmail*, while the latter opened with a level-headed essay on the art and craft of direction, featuring a celebrated account of the way he shot the knifing of Monsieur Verloc in *Sabotage*, and a biographical note that omits mention of *The Mountain Eagle* and erroneously gives his date of birth as 1900.

Thus from the war years onward I followed Hitchcock's career as it unfolded: the post-Selznick liberation and return to England with Ingrid Bergman to make *Under Capricorn;* his response to 3-D (*Dial M for Murder,* not shown stereoscopically in Britain until 1983, but the only one that struck us as truly original) and then the widescreen (VistaVision only); and his exploitation of TV (*Alfred Hitchcock Presents,* a brilliant way of keeping his name before the public without compromising his theatrical work). An admirer of his films from childhood, I came to recognize a greater complexity in his work only as he and I got older. By the late 1950s I was working as a radio producer, and he appeared on several programs of mine, unforgettably revealing at the end of an interview about *North by Northwest* in 1959 that his next film, *Psycho,* "will be my first horror picture." What really focused and crystallized my thinking at that time was being introduced to the work of French critics (the idea of Hitchcock as a Catholic artist and the concept of transference of guilt) and the appearance of Claude Chabrol and Eric Rohmer's *Hitchcock,* which I read in French with some difficulty in 1960. The launching of the auteur-oriented magazine *Movie* in Britain in 1962, several of whose contributors took part in my radio shows, involved me with British

enthusiasts, culminating in the publication in 1965 of a book by
one of its editors, Robin Wood's *Hitchcock's Films*, the first proper
study of the Master in English. Despite it being a modest paperback,
the *Observer* was persuaded to let me write an admiring review of
Wood's wholly original work, which he was to expand and modify
over the years (notably in connection with the Master's sexuality). It
was followed two years later by François Truffaut's book-length interview, *Le Cinéma selon Hitchcock,* along with the Chabrol-Rohmer
book (first translated into English as *Hitchcock: The First Forty-Four
Films* in 1979 just before Hitch's death). These three books were to
inspire first a stream and then a torrent of articles and monographs
that would become the largest body of writing on any single filmmaker. I myself have made a few contributions, including a lengthy
obituary for the *Observer* (4 May 1980). I called him "our greatest
filmmaker," fully the equal of "our greatest living novelist," his fellow
Catholic Graham Greene, who as a film critic was "never generously
disposed to Alfred Hitchcock" possibly because of the close parallels
between their careers. "There will never be another career quite like
his," I added, "growing up with a new art, learning its every aspect as
a young man, then living through the transition to sound, the arrival
of TV and the widescreen, the relaxation of censorship, and staying at
the top for fifty years, changing with the times, catering to new tastes,
but remaining his own man."

Kerzoncuf and Barr's *Hitchcock Lost and Found* takes us directly
into Hitchcock's career at all levels and into our own experience of
that period. His career is an enormous jigsaw puzzle of which we now
have most of the pieces. Only two largish segments—the absent feature *The Mountain Eagle* and the uncompleted *Number Thirteen*—
are wholly missing but likely to turn up in a mislabelled canister in
some archive or in a cabinet in a long-abandoned cinema. Hitchcock
dismissed them in interviews in a somewhat embarrassed way, but was
not in a position of demanding that they never be published (*Number
Thirteen*) or republished (*The Mountain Eagle*). Similarly he never
did anything like repressing his early work, as Greene did with his
second and third novels, or going back to excise famously quotable
lines and passages from his 1930s work, as did W. H. Auden, a poet

and would-be filmmaker, who in *Letters from Iceland,* the 1937 book he cowrote with Louis MacNeice, expressed his considerable admiration for Hitchcock.

Other observers may learn different things from *Hitchcock Lost and Found,* but my principal ones were these. The account of the apprentice years before the debut in *The Pleasure Garden* is further detailed proof of Hitchcock's assiduity as a student. With relatively little formal education, he never gave up observing, learning, absorbing. The answer to the question posed in Jack Sullivan's book *Hitchcock's Music,* as with so many aspects of the Master's encyclopedic knowledge, is that the man listened and remembered. The authors properly single out Hitchcock's bibliographer Jane Sloan as calling him "a sponge," a compliment in this case that identifies the way he absorbed and used knowledge. It becomes clear that three insufficiently appreciated filmmakers of the early 1920s influenced him, and their work demands greater attention—Graham Cutts as mentor, Eliot Stannard as collaborator, and the little known, intriguing director Henry Edwards, who appears to have preceded Hitchcock in articulating the difference between surprise and suspense. Among the numerous minor but crucial moments in this area is the revelation of the uncredited appearance in *North by Northwest* of Graham Cutts's daughter, Patricia, as the woman through whose bedroom Cary Grant escapes on his way to pursue the spies in South Dakota. An evocation of his early days in the cinema, it adds to the film's list of resonant references that include those to *The Man Who Never Was* (the ingenious World War II deception scheme devised by Ivor Montagu's brother Ewan) and to the Whittaker Chambers–Alger Hiss espionage affair that promoted the career of Richard Nixon.

The section on the war years is fascinating for confirming that Hitchcock had observed American behavior as closely as those other recent immigrants Billy Wilder and Fritz Lang. This knowledge enabled him to re-edit *Men of the Lightship* and *Target for Tonight* for U.S. audiences without robbing them of their essential British character. Together with the wartime Hollywood features (most notably *Foreign Correspondent, Saboteur,* and *Lifeboat*) and the two movies he made in Britain for screening in liberated France (*Bon Voyage* and

Aventure Malgache), they wholly refute the charge of lacking patriotic fervor so unfairly brought against Hitchcock by Michael Balcon. They also confirm that whatever he subsequently claimed, he never failed to bring his full attention and imagination to bear on whatever enterprise he undertook, and in the case of *Aventure Malgache* to demonstrate how rapid and flexible he was in reacting to new and unexpected situations. These are just a few of the revelations that arise from pursuing the complete works. Each discovery, however small, throws fresh light on the oeuvre as a whole.

As I write there has been a recent, calculatedly provocative piece in the *Guardian*—humorously phrased but not so jokey in intent—about the desirability of severely abridging long movies, *Seven Samurai*, *L'Avventura*, and *Heaven's Gate* among them. I radically disagree with this and support the assembly of complete works, and some quarter of a century ago I discovered just how widespread was my feeling for the discovery and restoration of old and lost films. At the end of my weekly column in the *Observer* on 1 April 1990, the only occasion that date fell on a Sunday during my term of office, I wrote:

> The week's major event, of course, is this morning's one-off (for contractual reasons) screening at the National Film Theatre of Orson Welles's *The Magnificent Ambersons,* painstakingly restored to its original length by Kevin Brownlow, using the footage recently discovered in the RKO archives. The new material crucially changes the tone of the last third of the movie, giving it a political dimension and a tragic aspect only hinted at in the version released in 1942.
>
> Brownlow also came across a fragment of the score Welles commissioned from the then unknown Leonard Bernstein, who was in California at the time, convalescing and writing his clarinet sonata. RKO rejected Bernstein's music out of hand as too avant-garde. Those lucky enough to be at the NFT at noon today (all tickets were snapped up within an hour) will be able to judge for themselves, when Carl Davis conducts his augmented arrangement of the Bernstein frag-

ment as a prelude to the restored *Magnificent Ambersons.*
For them it should prove a day to remember.

April Fools jokes work best when people read about something they've
hoped or feared might occur, and this one was widely believed.
One leading producer made an angry call to Brownlow demanding
to know why he hadn't been invited, and a leading British author
bumped into my wife later that day and asked how the great event had
gone. The *Observer*'s then editor, whom I had neglected to let in on
the joke, insisted that I reveal the next Sunday what I had perpetrated.
I would now check the date if I read a news report of the discovery
of *The Mountain Eagle,* though by the time I did the piece would no
doubt have gone viral.

                                                        Philip French

Note on Citation Style and Images

We have aimed to keep the system of referencing as simple as possible, without sacrificing scholarly accuracy. Newspaper and trade press quotations are normally dated within the text rather than in endnotes. Details of less ephemeral articles are given in endnotes. Citations from books are referenced briefly in endnotes, but all books cited, or otherwise drawn on, are listed with full publication details in the bibliography. Information about certain specific online items is given in endnotes; fuller guidance to online material is given in the "Other Resources" section of the bibliography.

Unless otherwise indicated, images reproducing film stills are taken directly from the frame.

Introduction

In 2011 the discovery in New Zealand of a "lost Hitchcock film" made headlines around the world. The film was *The White Shadow* from 1924, earlier than any other surviving example of Hitchcock's work. Soon it had high-profile and crowded screenings in Los Angeles, London, and elsewhere. Something similar had happened in 1983 when publicity was given in *The Times* newspaper in London to the emergence from the vaults of the Imperial War Museum of a "missing Hitchcock," a compilation of footage of the Nazi concentration camps. Media from all over the world homed in on the story, and Channel 4 News quickly devoted a lengthy report to it, again using the tagline "the missing Hitchcock."

A current DVD edition of two short propaganda films directed by Alfred Hitchcock labels them prominently on the cover as "Lost World War II Classics of Espionage, Suspense and Murder." The two films, *Bon Voyage* and *Aventure Malgache* (both 1944), were never in fact lost, though for years they were denied public screenings. The concentration camps discovery of 1983 was an aborted documentary in which Hitchcock's official role as treatment adviser was relatively marginal. Likewise, the hype over the recent discovery of *The White Shadow* was excessive. The print was nowhere near complete, and its director was Graham Cutts. Hitchcock had worked on it as assistant director, writer, and art director, just as he had on other films made directly afterward, which already survived.

1

Each case is testimony to the intense and continuing public interest in Hitchcock's work. More than three decades after his death, he still seems a living presence: the subject of revivals and retrospectives, of a continuing flow of books and articles, and even of two feature films within the single year 2012, with Anthony Hopkins playing him in *Hitchcock* (directed by Sacha Gervasi), and Toby Jones in *The Girl* (Julian Jarrold). No other filmmaker has inspired so many "completists," enthusiasts anxious to know, and if possible to own, every film he directed. To collect his feature films, more than fifty of them, is by now not difficult. Almost all are easy to find on DVD, and only one remains unattainable—*The Mountain Eagle* (1926), his lost second film, which has acquired something of a Holy Grail status among archivists. But the appetite extends beyond the features, creating an excitement around any kind of fresh footage, and explaining the drive to exaggerate the "lost" or "missing" status of such footage, or the extent to which it genuinely belongs to Hitchcock himself.

We have no wish to denigrate this enthusiasm. If we did not share it, we would hardly have embarked on a project called "Hitchcock Lost and Found." Our aim has been to examine successive stages of Hitchcock's career in a level-headed way, finding out as much as possible about the material from his early years in the industry that still remains lost and providing solid data about a wider range of lost or neglected or otherwise problematic material. We have not come up with a print of *The Mountain Eagle,* but we have found one feature from his apprentice years that was thought to be lost, along with other bits and pieces, plus, we believe, enough new data and enough of a fresh perspective to justify the effort.

Intellectual justification is offered by the wise words of the American scholar Paula Marantz Cohen, writing in *The Times Literary Supplement* (5 September 2008): "The appeal of Hitchcock to the theorist and historian of film is impossible to overstate. To study him is to find an economical way of studying the entire history of cinema." To study Hitchcock in depth should indeed not mean simply to isolate and celebrate a supreme individual auteur, but to open up new insights into the medium and its history. He is surely the closest we have to a universal representative of this medium of cinema, spanning silent and sound, Hollywood and Europe, mainstream and experimental, montage and long-take, and indeed film and television. He remains both an instantly recognizable iconic figure and the focus of advanced theoretical study. His fifty-year career as director occupies half of the twentieth century, the century of cinema: with a satisfying neatness, it is precisely the *middle half,* 1925–1975 in terms of production, 1926–1976 in terms of release, with virtually no down periods along the way: from *The Pleasure Garden* to *Family Plot.*

Another American scholar, Jane Sloan, provides a second apt formula in the introduction to her formidably comprehensive *Alfred Hitchcock: A Filmography and Bibliography* (1995): "Far from the lonely romantic artist, he appears to have been more of a sponge, eager to adapt the point of view that would sell, and open to any idea that seemed good, insistent only that it fit his design."[1] The sponge metaphor is well chosen. She is talking primarily of Hitchcock's later years, when he was an established director with an established identity and a "design" into which new projects would fit, but the notion applies equally to his early experience, which we examine in new detail in chapter 1, "Before *The Pleasure Garden.*" The sponge concept can be a negative one—a "sponger" exploits people—but also positive: to sponge is to absorb. This is what Hitchcock did from the beginning of his time in the industry: absorb all he could from a variety of collaborators and contemporaries, and process it in his own distinctive creative ways, with spectacular long-term results.

Most of our research has come to focus on three periods, the first parts of three successive decades: the apprenticeship of the early 1920s; the unstable period of the early 1930s, involving response to the new technologies of synchronized sound and of primitive television; and the early 1940s, during which Hitchcock did a wide range of topical war-effort work on both sides of the Atlantic in the margins of his first Hollywood features. Much of the product from all three periods seemed of ephemeral value at the time. The whole issue of preserving and archiving films did not begin to be seriously addressed until the 1930s. Companies had been famously cavalier in junking silent films when dialogue film took over, and early dialogue films in turn soon came to seem crude and dispensable once the new system settled down. The kinds of topical war items that Hitchcock worked on served short-term propaganda purposes and were quickly forgotten. Of course we now recognize all these categories of film, not only Hitchcock's work, as having far more than ephemeral value, and we are indebted to those visionaries who were responsible for at least selective preservation.

While we touch on a few "Lost and Found" items outside these three main periods, we do not attempt to be comprehensive, especially when we have little or nothing to add to material already available elsewhere. Once Hitchcock starts to direct in his own right, the narrative of his career immediately becomes less obscure. The silent films he made between *The Pleasure Garden* and *The Manxman* (1929) have been the subject of recent high-profile restorations by the British Film Institute (BFI), based on the collection and collation of prints from a diversity of sources and culminating in screenings all over the world from 2012 onward. Insofar as there is "lost and found" material here, it has already been quite fully discussed, and we therefore skip over this period and go straight from 1925 to a range of much less familiar material that follows the industry's conversion to sound. The BFI's website now carries extensive information on those nine silents, supplied by two of the team responsible for the restorations, Bryony Dixon and Kieron Webb.[2]

As we were completing this text, the American scholar Dan Auiler, already author of two books of Hitchcock research, published *Hitchcock Lost* (2013). This includes a full roundup of data, both on the one lost Hitchcock silent, *The Mountain Eagle,* and on his project of the late 1960s—known both as *Kaleidoscope* and as *Frenzy,* a title he would soon attach to another film altogether—for which much footage was shot before it was abandoned. That *Frenzy* project is like an echo of Hitchcock's first directorial effort, *Number Thirteen* from 1922, likewise abandoned after extensive shooting. Auiler devotes an early paragraph to *Number Thirteen,* simply stating that little is known about it apart from a single still. Well, there was a lot more waiting to be found—though not yet the film itself—as is set out in the course of chapter 1. He enables us to leave gaps in this book, while we fill in some of the gaps in his. The two are complementary, forming testimony, along with so much else, to the attraction of Hitchcock as a subject, and to the value of trying to build up an ever-fuller picture of his remarkable career.

"We are seeking to find some solution whereby successful films may be saved from premature and needless oblivion. . . . *Every* art must have its classics if it would obtain or retain either dignity or respect." This appeal for a system of film preservation is one of the first to be seriously articulated. It comes from an article titled "The Life of a Film," fourth in a five-part weekly series called "The Art of the Kinematograph" by the pioneer British screenwriter Eliot Stannard, published prominently on 13 June 1918 in the leading trade paper, *The Kinematograph and Lantern Weekly.* The paper's name is a reminder of the sheer youth of the cinema, then, as an independent medium; it would not drop the word *Lantern,* referring to the older medium of the lantern-slide show, from its title until late 1919. The Imperial War Museum in south London had by then started to build up a collection of film footage from the Great War for purposes of historical record, but systematic attempts to collect and preserve a wider range of films had to wait until the mid-1930s.

Alfred Hitchcock's career is closely bound up with the history of this film archive movement. Born in 1899, he was by 1918 a keen student of films and of the trade papers, and he entered the industry not long afterward. Soon he was involved in a range of developments in film culture, as well as in film production, that were in effect building up pressure for the creation of archives: he was an early member of two London organizations dedicated to raising the status of the medium, the Kinema Club for professionals (1921–1924), and the Film Society for a wider membership (from 1925). His own early films as director would become priority acquisitions for archives set up in Britain, America, and Europe.

On the first nine of those films, the silent ones, starting with *The Pleasure Garden* in 1926, his regular screenwriter was the very man who had made that appeal in 1918 to save films from oblivion, Eliot Stannard. There is a profoundly satisfying neatness about the way the story of the growth of film archives has played out over nearly a

Figure A.1. The widely circulated BFI poster, featuring Anny Ondra from *Blackmail* (1929). (Courtesy of the British Film Institute)

century since Stannard's prophetic article, with the films of that soon-to-be collaborator of his being a consistent thread in the story, and their joint body of work providing a climax to the story, as of 2012.

Archives do indispensable work in acquiring and preserving films; in turn, the preserved material helps the archives, mainly via screenings, to generate publicity, prestige, and new income, creating a form of "virtuous circle." This happens with a wide range of material, but Hitchcock is arguably the prime example.

His films were the basis of cinema's contribution to the "Cultural Olympics" project, mounted in 2012 in parallel with the London Olympic Games of that year. The BFI, home of the archive that began life in 1935 as the National Film Library, put on a complete and well-publicized Hitchcock Retrospective, using mainly its own prints; the series was exported in full for screenings at the Irish Film Institute in Dublin, and in part to other countries and regions. Integral to the enterprise was the launch of restored prints of all nine of the Stannard-Hitchcock silents, backed by a successful appeal for donations. These silents, enhanced by the live performance of new scores, were soon being widely screened elsewhere as a self-contained series; meanwhile, other archives in other countries continue to exploit their own holdings of Hitchcock prints. It is the culmination of a linked process of preservation and exhibition that goes back a long way.

There is scope for a separate book on Hitchcock and the archives, tracing how and when and where each archive obtained its prints, and what it did with them. This would complement, and overlap with, the work of Robert Kapsis in *Hitchcock: The Making of a Reputation* (1992), in which he traces the development of Hitchcock's public and critical image over the decades; it would also encourage the drive to keep searching, on the back of the dramatic story of the discovery in the New Zealand archive of footage from *The White Shadow*. Here, we do no more than briefly note the historical importance of Hitchcock's films to the growth of archives in three important cities: Paris, New York, and London.

The BFI was set up in 1933. Its second Annual Report in 1935 highlighted the National Film Library as a priority, based on the "well-known and much-deplored fact that a large number of films of outstanding value, either for their importance as examples of film technique or as historical documents, had disappeared, and were daily disappearing, through the lack of any central body interested in their preservation." The Institute would therefore "maintain a library with multiple functions. Within the limits of what is technically and financially possible, it would preserve for records a copy of every film printed in England which had a possible documentary value; it would make available films of interest to students; it would distribute films not available through the ordinary agencies; and it would maintain an up-to-date catalogue of films of cultural and educational interest." The word *documentary* here is not to be taken in a narrow sense; it could easily have been replaced by *historical,* since the reference is equally to dramatic fiction.

The new film library depended primarily on donations; when a budget became available for buying prints, it did not stretch very far.

Among the first batch of films was one donated by John Maxwell of British International Pictures (BIP), a print of the sound version of *Blackmail* (1929), which headed the list of eleven films acknowledged in the 1936 report. A column in *The Times* (20 February 1936) likewise singles out *Blackmail,* and names Hitchcock. Three years later (30 May 1939), *The Times* again foregrounds Hitchcock at the start of its report: "During the past year the British Film Institute has acquired for preservation in its National Film Library some 300 films. Among them is a particularly interesting group of British films made just before the advent of the talking picture. Two of these, *The Lodger,* produced in 1926, and *Downhill,* produced in 1927, represent the early work of Mr. Alfred Hitchcock, whose technique in recent years has been highly praised by experts both in England and in America."

Neither the BFI nor *The Times* is consistent from this point in listing all acquisitions, but Hitchcock films are noted at regular intervals. By the time a film theater was opened on the South Bank of the Thames in the early 1950s, a high proportion of his British films were held. One of the early seasons was "Three British Directors—a series of nine programmes devoted to the work of three notable British directors: Anthony Asquith, Alfred Hitchcock and Carol Reed." Three films by each of them were shown, the Hitchcock ones being *The Man Who Knew Too Much* (1934), *Sabotage* (1936), and *Young and Innocent* (1937). Extracts were added from *Downhill* (1927), *Easy Virtue* (1927), *Murder!* (1930), *Number Seventeen* (1932), *The 39 Steps* (1935), *The Lady Vanishes* (1938), and—surprisingly—the wartime French-language film *Bon Voyage* (1944). From this point on, Hitchcock quickly overtook both Asquith and Reed in frequency of screenings, starting with a seven-week season in 1953 and culminating in the massive Retrospective of 2012.

Two Hitchcock films had quickly become part of the BFI's solid historical and educational repertoire: *The Lodger* as one of four silent films representing "The British Film," and *Blackmail* as one of five films representing "The Beginning of Sound." The same two films were integral to the early repertoire of the Museum of Modern Art (MoMA) in New York, within its distribution package titled "The Film in England": *The Lodger* as one of three silent films, and

Blackmail as one of a quartet of sound films that also included *Juno and the Paycock* (1930). Hitchcock himself had been instrumental in providing prints, thanks to his and his wife Alma Reville's long-standing friendship with Iris Barry, an English film critic who had moved to New York in 1930 and initiated the film department at MoMA in 1933. Barry helped them to adjust to life in America in 1939, exchanging warm letters with Alma (copies of which are held in the MoMA archives), helping to host an early lecture in New York by Hitchcock, and pressing enthusiastically for a follow-up exhibition of sketches and stills and documents. Sadly, Alma had to tell her that a lot of material had been junked before they left England, and the exhibition did not happen, at least not then.

Barry was succeeded at MoMA in 1951 by Richard Griffith, who was less in sympathy with Hitchcock; it was he who updated Paul Rotha's landmark work of history, *The Film till Now* (first published in 1930), for its new edition in 1949, and his comments on Hitchcock's work of the intervening years were mainly negative. But Griffith failed to hold back the tide: it was MoMA that, despite his reservations, launched the first major American tribute to Hitchcock in 1963, which was put together by Peter Bogdanovich, linked to the release of *The Birds,* and supported by an interview-based book. In 1999, to mark the centenary of Hitchcock's birth, MoMA mounted another comprehensive retrospective, accompanied by an exhibition, full details of which are still displayed on its website (http://www .moma.org/interactives/exhibitions/1999/hitchcock/overview.html).

Not long before the first big MoMA event, in May–June 1960, La Cinémathèque française in Paris had put on an intensive "Hommage à Alfred Hitchcock," which included more than thirty films, drawing on prints from London and elsewhere as well as its own. In 1968 Hitchcock was one of many filmmakers to come to the defense of his friend Henri Langlois, who had cofounded the Cinémathèque with Georges Franju in 1936, when the French government attempted to dismiss him as director. It was famously the regular programming of Hitchcock's films among Langlois's postwar repertoire that had helped to lay the foundation for the celebration of Hitchcock's work in the magazine *Cahiers du Cinéma,* and in the books by the *Cahiers* writers and future filmmakers Claude Chabrol and Eric Rohmer, and later by François Truffaut, who had filled in some of Langlois's gaps by viewings in the Belgian archive.

To sum up, Hitchcock's films and the archives have had, over the years, a profitable form of symbiotic relationship, which continues long after Hitchcock's own death. We have drawn on a range of these archives both indirectly, through having access to the films in the public domain that they, as well as some of the production companies, have been responsible for preserving, and also directly, gaining access through them to films not as yet so widely available. These include many of the films, held in part or whole by the BFI, that Hitchcock worked on before his official debut as director with *The Pleasure Garden*—but also various subsequent items.

We now go back to the early 1920s, to the early stages of Hitchcock's career that those archival holdings help to illuminate.

1

Before *The Pleasure Garden*
1920–1925

Hitchcock directed his first feature, *The Pleasure Garden* (1926), at the age of twenty-five, the same age that Orson Welles was when he made *Citizen Kane*. Like Welles, he was celebrated at the time, though on a lesser scale, as something of a "boy wonder." Unlike Welles, however, he already had extensive film industry experience. The records indicate that before *The Pleasure Garden* he had worked on twenty-one films. Not one of these is known to survive in full in its original English-language version, and commentators have understandably tended to skim over this period with a few speculative remarks about what he is likely to have done and to have learned, based mainly on what he told people decades later. But enough remains, in both film and document form, to reward fuller investigation.

Hitchcock's early experience in cinema divides neatly into three stages, each centered on Islington Studios in North London, and each containing "lost and found" material:

1. Famous Players-Lasky British (FPLB), eleven films, 1920–1922
2. Transitional, five films, 1922–1923
3. Michael Balcon and Gainsborough, five films, 1923–1925

Hitchcock's first employer in the industry was American: the short-lived British branch of Famous Players-Lasky (FPL), which was headed in California by Adolph Zukor and would later adopt the more familiar name of Paramount. After converting a power station at Islington into a well-equipped film studio, FPLB began production in mid-1920 and made eleven films there before moving out early in 1922. Hitchcock worked on all of these films. Employed initially as a freelance designer of intertitles while retaining his day job with Henley's Engineering Company, he was subsequently taken on to the staff and used not only for titles but for a range of other subsidiary jobs. Patrick McGilligan gives the precise date of 27 April 1921 as Hitchcock's last day at Henley's, which means he was a full member of staff for around half of the time during which FPLB was in active production.[1]

After FPLB pulled out, Hitchcock stayed on at Islington for more than a year as part of a skeleton staff retained by the company while it rented out the studio as what would now be termed a four-wall facility. During this time he evidently worked on five films—it is possible that there were additional unrecorded titles—of a more varied character than the eleven FPLB ones. These included his own two initial efforts as a director, both of which were in different ways frustrated.

In April 1923 the young British producer Michael Balcon moved in at Islington with his new company Balcon-Freedman-Saville, which before long was rebranded as Gainsborough Pictures and bought the studio from FPL. Balcon had at once recognized Hitchcock's value, using him as writer and art director on a series of five films, all of them directed by Graham Cutts. Hitchcock had already, as a staff member at Islington during the transitional period, worked in minor capacities on two films made by Cutts before he teamed up with Balcon, and it was after the last of these seven Cutts collaborations, *The Prude's Fall* (1925), that he was entrusted by Balcon with a film of his own.

The film from this pre–*Pleasure Garden* period that has had the most publicity is, thanks to its dramatic rediscovery in 2011, *The White Shadow* (Graham Cutts, 1924), the second of the Balcon productions, but other solid material survives from all three stages. The eleven FPLB films are commonly said to be lost, but at least one of them survives in full, though only in a Dutch version. Of the five films of the transitional period, one feature survives, again in a Dutch version, along with half of a shorter film of which Hitchcock was codirector. Of the five films of the initial Balcon period, two survive, each in a German version, and two others survive in part, including *The White Shadow*. Between them, these items—not only the found material itself but what can be discovered about the films that are still lost—allow one to build up a fair picture of the work that the young Hitchcock was doing, and of the context in which he was doing it.

Famous Players-Lasky British: Eleven Films, 1920–1922

Table 1.1 covers the total output of Famous Players-Lasky British during its time at Islington: eleven films, to all of which Hitchcock contributed.

Lost: Original English Versions of All Eleven Films
Found: *The Man from Home* (George Fitzmaurice, 1922)

(Only the Dutch version, which does not preserve the intertitles designed by Hitchcock)

Hitchcock told an interviewer in 1966: "You have to remember that I was American-trained. When you entered the doors of that studio, you could have been in Hollywood. Everyone was an American. The writers were American, the directors were American."[2] Table 1.1 bears this out. On the eleven films, there are five Hollywood directors, all male, and five Hollywood writers, all female, two of them married to their directors (Lovett to Robertson, Bergère to Fitzmaurice). In addition, a number of cameramen and other technicians, plus a few actors, came over from Hollywood, the mix of American and British cast members being calculated to help market the films in both countries. The most frequently used actors, with six roles each, were Mary Glynne (British) and David Powell (American—though he was, like Donald Crisp, British by birth), but neither became a big star; Powell died as early as 1925.

Table 1.1. Total Output of Famous Players-Lasky British at Islington

Title and First Review Date*	Director and Locations	Writer and Source	Cast
The Call of Youth 2 Dec. 1920	Hugh Ford	Eve Unsell H. A. Jones (original)	Mary Glynne, Marjorie Hume
The Great Day 2 Dec. 1920	Hugh Ford *France locations*	Eve Unsell Louis N. Parker and George R. Sims (P)	Arthur Bourchier, Meggie Albanesi
The Princess of New York 30 June 1921	Donald Crisp	Margaret Turnbull Cosmo Hamilton (N)	Mary Glynne, David Powell
Appearances 7 July 1921	Donald Crisp	Margaret Turnbull Edward Knoblock (P)	Mary Glynne, David Powell
Dangerous Lies aka *Twice Wed* 29 Sept. 1921	Paul Powell	Mary O'Connor E. Philips Oppenheim (N)	Mary Glynne, David Powell
Mystery Road 3 Nov. 1921	Paul Powell *Riviera locations*	Margaret Turnbull and Mary O'Connor E. Philips Oppenheim (N)	Mary Glynne, David Powell, Ruby Miller
Beside the Bonnie Brier Bush aka *Bonnie Brier Bush* [or "...Briar..."] 1 Dec. 1921	Donald Crisp *Somerset locations*	Margaret Turnull Ian McLaren (P + N)	Mary Glynne, Donald Crisp
Three Live Ghosts 16 Mar. 1922	George Fitzmaurice *London locations*	Margaret Turnbull and Ouida Bergère Frederic S. Isham (P)	Anna Q. Nilsson, Clare Greet, Edmund Goulding
Love's Boomerang aka *Perpetua* 22 May 1922	John S. Robertson *France locations*	Josephine Lovett Dion Clayton Calthrop (N)	David Powell, Ann Forrest
The Man from Home 10 Aug. 1922	George Fitzmaurice *Italy locations*	Ouida Bergère Booth Tarkington (P)	James Kirkwood, Anna Q. Nilsson
Spanish Jade 21 Sept. 1922	John S. Robertson *Spain locations*	Josephine Lovett Louis J. Vance (P + N)	David Powell, Evelyn Brent

Note: P = play; N = novel.
* Review dates refer to the British trade paper *Kinematograph Weekly* (commonly abbreviated as *Kine Weekly*).

Overall, the enterprise made only a modest impact on critics and public on either side of the Atlantic, and it came as no surprise when FPL cut its losses by withdrawing from its British base. It did, however, leave a legacy in the form of a well-equipped studio, and of the experience given to one junior employee in particular.

So what can we infer that Hitchcock learned from this period of "American training"? For a start, it gave him status as an authentic film industry professional. On 23 July 1921, less than three months after he joined the full-time staff at Islington, an article on the principles of titling appeared in *Motion Picture Studio (MPS)* under the byline of "A. J. Hitchcock, Title Designer for Famous Players-Lasky British." This weekly paper is especially useful for its focus on British production; other papers such as *Kinematograph Weekly (KW)* and *The Bioscope* served exhibitors by covering the full international range, with an inevitable emphasis on Hollywood imports. *Motion Picture Studio* was launched in June 1921 as a spin-off from *KW* before, disappointingly, being absorbed back into it in February 1924. It is again in *MPS* (21 January 1922) that we find the name of "Hitchcock A. J." as a founder-member of the Kinema Club, an ambitious new venture that was "open to all those engaged in the production of British films." Opened in December 1921, the club occupied a prime site in Central London and offered a busy program of social and sporting events as well as discussion of film topics. Hitchcock no doubt took the chance to use the restaurant with its "expert menus by an excellent French chef," and to mix with other professionals: that first list of some four hundred members includes the names of most of those who were by then prominent in British production. The club would, however, like *MPS*, be wound up in 1924, a bad year altogether for British cinema.

The membership list does not include any of the Americans from FPLB; their presence was only temporary, and the last of them were already preparing to move out. But Hitchcock had clearly been making the most of his access to them at Islington.

In the authorized biography, John Russell Taylor describes the team of writers who "ran a little factory whipping the material into shape, mostly from pre-existing plays or novels. . . . There was little these ladies did not know about the technique of screen writing, and in Alfred Hitchcock they found an eager and attentive pupil."[3] We can be certain that he was equally attentive to the team of five experienced directors, who included Donald Crisp, George Fitzmaurice, and John S. Robertson. Crisp provided a close link to D. W. Griffith, with whom he had recently worked both as assistant and as actor. Fitzmaurice is claimed by Donald Spoto to have impressed Hitchcock with the preplanned discipline of his working methods. Robertson must have impressed him as well, since in 1939 Hitchcock named two

Hitchcock's Top Ten Films

In 1939, soon after arriving in America, Hitchcock was persuaded by the press to name his ten favorite films. Although it was claimed that they were "thoughtfully selected," it is not clear how much time he took over the selection, or how far he was being deferential to his hosts in naming only one film from anywhere else but Hollywood. It is striking, anyway, that only one is a dialogue film.

Forbidden Fruit (Cecil B. DeMille, 1921)
Sentimental Tommy (John S. Robertson, 1921)
Scaramouche (Rex Ingram, 1923)
Saturday Night (Cecil B. DeMille, 1923)
The Isle of Lost Ships (Maurice Tourneur, 1923)
The Enchanted Cottage (John S. Robertson, 1924)
Variety (E. A. Dupont, Germany, 1925)
The Gold Rush (Charles Chaplin, 1925)
The Last Command (Joseph von Sternberg, 1928)
I Am a Fugitive from a Chain Gang (Mervyn LeRoy, 1932)

From the *New York Sun*, 15 March 1939, quoted by McGilligan, *Alfred Hitchcock*, 234.

of his films in a list of ten favorites that he was induced to provide for the New York press soon after moving from Britain. One was made shortly before Robertson's brief time at Islington, the other shortly after: *Sentimental Tommy* (1921) and *The Enchanted Cottage* (1924), based, respectively, on plays by J. M. Barrie and Arthur Wing Pinero, authors who had made a strong early impact on Hitchcock as theatergoer.[4]

More specifically, we know that Hitchcock was picking up insights into photography, art direction, and editing. He told François Truffaut that he had already been impressed by the higher

Figure 1.1. Two-page advertising spread for *Dangerous Lies* (Paul Powell, 1921) in *Kine Weekly*, 22 September 1921. (Courtesy of the Cinema Museum, London)

quality of lighting in American films, and now he had the chance to observe and meet camera experts from Hollywood. The memoir of one of them, Arthur Miller, describes a collaboration with Hitchcock on *Three Live Ghosts* (George Fitzmaurice, 1922) when they went together on an expedition to find props for dressing an important set; so by then he was doing more than designing titles.[5] In the British trade directory *Kine Year Book* for 1926—the first year he appears in it—Hitchcock describes himself as having started "in editorial department of F.P.L." This refers to the work of script editing and titling rather than to the actual mechanics of cutting film, but his work on titles was allowing him to play with basic principles of film editing that he would later develop in his exploitation of the Kuleshov effect: as he recalled to Taylor, "you could change the way audiences read an action or an expression by changing the intertitle."

While none of Hitchcock's own title designs have yet been un-earthed, he often recalled them in interviews. For instance, as early as 1930 when he was already harking back to the lost world of silent film, he remembered: "I was doing art titles for Famous Players at their London studio . . . drawing guttering candles behind the an-nouncement of a mother's death, and sketching hour-glasses to deco-rate captions about the passing of time. Yes, you may smile, but nine years ago it was considered advanced technique."[6]

To Truffaut in the 1960s, he recalled that a caption about a char-acter leading a fast life might be illustrated by the image of a candle burning at both ends.[7] In his article of July 1921, "Titles—Artistic and Otherwise," the closest he gets to anything specific about his own practice is this: "Symbols are the most effective subjects, provided they are not too subtle. . . . But beware of repetition. The hour glass and scales of justice, their day is ended. A fair example of the use of sym-bols can be seen in Paul Powell's production, *Dangerous Lies* [1921]." The advertisement for the film shown in figure 1.1 may give a hint of what he was referring to.

As the image suggests, it is a story of temptation and adultery. Did Hitchcock, with his experience of advertising, help to design the poster? Was the poster picking up a serpent motif devised by him for use in a title card? Either (or both) seems plausible. And we do now, thanks to research by Christopher Philippo, have a firm description of one of his designs for the same film, from a local American news-paper, *Utica Morning Telegram,* on 3 December 1921.[8] The article "*Dangerous Lies* Is Coming to Utica" stated: "One of the titles of the picture describes the influence of a young girl in the household of a man whose interests are entirely centered in musty folios of first editions. For this A. J. Hitchcock, art designer, had evolved as an ac-companying design a ray of sunlight resting on a file of dusty books. He made a rough sketch of his idea and sent it to his staff of artists with other material to be put into execution." The story, probably based on publicity material supplied by FPL, goes on to describe mis-understandings in following Hitchcock's outline, before the correct title card is produced. It gives a nice glimpse of Hitchcock's mode of working at this very early stage, producing simple sketches for others to work from—as he would later do in, for instance, sketching shot-by-shot storyboards.

The one surviving FPLB film, *The Man from Home,* contains in its Dutch form no pictorial title. It does, however, contain a playful insert that it is tempting, and quite plausible, to ascribe to Hitchcock (figs. 1.2 and 1.3). He later spoke of having graduated quickly to this sort of work, directing a variety of inserts and pick-up shots—and this film is one of the final pair of FPLB productions.

The American protagonist, played by James Kirkwood, newly arrived in Italy, wants ham and eggs for breakfast. Unable to make himself understood, he puts over the egg concept in a drawing. The simplicity of the curves, and the rapidity of their sketching, evokes the Hitchcock self-portrait that would become so familiar. It is a separate insert, so Hitchcock could easily have handled it, designing and directing the sketch for a third party to execute; the left hand, with a ring on its little finger, is not that of the actor, since in other shots of him no ring is visible.

This whole scene is suggestive in a further way. The visitor automatically expects the Italians to speak his language and to serve him an American breakfast; when they fail to do so, he ends up marching into the kitchen, pushing the staff aside, and getting it for himself (fig. 1.4). It is a crude version of what, in essence, Famous Players-Lasky was doing in its British venture: insisting on things being done the American way.

The company had begun by professing a policy of partnership that would foreground British stars and locations and bring on other British talent, but this became increasingly tenuous. The last three of the eleven films have virtually no British element. *The Man from Home* is set entirely in America and Italy and has British players only in a few subsidiary roles, notably Annette Benson (later to work with Hitchcock in *Downhill* [1927]) as an Italian fisherman's wife. Islington provided a studio for shooting interior scenes—and inserts and intertitles—that could just as well have been in Hollywood. One of the reasons for creating the Islington outpost had always been that it was a more convenient base for European location shooting; the final trio of films exploited this, but in itself this was not sufficient

Figures 1.2–1.3. Sketch insert from *The Man from Home* (George Fitz-maurice, 1922; Famous Players-Lasky). (Courtesy of Nederlands Film Museum [EYE])

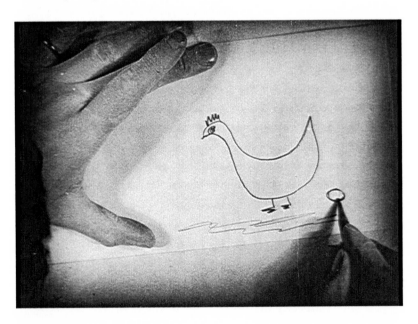

Figure 1.4. The American shows the natives how to do things his way. *The Man from Home* (George Fitzmaurice, 1922; Famous Players-Lasky). (Courtesy of Nederlands Film Museum [EYE])

justification. To judge from the reviews on both sides of the Atlantic, the ten lost films were seen, like the surviving *Man from Home,* as falling between two stools, not attractive enough either to British or to American audiences.

This is not to question the importance of Hitchcock's initial FPLB training. The very fact of experiencing Hollywood's "cultural imperialism" from the inside at this formative time must have helped in a double way: giving him a high-level technical grounding and also an intimate understanding of the dominant machine against which British cinema had to find some way of asserting and defining itself—emulating its professionalism but building on it to create something distinctively and attractively British. It was precisely this aspiration, this blend, that was becoming an ever more urgent preoccupation in 1920s Britain. Both within the film industry and beyond, the need for

Famous Players-Lasky British: Some Figures

The Margaret Herrick library in Beverly Hills holds files for all eleven of the Famous Players-Lasky British productions, deriving from 1941 when Paramount was taking stock of the options for remaking properties it owned. A member of the staff read the scripts and delivered a verdict, usually a negative one. For six of the eleven films, the files included the financial record, set out in bare summary form, as in the following list. It is not clear how costs of distribution, advertising, and so on, would have been factored in, but from any angle the figures look grim, and they help to explain why the company pulled out of Britain so quickly. Only *Dangerous Lies* earned significantly more than it had cost, with two others narrowly breaking even; *Mystery Road,* widely condemned for tastelessness, was a disaster.

APPEARANCES

Negative cost	167k
Domestic sales 81 + Foreign sales 43	124k

MYSTERY ROAD

Negative cost	302k
Domestic sales 69 + Foreign sales 44	113k

DANGEROUS LIES

Negative cost	118k
Domestic sales 88 + Foreign sales 72	160k

THE PRINCESS OF NEW YORK

Negative cost	136k
Domestic sales 75 + Foreign sales 63	138k

LOVE'S BOOMERANG

Negative cost	177k
Domestic sales 118 + Foreign sales 60	178k

SPANISH JADE

Negative cost	174k
Domestic sales 103 + Foreign sales 50	153k

radical action to counter American dominance of the home market was recognized, the eventual result being the legislation passed in 1927 to protect British production, largely through the system of an imposed quota. Hitchcock was already exceptionally well placed to benefit from the new system and to help, in a modest way, to make it work.

Soon after the studio opened, the American writer-producer John Emerson—who was married to the author Anita Loos—visited Britain and wrote, for trade papers on both sides of the Atlantic, a candid account of what he found. After spelling out the crippling technical deficiencies of the established English studios, he noted: "There *is* a model studio in England, which few of the producers have visited. At the risk of being accused of bias, I can state that the Famous Players-Lasky studio, built in London under the direction of Milton E. Hoffman, is as good as any studio in America. . . . Without a doubt this studio will turn out pictures of the highest order—at least from a technical standpoint. No matter how good British writers, actors or directors may be, they cannot work without their tools" (*Kine Weekly*, 26 August 1920). The technical assets of the studio—dimensions, power, equipment, and so on—were complemented by an organizational machinery run on quasi-military lines by its general manager, the Englishman Major C. H. Bell. Hitchcock admired and relished the high professionalism of the organization into which he was now absorbed, along with the slickness of its product.[9]

Since we now have the one full-length example of this product in *The Man from Home*, it is worth looking at it in a bit more detail. Though no masterpiece, it demonstrates the well-oiled structural efficiency and high production values of the American machine at this period. Its narrative outline is clean and purposeful: the American couple are separated when the woman, Genevieve, goes to Italy and falls for another, untrustworthy, man; the American comes over and sorts things out, with the final shot celebrating the couple's union. Subplots are neatly integrated. The film takes full pictorial advantage of its coastal locations, always taking care to integrate the characters into them. The most spectacular scenic image, a high-angle long shot, is, typically, motivated by being revealed as the point of view of the jealous American (figs. 1.5 and 1.6).

Earlier in the film this American, still at home, has received a letter from Genevieve in Italy. To accompany the pleasure of reading it, he puts on a record of the song "Sweet Genevieve." The letter brings bad news. After reading it, he slumps back; cut to the record coming to an end (figs. 1.7–1.9). The live musical accompaniment that was standard at the time would no doubt have made a point of exploiting these cues, but the visuals are eloquent in themselves, providing an effect analogous to the use of pictorial symbols in intertitles that Hitchcock had discussed in his 1921 article.

Like the sketch of the hen and the egg illustrated in figure 1.3, these two inserts were possibly, even probably, shot by Hitchcock himself, by now the all-purpose studio assistant. The effect looks ahead to the emotionally expressive use of objects in his own early films. For instance, in a similar scene of disappointment in *The Ring* (1927), the boxer pours champagne to celebrate a victory and the bubbles fizz in close-up, but his wife stays out with another man, and we cut back from the dejected group to show that the champagne has gone flat.

Typical of the economy of *The Man from Home* is the fact that, without ever feeling static, it is virtually devoid of camera movement. Not counting some brief shots of characters in a moving car, it contains just three unobtrusive panning shots. This may have been the preferred style of its director, George Fitzmaurice, who is known as an early exponent of the preplanned storyboard technique. Again, Hitchcock would absorb this strategy, moving the camera very rarely in his early films, including *The Lodger* (1926). While his camera style would become more varied, it was firmly grounded in this basic cinematic skill of creating movement within and between fixed-frame shots. Fitzmaurice provided something of a master class in this, building on what D. W. Griffith had done in his pioneering short films for Biograph. The other FPLB films, if we had them, might prove to operate in similar ways.

It was also during his time with FPLB that Hitchcock met his future wife, Alma Reville, though they did not, it seems, yet become close; she did not, as he did, stay on at Islington after the company ceased its own production. On 6 May 1922, *MPS* carried this advertisement: "Alma Reville, the continuity writer, late of Famous-Lasky, has fully recovered from her recent illness, and is now at liberty to

Figures 1.5–1.6. A scenic image as point-of-view shot. *The Man from Home* (George Fitzmaurice, 1922; Famous Players-Lasky). (Courtesy of Nederlands Film Museum [EYE])

Figures 1.7–1.9.
A letter from
Genevieve
brings bad news.
*The Man from
Home* (George
Fitzmaurice,
1922; Famous
Players-Lasky).
(Courtesy of
Nederlands Film
Museum [EYE])

accept engagements." We know from her daughter's book about her that this period out of work dragged on, and we know that Hitchcock himself, when appointed by Balcon as assistant director on *Woman to Woman* (Graham Cutts, 1923) nearly a year after that advert appeared, surprised her by telephoning her, out of the blue, to offer employment as editor. She was thus not involved at all in the intermediate phase of his Islington apprenticeship.[10]

Islington Interlude: Five Films, 1922–1923

The last of the eleven FPLB productions, *The Man from Home,* was completed in mid-February 1922. The first film of Michael Balcon's company, *Woman to Woman,* began shooting in mid-April 1923, with Hitchcock now taken on as an integral part of the creative team. Table 1.2 gives details of the films that are known to have been shot at Islington in the interim fourteen months, while he remained a relatively humble member of the studio's staff.

Tell Your Children (1922) looks back to the FPLB period and may originally have belonged to FPLB's schedule; its director, Donald Crisp, had been a central figure there, and filmographies have always counted it as the last of the twelve films for which Hitchcock did titles. In contrast, the next two films look ahead, in that they link Hitchcock for the first time with two important collaborators: respectively, Graham Cutts, director of both, and Eliot Stannard, writer of the second. But obviously the most eye-catching films of the five, as his first directorial efforts, are *Number Thirteen* (begun in 1922) and *Always Tell Your Wife* (1923).

We now take the five projects in order.

Lost: *Number Thirteen* aka *Mrs. Peabody*
Hitchcock's role: director

This uncompleted production was evidently too much of an independent venture to be noticed in the trade papers. No firm dates for it have been established, but the likeliest one is early 1922, soon after FPLB ceased production. There is a triple continuity from the FPLB period:

Table 1.2. Films Shot at Islington during Interim Period			
Shooting Date, Title, and Review Date*	Director and Company	Writer and Source	Cast
? early 1922 *Number Thirteen* aka *Mrs. Peabody* Unfinished, no review	Alfred Hitchcock	Elsie Codd (original)	Clare Greet, Ernest Thesiger
? May–June 1922 *Tell Your Children* aka *Lark's Gate* 21 Sept. 1922	Donald Crisp *International Artists*	Leslie H. Norman and Margaret Turnbull Rachel Macnamara (N)	Walter Tennyson, Doris Eaton, Margaret Halstan
July–Aug. 1922 *Flames of Passion* 16 Nov. 1922	Graham Cutts *Grahame-Wilcox*	Herbert Wilcox (original)	Mae Marsh, C. Aubrey Smith
Sept.–Oct. 1922 *Paddy the Next Best Thing* 1 Feb. 1923	Graham Cutts *Grahame-Wilcox*	Eliot Stannard Gertrude Page (N)	Mae Marsh, Marie Ault
Feb. 1923 *Always Tell Your Wife* No review found	Hugh Croise and Alfred Hitchcock *Hicks Productions*	Hugh Croise Seymour Hicks and E. Temple Thurston (P)	Seymour Hicks, Ellaline Terriss, Gertrude McCoy

Note: P = play; N = novel.
* Review dates refer to the British trade paper *Kinematograph Weekly* (commonly abbreviated as *Kine Weekly*).

the use of one of the company's cameramen, Joe Rosenthal Jr.; of Clare Greet (from *Three Live Ghosts*) in the lead; and of a female writer, employed at Islington, who had worked with Chaplin and who thus, Hitchcock recalled, had enough prestige to help get the project off the ground. But despite subsidy from Clare Greet and from a Hitchcock relative, money ran out.

Although no trace of any surviving footage has been found, we now have a lot more information than is offered in the biographies: the writer, the plot, stills, and the film itself.

First, the writer. John Russell Taylor names her as Anita Ross. Patrick McGilligan is more cautious: "*Number Thirteen* was written by a woman employed at Islington, her precise identity unknown, whose background included a vague prior affiliation with Charles Chaplin."[11] Hitchcock had, however, identified her in talking to Peter Bogdanovich in 1972: this detail did not make it into the published version of the interviews, but in the full recording he can be heard to name her clearly as Elsie Codd.[12] Codd had indeed worked with Chaplin: she was his British publicist in the late teens and joined him in Hollywood in 1919 before returning to England to handle publicity for FPLB and to write extensively for *Picturegoer* magazine, mainly on Chaplin. In January 1922 she wrote for *Kine Weekly* what was billed as being the first article in a regular series, "Through a Woman's Eyes." It features FPLB's John S. Robertson, but no other articles follow, which is frustrating, since her own script was being filmed by Hitchcock around this time, and that experience would surely have been worth a story or two.[13]

Second, the plot. Hitchcock was always reticent with later interviewers, simply expressing relief that no traces survived. But in 1930 he had revealed more: "Clare Greet and Ernest Thesiger played the leading parts. The plot consisted of the dream of a charlady who, having bought a lottery ticket, optimistically dreamed of wealth. All her friends were honoured guests at her mansion—a gentleman who had been particularly kind to her being permitted to wear a diadem from morning to night—and all her enemies became her servants."[14] Elsie Codd had been present at the shooting of Chaplin's *The Kid* (1921), even appearing in it as an extra, and her story sounds as if it was influenced by the extended heavenly dreamland sequence toward the end of that film.

Third, stills. New ones have been found, to add to the few already in circulation. The latter include an image of Hitchcock directing on location in Rotherhithe, south of the Thames, where the pub, The Angel, still survives, but the congested housing does not (fig. 1.10).

The male lead, Ernest Thesiger, had recently played Cameron in the original stage production of J. M. Barrie's *Mary Rose*, which may be what brought him to Hitchcock's attention; he went on to write autobiographies and to have his archive lodged in the Theatre Department at Bristol University. Neither the published autobiography nor its unpublished sequel contains any reference to the film or to Hitchcock, but the Bristol archive does contain some unfamiliar stills, three of which are reproduced here for the first time (figs. 1.11–1.13).

Figure 1.10. Shooting *Number Thirteen* in 1922. Rotherhithe location, with Hitchcock kneeling, far right. From *Cinema Studio*, 7 December 1949. (Courtesy of the Cinema Museum, London)

Fourth, the film itself. Hitchcock told his 1930 interviewer cryptically: "Unfortunately as a production unit we were so inexperienced that we made it as straight comedy instead of farce; so it was shelved." It was shelved without being completed, but it was taken off the shelf for inspection in 1925. By then there were two reasons for reviving it: Hitchcock was now an official Gainsborough director, whose first film, now completed, was about to get him good publicity; and legislation was imminent to protect the British film industry by, among other things, establishing a minimum quota of British films for showing on British screens—*Number Thirteen* might be in a position to profit from this. Michael Balcon asked Adrian Brunel to have a look at it.

Brunel was another bright young man whose early career developed in parallel with Hitchcock's own. In addition to directing, he ran a company in partnership with Ivor Montagu that specialized in titling, re-editing, and general "doctoring" of problematic films. This was Brunel's verdict, written to Balcon on 11 November 1925 at the

Figures 1.11–1.13. Production stills from *Number Thirteen*. (Courtesy of Bristol University Theatre Museum, Ernest Thesiger Collection)

time when Hitchcock was away in Europe shooting his second feature
for Gainsborough, *The Mountain Eagle* (1926):

> My dear Mick
> With regard to the Hitchcock comedy, I have now collected
> this from Wainwright. I have talked this over with Hitch
> himself and we agree that it will not be a cheap proposition,
> as so much new stuff will have to be shot. As it stands now it
> is about 3,400 ft, much of which must come out.
>
> I have several ideas for expanding it, but I would ask you
> to see the picture first if you can possibly manage it.
>
> Please do not think that it is through lack of interest that
> I have not brought the matter up before. I have not pressed
> the question as I knew that it would entail more money than
> you anticipated to put the film right. But now with the Quota
> coming into force, the whole situation is different.
>
> Yours: Adrian[15]

The film referred to can only be *Number Thirteen*. The other
uncompleted comedy on which Hitchcock had worked, *Always Tell
Your Wife,* was more of a Seymour Hicks project than a Hitchcock
one, and its length, as a two-reeler, would never have approached
3,400 feet (between thirty and forty minutes, depending on running
speed). Balcon may or may not have taken up the invitation to view
the footage, but there is no evidence that the idea of finishing it was
taken any further.

The Wainwrights referred to in Brunel's first paragraph were associated both with film laboratories and with film distribution. The
best hope for discovery of *Number Thirteen* seems to lie in tracing
what happened to the material in their vaults.

Lost: *Tell Your Children* (Donald Crisp, 1922)
Hitchcock's role: intertitles, studio assistant

All sources agree that Hitchcock did intertitles for *Tell Your Children*
as well as for the eleven FPLB films. It was made by the same writer-

director team, Margaret Turnbull and Donald Crisp, who had been working together at FPLB, and it may have been one of the company's intended projects, abandoned when it decided to pull out. In the event, *Tell Your Children* was made, after some delay and switching of plans, at Islington for International Artists. After his four films at Islington—this one and its three FPLB predecessors—Crisp directed no more films, but he continued his acting career into the 1960s.

Reviews were mainly negative. *Kine Weekly* (21 September 1922) reported: "This is still another attempt to put on the screen the dangers of allowing children to remain ignorant of the basic facts of sex. It is difficult, if such a theme is to be treated so as to avoid all offence, to make it either interesting or convincing, and in this case it has succeeded in being neither. The story is improbable and mechanical, and long before the end becomes wearisome. . . . It is not helped by the way the continuity goes all to pieces on several occasions. Only a moderate attraction for most halls." By the time of its release, Hitchcock was involved with more promising projects of a different kind.

Survives: *Flames of Passion* (Graham Cutts, 1922)
Hitchcock's role: studio assistant, possible work on sets

This is the first film involving the young Alfred Hitchcock that is in any kind of current circulation: the British Film Institute (BFI) has made the archive print freely available at its Mediatheque installation on the South Bank of the Thames. Viewers can access the film on demand, complete with its short sequences in two-tone Prizmacolor, accompanied by an English translation of the Dutch version's intertitles. These cannot, of course, reproduce the original titles either verbally or pictorially, but it is not as if Hitchcock had been responsible for these titles; neither he nor anyone else has claimed that he was. The production did make use of the skeleton staff at Islington to which he belonged, however, and it can be assumed that he assisted with a variety of tasks, including work on the sets, which included an impressive reproduction of the courtroom at the Old Bailey for the film's protracted final scenes.

Flames of Passion brought Hitchcock together for the first time with the director Graham Cutts, the first of seven collaborations in which he took on progressively more influential roles before leaving to direct on his own account. This film alone shows how foolish it is to dismiss Cutts, as many have been happy to do, as some kind of hack director whom Hitchcock and (later) his wife had to "carry." Far from being a step down for Hitchcock after the American collaborations—the eleven FPLB films and then *Tell Your Children*—this can be seen as a step up. The imported Hollywood star, Mae Marsh, had greater stature than any of those used in the FPLB films, and the film's reception was, in Britain especially, more positive than for any of them, setting up Cutts as a high-profile and bankable director, one equipped to make full use of the superior Islington facilities.

The Mae Marsh character, neglected by her father, has a brief romance with the family's much older chauffeur (Herbert Langley). The chauffeur's wife (Hilda Bayley) adopts the resulting baby, which neither she nor the chauffeur knows to be his. Marsh then marries a new father figure, a lawyer played by C. Aubrey Smith (who would be used by Hitchcock in his first Hollywood film, *Rebecca* [1940]). The chauffeur declines into drunkenness and kills the baby. At his trial, Smith is the prosecutor; at the climax, the chauffeur's wife reveals all, and Smith resigns his post.

Certain elements in the film can be related to Hitchcock's own work as a director, whether we want to take this as evidence of influence, or simply of affinity. The trial's climax will be echoed in *The Manxman* (1929), another silent melodrama of concealed parentage, which ends with the Judge (Malcolm Keen) likewise forced into resignation. Hitchcock will cause the Old Bailey setting to be re-created in equally elaborate and well-publicized detail in Hollywood twenty-five years later for *The Paradine Case* (1947). And there will be formal echoes as well. A crucial scene is one in which the chauffeur attacks his wife (figs. 1.14–1.16). The images have the same kind of brutal shot-reverse-shot intensity that Hitchcock will from time to time create, even as late as the marital rape scene in *Marnie* (1964; figs. 1.17–1.19) and the strangling in *Frenzy* (1972).

Figures
1.14–1.16.
Hilda Bayley
and Herbert
Langley
in *Flames
of Passion*
(Graham Cutts,
1922; Grahame-
Wilcox
Productions).
(Courtesy of the
BFI National
Archive)

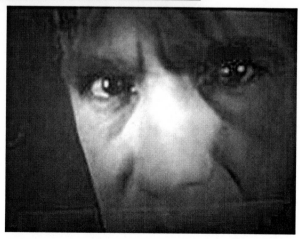

Figures 1.17–
1.19. Tippi
Hedren
and Sean
Connery in
Marnie (1964;
Universal
Pictures).
(© Geoffrey
Stanley Inc.)

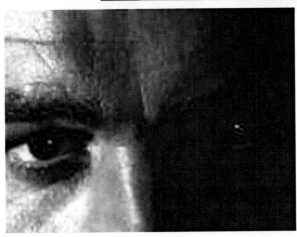

Lost: *Paddy the Next Best Thing* (Graham Cutts, 1923)
Hitchcock's role: studio assistant, possible work on sets

Paddy the Next Best Thing was directed by Cutts immediately after *Flames of Passion*, again for Grahame-Wilcox. *Kine Weekly* noted on 5 October 1922 that "the company has again taken the Lasky studio at Islington, with the whole of its technical staff." Again, the film aimed high, retaining Mae Marsh and deploying a generous budget. It became a commercial success in the United States as well as in Britain, where it had an early reissue, a rare privilege at the time. It is another frustration to find no surviving trace of *Paddy*, since it constitutes for Hitchcock the first cinematic link both with Ireland, the country of his maternal grandfather's birth, and with Eliot Stannard, who worked on the script of this film and, later, of all Hitchcock's nine silent films up to *Blackmail* (1929).[16]

According to *Kine Weekly,* the company went to the West of Ireland to shoot location footage in September 1922. However, in October it reported:

> Work done during the last five weeks on Paddy The Next Best Thing has been so much wasted effort. Herbert Wilcox, of Graham-Wilcox Productions, tells us that the photography has not been up to the standard that he and Graham Cutts had set up, and rather than put out any work that does not satisfy them as being absolutely beyond reproach, they faced the heavy loss entailed and scrapped everything that has been done. . . . So Mae Marsh and her colleagues are once again busy at the Islington studios on the interiors, and all those interested are praying for the bright weather of the past few days to continue until the location work has been done again.

It does not seem that they returned to Ireland, nor is it clear whether or not Hitchcock, as a member of the studio staff, would have accompanied them to the original Irish locations.

The review in *The Times* (27 January 1923) called the result "a very sentimental film which is excellently produced and cleverly acted," notably by Mae Marsh as Paddy, who moves from her Irish home to London and back to Ireland: "She ensnares the hero (Mr Darby Foster) in the first few feet of the film, but neither of them seems to realise their reciprocal attraction until the very end. Miss Marsh's acting, however, carries the film through triumphantly, and the audience last night applauded the film heartily." For *Kine Weekly* (1 February 1923), "there is not a dull moment in the entire picture. . . . This is another film which marks a milestone in the improvement of British screen art." Cutts was at once taken on as leading director by the ambitious company, headed by Michael Balcon, that moved into Islington shortly afterward. This film had meanwhile introduced Hitchcock not only to Eliot Stannard but to two character actresses of whom he would subsequently make effective use, Marie Ault (*The Lodger,* 1926) and Marie Wright (*Murder!,* 1930).

Found in Part: *Always Tell Your Wife* (1923)
Hitchcock's role: production manager, and director after taking over halfway through

Unlike *Number Thirteen, Always Tell Your Wife* survives in part and had some good trade paper coverage in the pages of the weekly *Motion Picture Studio.* In the issue for 21 October 1922, the columnist "Megaphone," in his weekly feature "High Lights," notes the plan of the stage actor Sir Seymour Hicks to turn to film work: "He has contracted to turn out a dozen two-reelers at the rate of one a month. Ellaline Terriss [his wife] will be his leading lady. Well, there is a dearth of good screen comedy, and if Seymour Hicks is as funny before the camera as before the footlights, his contribution will be very welcome."

Megaphone follows up on 30 December: "I was more than usually interested in the news from Hugh Croise that he is now producing a new series of screen comedies starring Seymour Hicks and Ellaline Terriss. . . . Croise has made the adaptations of the comedies himself, and at Islington Studios he will have a capable right-hand man as production manager in the person of A. Hitchcock. The first scenes

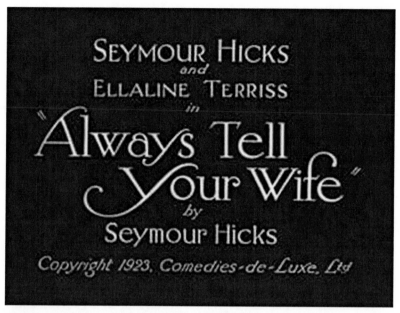

SEYMOUR HICKS
and
ELLALINE TERRISS
in
"Always Tell
Your Wife"
by
Seymour Hicks
Copyright 1923, Comedies-de-Luxe, Ltd

Figure 1.20. Opening title from *Always Tell Your Wife* (1923; Comedies-de-Luxe). (Courtesy of the BFI National Archive)

will be made on Monday, January 1—a good New Year start for all concerned." This is the earliest trade paper naming of Hitchcock that has so far been found, other than his July 1921 article as a title specialist, and his unobtrusive listing early in 1922 as a Kinema Club member. In the same issue, in the feature "Cameramen at Work," it is noted that "Claude McDonnell has started with Hugh Croise at the F.P.-Lasky Islington Studios." (McDonnell was already an experienced cameraman, and he would work on several subsequent feature films at Islington directed by Graham Cutts and, later, by Hitchcock himself: *Downhill* and *Easy Virtue* [both 1927].)

However, things now begin to go wrong. The next week (6 January 1923) Megaphone reports that "Hugh Croise has had bad luck at the outset of his productions featuring Mr and Mrs Seymour Hicks. Ellaline Terriss has been seized with illness and work is practically suspended for the next week or so. Here's wishing her a speedy recovery!" Nothing more is heard until 24 February, when the first of Hicks's "two-reel comedies" is listed as being in its second week of shooting. On 3 March it is in its third week, with Gertrude McCoy added to the cast, and on 10 March it is "being cut." For the next few weeks, in the formal summaries of studio activity that were presumably supplied by the companies themselves, there is no record of progress. The issue of 21 April still says "first one being cut," but on another page the paper's regular humorous column includes, under the cryptic heading of current "Mysteries," "Seymour Hicks's first film results"; so questions were clearly by now starting to be asked. The same issue notes that *Woman to Woman* has begun shooting at Islington, that its star Betty Compson is due to arrive from America soon, and that "A. J. Hitchcock is responsible for the adaptation and continuity."

No more is heard of this or of any subsequent Hicks comedy. The projected series has dwindled to one; if this one film ever had a release, it was a late and unpublicized one, even though at that time short comedies remained a popular feature of film programming, and Hicks's chosen writer-director, Hugh Croise, was an experienced maker of them both before and after. The single Hicks film is not even given a title at the time, but records and reminiscences confirm it as *Always Tell Your Wife* and show that Hitchcock took over direction halfway through. Hicks recalled the circumstances in his 1949 autobiography:

> Half way through the production the director was taken ill and I was at my wit's end to know what to do. Being on the verge of throwing the whole thing up, I was interested when a fat youth who was in charge of the property room at the studio volunteered to help me. It seemed a forlorn hope, but as I liked the boy and as he seemed tremendously enthusiastic and anxious to try his hand at producing, we carried on as co-directors and the picture was finished. Who do you think that boy was? None other than Alfred Hitchcock.[17]

Other sources, including Hitchcock in interview, suggest that the reason for Croise's departure was not illness but a row, and this is borne out by a trenchant item published in the weekly *Entertain-*

ment World on 3 March 1923, when the film was in its third week of production. It comes from a weekly column of film gossip by Penrhyn Blade:

> Hugh Croise had some caustic remarks to make on the subject of West End stars when I ran into him at the Kinema Club yesterday.
>
> "A few years ago," he said, "the stage star regarded the film artist with an attitude of lofty contempt. Then, when they realised the box-office receipts at the theatres were falling off and there was money to be made in the studio, they were anxious to get into the game.
>
> "But the trouble is that they have the same contempt for the film today as they had years ago. They will not take the trouble to learn its special technique which is quite different from and about ten times more difficult than the stage. They think they know everything and refuse to take any lessons in acting from the producer. The result of this attitude is painfully obvious when the film is seen on the screen."[18]

The dates establish that Croise must, beyond doubt, be talking about Hicks. He himself was in good enough health to continue his progress through successive rounds of the Kinema Club's lengthy billiards tournament, which he won in early June, and to start on an unrelated new series of comedies in July. Meanwhile, Hitchcock took over the Hicks film; and one reel of it survives, in the archive of the BFI.

Was the film ever released, and if not, why? Why did the series cease so abruptly? How did the film find its way into the British archives, and why only half of it? Does it include any footage shot by Hitchcock, or it is just Croise's work? These are questions still to be resolved. But the half that survives is the first reel of two, and the film may well have been shot in sequence, which would mean that this is Croise's material, or at least mainly so, rather than Hitchcock's. It bears out Croise's point about unadapted theatricality: the action is mainly shot frontally, as if for a theater audience, and Hicks does not hold back on large-scale gesture.

Figure 1.21. Frontal composition: Seymour Hicks with the blackmailer. *Always Tell Your Wife* (1923; Comedies-de-Luxe). (Courtesy of the BFI National Archive)

It would be of great interest to see whether Hitchcock completed the film in the same style for the sake of consistency, or in a more cinematic style for the sake of quality—assuming Hicks allowed it. But the first half does provide one indisputable Hitchcock shot, the insert of a telegram sent to Hicks by an old flame—the device that sparks off the plot, based on Hicks's frantic struggle to stop his wife from discovering the episode from his past. The initial version of the telegram, before its transcription by the Post Office, is given in Hitchcock's own handwriting (see figs. 1.22 and 1.23).[19]

Given his previous Islington experience in title design, Hitchcock may also have taken responsibility for the film's handsome main title and for the intertitles. At the end of the surviving first reel a friend offers to divert the wife so that Hicks can be free to go out to dine with the importunate old flame: "Your wife will dine with us—you can get up and go out and be back in bed before she returns." It is easy to imagine the kind of primitive suspense scene, based on Griffith-like

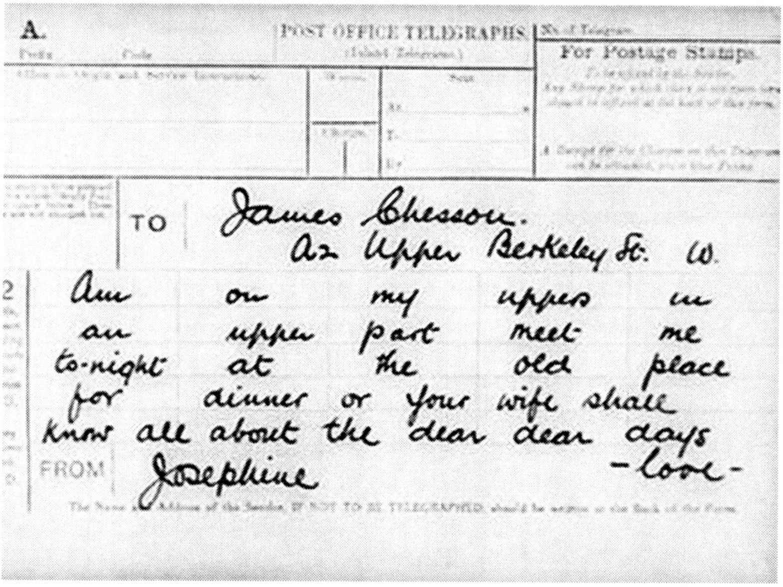

A.

POST OFFICE TELEGRAPHS

For Postage Stamps.

TO James Chesson.
42 Upper Berkeley St. W.

Am on my uppers in an upper part meet me to-night at the old place for dinner or your wife shall know all about the dear dear days

FROM Josephine -love-

Figure 1.22. The telegram insert written by Hitchcock from *Always Tell Your Wife* (1923; Comedies-de-Luxe). (Courtesy of the BFI National Archive)

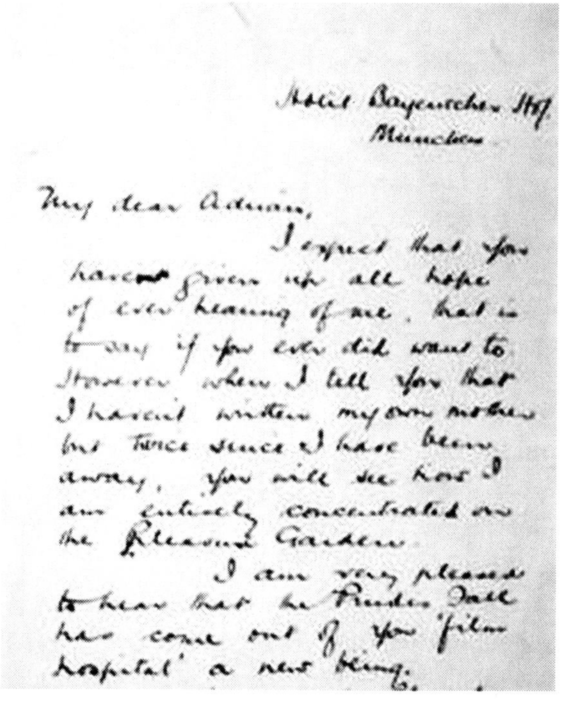

Hotel Bayerischer Hof
München

My dear Adrian,
I expect that you haven't given up all hope of ever hearing of me, that is to say if you ever did want to. However when I tell you that I haven't written my own mother but twice since I have been away, you will see how I am entirely concentrated on the Pleasure Garden.
I am very pleased to hear that the Prude's Fall has come out of your 'film hospital' a new thing.

Figure 1.23. The start of an undated letter written by Hitchcock to Adrian Brunel sometime between June and August 1925 during the shooting of *The Pleasure Garden*. (Courtesy of the BFI Library Special Collections, Adrian Brunel)

crosscutting, that could have followed. However, if the film kept to
the original theatrical outline, the chance for such crosscutting would
have been limited. This is how *The Times* had reviewed the play on
23 December 1913, when it was part of a vaudeville-style mixed bill
in London:

> The principal item in the Christmas programme at the Coli-
> seum is *Always Tell Your Wife,* a new one-act play by Mr E.
> Temple Thurston. In this Mr Seymour Hicks plays a young
> husband who, in order to be finally free of a pre-marital
> entanglement, is intending to give the lady dinner at a restau-
> rant where he and his solicitor are to see the matter through
> together. In order to conceal his doings from his young wife
> (Miss Ellaline Terriss) he feigns a severe cold and goes to
> bed—putting on his pyjamas over his dress clothes—until
> his wife shall have left the house. Thanks to the telephone,
> however (which plays a very large part in the play), the wife
> gets wind of the engagement, and the secret of the supposed
> cold, and on the advice of a friend (conveyed by telephone)
> proceeds to "soak" or punish her husband with all manner of
> tortures—mustard baths, mustard leaves, inhalers, thermom-
> eter, and what not—until the time comes for her to end the
> joke by revealing (on the telephone) that she knew all along
> his cold to be a sham. There is any quantity of farcical fun
> in the play, and the pair romp through it in their well-known
> vivacious and vigorous style.

The author credited here, E. Temple Thurston, was an authentic
playwright, not a Hicks pseudonym; the film credits Hicks as author
instead, and Hugh Croise had done a further screen adaptation, so it
is possible that the plot had changed.[20] There is no evidence that the
film was ever submitted to the censor, given a trade show, or exhibited
to the public. But Hitchcock is unlikely to have taken a close interest
in its eventual fate, since he was soon involved in scripting a far more
ambitious Islington production, *Woman to Woman,* for Michael
Balcon.

Michael Balcon and Gainsborough:
Five Films, 1923–1925

All five films of this period are directed by Graham Cutts, using Islington Studios and sometimes locations in England and Europe. The last three are credited to the newly formed production company, Gainsborough (see table 1.3).

Since none of these five films has yet been found in its original form, we cannot tell how Hitchcock's name featured in the credits. Foreign-language versions carry little information, and the Dutch version of the pre-Balcon *Flames of Passion* even credits the wrong director, Maurice Elvey instead of Graham Cutts. It is clear from the trade press, however, that in each case it was A. J. Hitchcock who adapted the original material for the screen. The press does not say much about additional contributions, but other evidence, including Balcon's memoir *A Lifetime of Films,* supports Hitchcock's claim that he also acted consistently as art director and assistant director. In view of the way in which Cutts, director of all five of these films, has often been written out of history by Hitchcock partisans, it is ironic that at the time he was routinely foregrounded at Hitchcock's expense. The production company handled a tribute paid to the third

Title and Review Date*	Source	Cast
Woman to Woman 8 Nov. 1923	Michael Morton (P)	Betty Compson, Clive Brook
The White Shadow 21 Feb. 1924	Michael Morton (original story)	Betty Compson, Clive Brook, Henry Victor, A. B. Imeson
The Passionate Adventure 21 Aug. 1924	Frank Stayton (N)	Alice Joyce, Marjorie Daw, Clive Brook, Victor McLaglen, Lilian Hall Davis
The Blackguard 23 Apr. 1925	Raymond Paton (N)	Jane Novak, Walter Rilla, Bernhard Goetzke
The Prude's Fall aka *Dangerous Virtue* Late 1925 (no review)	Rudolf Besier and May Edginton (P)	Jane Novak, Julanne Johnston, Warwick Ward, Miles Mander

Table 1.3. Films Shot at Islington with Michael Balcon/Gainsborough

Note: P = play; N = novel. All five films were directed by Graham Cutts and written by Hitchcock.
* Review dates refer to the British trade paper *Kinematograph Weekly* (commonly abbreviated as *Kine Weekly*).

Figure 1.24. Advertisement for *The Passionate Adventure* (Graham Cutts, 1924) in *Kinematograph Weekly,* 10 July 1924. (Courtesy of the Cinema Museum, London)

film of the five, *The Passionate Adventure* (1924), by the author of the original novel, Frank Stayton, by billing it as a letter to Cutts (fig. 1.24). A close look, however, shows it to be addressed to "Messrs Graham Cutts and Hitchcock" and to pay tribute equally to script and direction. The text reads: "Gentlemen: I should like to place on record my sincere appreciation of the treatment you have given to 'The Passionate Adventure.' The production is in my opinion an artistic triumph, vital, vivid, intimate, interesting and human. You have treated my work with such respect, and so maintained the atmosphere I tried to create, that I feel intensely grateful. I was held every moment, thrilled and excited."

This was the first film to be produced by Gainsborough Pictures, the new company set up by Balcon in 1924 with what would become

Figures 1.25–1.26. "The Gainsborough Lady" and "the Gainsborough Man." Advertisements in *Kine Weekly*, 13 March 1924. Graham Cutts does not even need to be named. (Courtesy of the Cinema Museum, London)

the very familiar trademark image of "the Gainsborough Lady" (fig. 1.25). The company's early advertising balanced this image with one of "the Gainsborough Man," a title for which at that time there could be only one candidate (fig. 1.26).

Altogether, Hitchcock got little publicity prior to *The Pleasure Garden,* but this may not have bothered him, since he was gaining such solid experience and impressing those who mattered, notably Balcon. And when the press did start to notice him, it was in a big way.

Lost: *Woman to Woman* (Graham Cutts, 1923)
Hitchcock's role: scenario, adapted from the play by Michael Morton; art director and assistant director

Woman to Woman is the only film of the five from which nothing has been found, although the 1929 sound remake, directed for Gainsborough by Victor Saville, does survive, with the same plot and the same star in Betty Compson.

David, an English army officer on leave from the trenches, falls in love with Dolores, a French dancer, but is called back to the front before they can marry. Shellshocked in the next attack, he loses his memory and goes home to acquire an English wife. Years later, he meets and recognizes Dolores and is introduced to the son of their liaison. Eventually Dolores defies doctor's orders by continuing to dance, and she dies; the cold wife has by now softened toward her and agrees to adopt the child as her own.

The film was a spectacular success both critically and commercially, consolidating Cutts's stature as a major figure. The tribute paid to it by the cosmopolitan Irishman Rex Ingram, director of the recent *Four Horsemen of the Apocalypse* (1921), was quoted by *Kine Weekly* on 8 November 1923: "I have just seen a British film, *Woman to Woman,* one of the best and most sincere films I ever saw in my life. They have never produced in America a better film than *Woman to Woman.*" A reviewer in the same issue stated that "no praise is too high for the artistic direction and the eminently human way in which Graham Cutts has unfolded the story." He went on to note that "the scenarist's name is not mentioned, but he certainly deserves a fair share of praise in the success of the picture." Though the name of A. J. Hitchcock had been given in some of the advance publicity, it evidently did not make it onto the credit titles. Reviews also made

Figure 1.27. A cartoon drawing depicting Hitchcock and Graham Cutts in *Motion Picture Studio*, 18 April 1923. (Courtesy of the BFI Library)

much of the lavish sets, including a French nightclub based on Hitchcock's research in Paris, but again no credit was given. However, he had received some acknowledgment in the lengthy production report from the floor at Islington in *Motion Picture Studio* (18 April 1923). Naturally Cutts is dominant in the headline, the report, and the pictorial accompaniment (fig. 1.27), but his assistant is there too and had talked to the journal's reporter: "A. J. Hitchcock, who, incidentally, adapted the play into scenario form, described to me his researches which were necessary before the set, an exact replica of the original, could be accurately reconstructed." This image may be the first one of Hitchcock to have appeared in the press.

Although no trace of *Woman to Woman* survives, there is an unusually full account of its narrative in an American collection from 1924, *Representative Photoplays Analyzed*. The collection "is devoted to the exposition and analysis of more than one hundred representative photoplays drawn from every source. Here the student will find a synopsis of each story and a detailed analysis together with the necessary comments on the story's worth." The analyst is Scott O'Dell, identified as being "formerly member technical staff Famous Players-Lasky, instructor in Photoplay Technique, Palmer Institute of Authorship." There is no evidence that his FPL employment took him to the British outpost, where his path and Hitchcock's would have crossed. The institute itself, located in Hollywood, is the publisher.[21]

The name of the screenwriter, Alfred J. Hitchcock, is one of four given at the start of the section on *Woman to Woman,* alongside those of Betty Compson, Graham Cutts, and Michael Morton. A three-page synopsis follows, including a different ending made for America: Dolores rallies and lives, and is finally free to marry David. O'Dell notes:

> This was in conformity with the popular demand for a happy ending. Whether or not the picture has gained in audience appeal by sacrificing dramatic strength and plausibility for a happy ending is open to conjecture. In the American version the anti-climax action was decidedly weak.
>
> Another point which may interest the student was this: In many states the censors refused to permit the picture to be shown unless David and Dolores were depicted as having been married before he left for the trenches. It is doubtful which was the lesser evil, to show Dolores as the mother of an illegitimate child or David as a bigamist.

Summing up, he writes that *Woman to Woman* "is one of the best British productions to be brought to this country and the analysis of it is well worth the consideration of the student in order that he may ascertain to what length producers and distributors are compelled to go to satisfy the demands of the censors and the public."

All this is of interest in telling us more about the context of this new stage in Hitchcock's career: the film's high-profile status, higher than that of any of the FPLB films, and the difficulties attached to any British attempt on the U.S. market. But O'Dell's analysis is suggestive in a further way, praising Hitchcock's crosscutting structure specifically for the way it creates suspense:

> We have seen the start of the love element, David's departure for the war and his injury, and we are aware of his marriage to his haughty wife. Then we see them in an intimate scene in which she refuses to bear him a son. Meanwhile, what of the little dancer? Believing that her lover is dead she flees to England, with the philosophical remark that "Her boy's father was an Englishman. His son shall be raised in England."
>
> Now suspense begins to rise for we know that sooner or later David and Dolores will meet. This foreknowledge on the part of the spectators cannot but develop a poignant suspense.

Found in Part: *The White Shadow* (Graham Cutts, 1924)
Earlier Titles: *Children of Chance, The Awakening, The Eternal Survivor*
Hitchcock's role: scenario, adapted from an original story by Michael Morton; art director and assistant director

The White Shadow is the film of which approximately half was recently discovered at the New Zealand Film Archive and widely publicized. While it was an exciting find, the negative reception the film received in 1924 is easy to understand.

Michael Balcon's autobiography is brutally honest: the company had signed Betty Compson from Hollywood on an expensive two-picture deal, and they were too caught up with *Woman to Woman* to make proper plans for the follow-up film, which had to start quickly. The money made on the first was lost in the fiasco of the second.[22] What Balcon does not mention is that the second film was initially announced as *The Prude's Fall,* already scripted by Hitchcock from a recent West End play. Possibly Compson, when she looked at the script, didn't care for it. (As we will see, *The Prude's Fall* turned out to be even more of a disaster when eventually made, with another

American star in Jane Novak fulfilling a two-picture deal.) The last-minute replacement was an original story by the author of the play of *Woman to Woman*, Michael Morton, hastily adapted by Hitchcock into a scenario.

Betty Compson plays twin sisters, one virtuous (Georgina), the other less so (Nancy). A wealthy young man, Field (Clive Brook), falls for Nancy, without realizing she has a twin. Predictable complications ensue. In the end, the strain causes Georgina, now in love with Field, to break down, and she maneuvers him back to Nancy. Then, in the words of the *Kine Weekly* synopsis, "Georgina dies and her soul passes into the body of the twin, thus altering her entire nature." This is evidently shown in pictorial fashion and is followed by a happy ending.

The surviving material all comes from the first part of the film, though there are gaps even in that. Visually it is impressive, with handsome interiors and exteriors at an estate in Devon and nightclub scenes in Paris. And of course the theme of the "double" has strong dramatic possibilities, and strong Hitchcockian resonances: in his book *Hitchcock's Motifs*, Michael Walker devotes eight pages to it. The idea of a double role for Compson may have been inspired by her Hollywood film *The Little Minister* (1921), set in a Scottish community of weavers. Since it is based on a play by J. M. Barrie, already a favorite author of his, Hitchcock is sure to have seen it. The daughter of a local lord, Compson's character takes on the alter ego of a gypsy, Babby, insinuating herself into the community and taking their side against employers and the Law. The film skillfully exploits the play between her two personae, in both dramatic and thematic terms. With a script needed at short notice, one can imagine Hitchcock suggesting another double role for her, or, if the idea came from Morton, welcoming the chance to develop a story of a comparable kind. He must also have been pleased to be able to return to this structure, with more time and finesse, and with the help of a more experienced writer in Eliot Stannard, in *The Pleasure Garden*, which develops out of the meeting of a similarly contrasting pair of young women, though not sisters.[23]

The White Shadow itself, however, at least in its surviving reels, fails to establish any vivid or subtle links or contrasts between the

Figure 1.28. Cutts and Hitchcock again sketched in *Motion Picture Studio,* 11 August 1923, on the set of *The White Shadow* (1924). (Courtesy of the BFI Library)

twins—nothing much seems to be at stake, and the Clive Brook character is a nullity. *Kine Weekly* was particularly hard on the script, and in this case the writer must have been grateful *not* to be named: "There is a complete lack of conviction in the way the sisters are mistaken for each other, and no attempt at a coherent and well-proportioned sequence of events. . . . It looks as though Michael Morton and the producer had made up the story as they went along." Because of the rush, they and Hitchcock may in effect have been doing just that.

Survives: *The Passionate Adventure* (Graham Cutts, 1924)
Hitchcock's role: scenario, adapted from the novel by Frank Stayton; art director and assistant director

The Passionate Adventure is one of only four films to survive in full, albeit in a German version, out of the twenty-one that Hitchcock was involved with before *The Pleasure Garden,* and it is the only one that has been the subject of sustained critical appraisal—by Christine Gledhill in her pioneering study *Reframing British Cinema 1918–1928.* Unusually, she approaches it as a Graham Cutts film, relating it to his previous work and to its wider context in British cinema rather than assuming that everything interesting in it must be retrospectively ascribed to the input of Hitchcock. She is able, decisively, to trace Cutts's signature right back to *The Wonderful Story* in 1921, made before even his first tenuous association with Hitchcock on *Flames of Passion*.

The novel by Frank Stayton gave Hitchcock as adaptor the chance to develop a more successful version of the narrative of the double than he had been able to in *The White Shadow*.

Like the Betty Compson character in *The Little Minister,* Clive Brook—here in his third successive role for this production team—has a respectable wealthy persona and an alternate low-life one: to offset the sterility of his upper-class marriage, he makes regular incognito visits to the East End of London. There he becomes involved with a woman whom he rescues from a bully played by another future Hollywood star, Victor McLaglen. Like *The Little Minister* and *The White Shadow*, the film has what is at least ostensibly a happy ending, as Brook's character returns to remake his marriage on a more honest basis than before.

In terms of Hitchcock's motifs, the most startling element in the film is the "Entry through a Window"—a recurring motif, given six pages by Walker, that generally has some kind of sexual resonance, as it seems to do here. Brook effects this entry late in the film, on his return home to his wife from another secret visit to the East End. Hitchcock's sets, for both the upper-class and East End scenes, are again impressive in their scope and detail. But the main element that stands out, in relation to his own subsequent films, is the strategy of "the look," deployed in varied and subtle ways. The sterility of the upper-class marriage is conveyed by the way the husband fails—in a shot-reverse-shot construction—to return the look of his wife as she goes upstairs to bed. The exchange of looks between the man and the East End woman is much stronger on both sides. The tensions culminate in a scene where she takes a bath behind a screen while he recuperates (figs. 1.29–1.32). This sequence will be echoed at the start of *The Pleasure Garden,* where the chorus girl played by Virginia Valli returns the voyeuristic gaze of the man in the front stalls, and

Figures 1.29–1.32. The mechanism of "the look" in *The Passionate Adventure* (Graham Cutts, 1924; Gainsborough Pictures). Clive Brook and Marjorie Daw. (Courtesy of the BFI National Archive)

in a different way in *Blackmail,* where Anny Ondra changes clothes behind the screen that separates her from the artist at the piano.

It seems unlikely that a script would have laid out this and the earlier sequences shot by shot, and there are in any case, as Gledhill demonstrates, continuities with Cutts's earlier films into which Hitchcock had little or no input. Rather than arguing that Cutts here influenced Hitchcock, or vice versa, we can at least point to a clear *affinity* between the two filmmakers, and to the strength of this particular collaborative venture. It is a British film of the 1920s that deserves to be given—like Anthony Asquith's *Shooting Stars* (1928), Miles Mander's *The First Born* (1928), and the various silent Hitchcocks— a high profile relaunch with orchestral accompaniment. All it lacks (so far, anyway) is a set of the original intertitles.

Survives: *The Blackguard* (Graham Cutts, 1925)
Hitchcock's role: scenario, adapted from the novel by
Raymond Paton; art director and assistant director

Like *Flames of Passion, The Passionate Adventure,* and several other Graham Cutts films in which Hitchcock was not involved, *The Blackguard* has long been available in the archives, but like them it has been little noticed—partly, perhaps, as a result of the cavalier claim made in John Russell Taylor's authorized biography *Hitch* that not a single Cutts-directed film survived. Like them, it has had no video or DVD release, nor have we found a version with the original English titles. To this extent it has been lost and needs rediscovering.

Again, Hitchcock filled multiple roles on the film: writing the script, this time from a novel by Raymond Paton; designing the sets; and directing the action on at least one of the sets, the most imposing one.

A second edition of Paton's novel was published as an early film tie-in, complete with stills from the film and seven pages of introductory material.[24] These do not once mention Alfred Hitchcock— another instance of the ironic pattern by which at the time he was marginalized, as important collaborators on the films he went on to direct would be marginalized in turn.

Figure 1.33. Michael's dream-vision of climbing to heaven. *The Black-guard* (Graham Cutts, 1925; Gainsborough Pictures). (Courtesy of the BFI National Archive)

He later spoke of the sets more than the script. This was a co-production between Gainsborough and UFA in Germany, shot at the UFA studios. It gave him the chance, which he never forgot, to observe F. W. Murnau working on *The Last Laugh* (1924) and to supervise construction of sets in the studio where Fritz Lang had recently shot *Siegfried* (1924)—indeed, he ordered the destruction of Lang's forest set in order to construct a spectacular dream sequence. This is the element in *The Blackguard* that is best remembered, partly because it so clearly prefigures the "stairway to heaven" that would provide the American title of the Michael Powell–Emeric Pressburger film *A Matter of Life and Death* (1946). The film's violinist hero, Michael Caviol, stunned early in his apprenticeship by a blow on the head from a bottle wielded by his drunken grandmother, has a dream-vision of climbing to heaven and being told that, if he is to become a great musician, he must sacrifice everything else (fig. 1.33). Talking to Charles Champlin in a TV interview in 1971, Hitchcock recounted in detail and with relish how he set up this elaborate shot himself and directed the several hundred extras by blowing a whistle.[25]

This elaborate set-piece scene is central to the film, being twice echoed later in the narrative, but there is no firm evidence that Hitchcock otherwise did more than to provide the scenario and to construct sets. He took advantage of UFA resources to create some other imposing settings, including interiors of a European cathedral and an English country mansion. A concert-hall setting was due to be modelled on the Albert Hall in London; a decade ahead of his use of the Albert Hall for the concert in *The Man Who Knew Too Much* (1934), Hitchcock had been anxious to get the details right. On 17 November 1924, Michael Balcon wrote a memo to Adrian Brunel, who later, in collaboration with Hitchcock, would fine-tune the now-lost English intertitles:

Dear Adrian

This is to remind you that in addition to the Albert Hall arrangements we discussed, Hitchcock wants good still photographs of one of the boxes, the whole organ and the orchestra.

As I have explained, we are most anxious to get the crowd scenes but even if we are not successful, the above photographs are still required.[26]

In the event, they did not go through with this, and the concert-hall setting is altogether more modest, but the Albert Hall itself was the venue for a spectacular launch of the completed film on 20 April 1925. The report in *Kine Weekly* three days later provides a vivid glimpse of the way things were done in those days for a big silent film like this one: "The reception of 'The Blackguard' by the huge Albert Hall audience on Monday is a tribute, not only to the picture, but to the fine presentation by W. and F. W. L. Trytel, who conducted the big orchestra, also composed the love theme of the film. . . . Vivian van Damm is to be commended on the effects, and Serge Morosoff upon a Russian ballet scene, 'The Forbidden Dance of the Elves,' which preceded the screening."

As a screenwriter, Hitchcock would specialize in adaptations of novels and plays that stayed close to the originals. This applies to all of the scripts for which he took credit, along with his wife, Alma Reville, in the early sound period—in strong contrast to the more radical adaptations made first as silents by Eliot Stannard and then as sound films by Charles Bennett. But among his own earlier scripts, *The Blackguard* is an exception. Paton's novel ranges so widely in terms of theme and geography, and has such elaborate mystical dimensions, that it was a surprising property for Gainsborough to choose, and it became a difficult challenge for Hitchcock to adapt. He did an effective pragmatic job, scaling it right down and eliminating altogether a framing narrative in which a third party recounts Michael's story. The improbability of having the virtuoso violinist Lewinski, who has trained Michael in Paris, become the leader of the Bolshevik revolution is simply brushed aside. His childhood sweetheart, Maria, married against her will to a horrible Russian duke, is rescued by Michael in a strong suspense climax. In the novel he is severely wounded, finds his way slowly back to Paris, and dies there, followed soon by her. Back in England, the son of their love affair, unknown to him, survives—an echo of the revelation of the son's existence in *Woman to Woman*. In the film he is wounded, but, in the words of the intertitle, "as if by a miracle Michael survived, despite his serious injury," and Maria survives too. There is no indication of how he extricates himself, but we next find him in Paris, ready for a happy ending. In the final shot of the film, they kiss (fig. 1.34).[27] If they are to have a child, it still lies in the future.

The film's title has at no point been explained. In the novel, whose full title is *The Autobiography of a Blackguard,* Michael is a ruthless operator, his whole career being based on his theft of a large fortune from an Englishman who subsequently kills himself. That element of the book is excised, as are the luridly described rape-and-slaughter extremes of revolutionary violence—both of these would have been problematic for the censor.

In the film, when the young Michael first conceives a passion for music, he goes to the cathedral to pray to the Virgin Mary for a violin. A hand on his shoulder rewards him: a painter will give him a violin

Figure 1.34. The final shot from *The Blackguard* (Graham Cutts, 1925; Gainsborough Pictures). (Courtesy of the BFI National Archive)

in payment for having him as a sitter (fig. 1.35). Later, he prays again, to find Maria, and his prayer is again answered (fig. 1.36). It is a classic formal symmetry, such as is found at (for instance) the start and end of Hitchcock's film *Young and Innocent* (1937). The first prayer is taken from the novel, but the second, of course, is not. The symmetry also prefigures the resolution of Hitchcock's film *The Wrong Man* (1956), when the prayer of the wrongly accused character played by Henry Fonda is answered by the appearance, superimposed upon his face, of the face of the real criminal. Perhaps Hitchcock's script specified this formal symmetry, perhaps it was Cutts's work, or some form of combination.

Michael Walker in *Hitchcock's Motifs* traces common elements through each of the films directed by Hitchcock, plus the single addition of *The Blackguard,* since he finds elements there that strongly anticipate the director's later practice. These come under the headings of "Painters" and of "Staircases." The latter entry discusses the heavenly staircase, but it could also have noted the significant staircase in another of Hitchcock's elaborate sets—that of the interior of the place

Figures 1.35–1.36. Praying to the Virgin Mary: Michael as a boy (Martin Hertzberg) and as an adult (Walter Rilla). *The Blackguard* (Graham Cutts, 1925; Gainsborough Pictures). (Courtesy of the BFI National Archive)

where the young Michael lives with his grandmother. Michael retreats to his upstairs space to get away from her and to focus on his musical ambitions. Walker refers in passing to *The Prude's Fall* for its briefly shown staircase, and he could also, as noted previously, have cited *The Passionate Adventure* for its "Entry through a Window," one of the most distinctive of all the Hitchcockian motifs that his book traces. His entry on "Painters" considers the psychology of the gaze in the early scenes in which the near-naked Michael acts as a model: first the homosexual subtext, not followed through as it is in Carl Dreyer's *Mikael* from the previous year of 1924; and then the way the film's central love relationship is set up. Maria gazes at Michael when she comes to the studio as a child. As Walker notes, "It is the (almost naked) Michael himself that the girl first looks at; the painted portrait she later sees as an adult is a reminder of this moment. Such an inversion of the far more familiar situation of a man looking with desire at a woman's portrait is quite striking."[28]

The mechanics of the gaze, rendered through point-of-view construction: this has been a recurring topic in studies of Hitchcock ever since Laura Mulvey's famous article "Visual Pleasure and Narrative Cinema" (1975).[29] It is hard to discriminate between Graham Cutts as director and Hitchcock as all-purpose lieutenant in scenes like these. We have already noted the centrality of the mechanics of the gaze to *The Passionate Adventure*. Where Walker is focused entirely on Hitchcock, Christine Gledhill, in her equally scholarly study of the context in which he was first shaping a career, gives convincing weight to Cutts. The index to her book has twenty entries for Hitchcock. Of these, eight come under the heading "Alfred Hitchcock: prefigured by earlier directors."

Survives in Part: *The Prude's Fall* (Graham Cutts, 1925)
Alternative Title: *Dangerous Virtue*
Hitchcock's role: scenario, adapted from the play by Rudolf Besier and May Edginton; art director and assistant director

The Prude's Fall was several times announced as an imminent project, only to be postponed: initially scheduled to follow *Woman to*

Woman as the second of the Cutts-Balcon films, it eventually became the fifth, the last on which Hitchcock worked. Reliable authorities such as Rachael Low, Denis Gifford, and Jane Sloan all date it as 1924, but shooting did not start until February 1925.

One reason for the confusion is that it seems to have been hardly shown. No British reviews have been found, even in the trade press; it is unique, or virtually so, for an ambitious production in having had no London trade show. *Kine Weekly* (29 October 1925) lists it in its monthly chart as being generally released in November, along with twenty-seven other films. One column in the chart gives the date of the film's original "Kine review"; for *The Prude's Fall* alone, this column is left blank. Clearly Gainsborough had gone to some lengths to shield the film from professional criticism and were in effect writing it off. The initial cut had been felt to need emergency treatment at the Brunel-Montagu "film hospital" (see the Hitchcock letter reproduced in figure 1.23) and emerged "a new being," but this was not enough to make it commercially viable. It had two minor trade shows, in Birmingham and Sheffield; these provincial shows were notoriously low-key and sparsely attended, and evidence of public screenings is minimal. Under the title *Dangerous Virtue* it had a limited release in America, trading on the star status of Jane Novak, but was badly received.

Three reels of the film survive in the BFI's archive, but these do not, unlike the material from *Always Tell Your Wife* and *The White Shadow,* include the beginning, which makes it hard to make full sense of it in isolation. At the Pordenone Silent Film week in the Hitchcock centenary year of 1999, it was shown as a free-standing item, without the kind of contextualization that would be given to the screenings there and elsewhere of *The White Shadow* in 2011, and understandably it made little impression. The surviving reels constitute all or most of the final half-hour of a film running twice as long, and make sense if we know the complicated backstory. In the absence of the normal trade paper reviews, the fullest source we have found is the Press Book held in the Jane Novak Collection at the Margaret Herrick Library in Beverly Hills. This summary is distilled from its long narrative: the surviving material is given in italic type:

The prude of the title is Beatrice, a young woman from a County family who is expected to marry her cousin Neville, a conventional Army officer. On a skiing holiday, she falls in love with a French philanderer, André le Briquet, but on their return to London he transfers his affections to her Russian friend Sonia. "Stranded in Europe, in common with so many victims of the Russian Revolution, Sonia had drifted with her mother, Countess Roubetsky, into the toils of Marc de Roqueville, an unscrupulous Continental adventurer, by whom she is used as a decoy for his gambling den." On the day of her marriage to André, the anxious Sonia writes an urgent letter, telling the story of her past, and entrusts it to Beatrice to hand over, but Beatrice's scruples stop her doing so till after the wedding. *When she finds out about this delay, Sonia panics and takes poison while the guests are celebrating. The broken-hearted André is set on vengeance, and on return from two years of work abroad sets about seducing and disgracing Beatrice, who still loves him. Finally, André realises that he returns her love, and Neville resigns himself to the prospect of the couple's marriage.*

What made it so unacceptable? The final twenty minutes are dialogue-heavy, and also what would have been characterized at the time as "sordid," hinging as they do on the attempt by André (Warwick Ward) to persuade Beatrice (Novak) to become his mistress: "Don't you think, Beatrice, that, loving as we do, marriage is an unnecessary formality?" From her protective cousin Neville (Miles Mander): "Once and for all, le Briquet, are you above board or not?" The casting of Ward and Mander creates little tension, since they are such similar types; Mander, representative here of a conventional decency, is more suited to the roles he would play for Hitchcock immediately afterward in *The Pleasure Garden*, as the caddish husband, and later in *Murder!*, as the drunken widower.

But the first few minutes of the archival print, less reliant on intertitles, are remarkable and reward close attention. The series of nine frame stills set out in figures 1.37–1.45 can stand as an example of the cinematic force and economy achieved by the Cutts-Hitchcock partnership at its best, a highlight of their final collaboration, even though few saw it. The nine stills in themselves tell a story vividly in strip-cartoon style, a shorthand version of the sequence as it unfolds in time.

Sonia, on her wedding day, has given Beatrice the letter to deliver to André explaining her past so as to have no secrets from him and to give him the chance, if he wants, to call it off. Having such a letter written, and then going astray, is a classic melodramatic device—in Thomas Hardy's novel *Tess of the d'Urbervilles* (1891), it ruins the life of Tess and her bridegroom Angel Clare. As the archival print opens, André has just read the letter; he realizes that he was meant to receive it before the wedding rather than after, and believes that Beatrice was trying to ensure that the marriage would be (like that of Tess and Angel) a miserable one. Her delay was, in fact, caused by selflessness, wanting to ensure there would be no obstacle to the marriage, and André is, in fact, unworried by the revelation of Sonia's past: he tears up the letter and goes happily to join her, leaving Beatrice humiliated. But Sonia already knows of the delay in delivering her letter, fears the worst, and has drunk poison.

This strong melodramatic situation is powerfully exploited in a passage of crosscutting that opens with Sonia (Julanne Johnston) looking in desperation into her mirror (fig. 1.37). From this point it runs for thirty-four shots and four intertitles. She picks up the phial of poison. Cut to the bitter exchange between André and Beatrice, six alternating shots and the title "I am going to Sonia." Back to Sonia, drinking the poison. Cut to the wedding guests, wishing "Long life and happiness to the bride." Back to Sonia, still the same set-up (fig. 1.37), a boldly protracted shot of nearly one minute as the poison slowly takes effect. Enter André, tearing up the letter: four alternating shots as she sees him (figs. 1.38 and 1.39). Then she collapses, he runs to catch her and grieves over her body (fig. 1.40), promising revenge (fig. 1.43) on the shattered Beatrice (fig. 1.44). Finally, back to the unsuspecting guests, raising their glasses in a toast to the bride and groom (fig. 1.45).

The flow of narrative has been skillfully intercut with detail

Figures
1.37–1.45.
Sonia's
death and its
aftermath in
*The Prude's
Fall* (Graham
Cutts, 1925;
Gainsborough
Pictures).
(Courtesy
of the BFI
National
Archive)

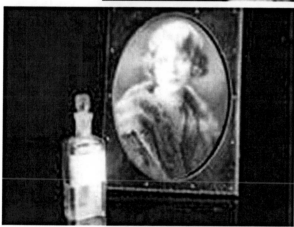

"I will avenge you, Sonia —
I will never rest until I have
made Beatrice pay, and suffer."

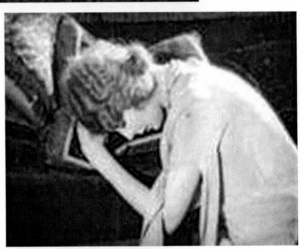

shots, including pieces of the torn-up letter fluttering to the ground; André's point-of-view shot (fig. 1.41) of the photo of Beatrice that we have already seen adjacent to Sonia in figure 1.39; and, as Sonia dies, a brief shot of a roulette wheel coming to a halt at zero (fig. 1.42).

The wheel is evidently not an arbitrary symbol: there is a further shot of a roulette wheel later in the film, and it seems certain that it must be echoing images from Sonia's "gambling den" past in the earlier scenes that are now lost. Even without this context, the way it is used recalls the shot of the gramophone record coming to an end in the scene illustrated (fig. 1.9) from the FPLB production *The Man from Home,* creating a neat link between the first surviving film and the final film of Hitchcock's career before *The Pleasure Garden.* It feels as if, in this high-intensity passage within a failed film, he is extending his grasp of the expressive use of visual motifs, and of crosscutting for emotion and for suspense, in preparation for his imminent move into directing in his own right. Perhaps he was still learning from Graham Cutts; perhaps, as he and his wife would claim decades later, he was already in effect acting as director; perhaps the crucial work of shaping the sequence was done by Adrian Brunel as part of the remedial work that Balcon organized and that Hitchcock acknowledged. Whatever the precise interplay between the three men's input, we can be grateful that the sequence is not lost but survives as a marker of the cinematic place that Hitchcock was coming from in 1925.

It is now widely accepted that Hitchcock owed much to Cutts's near-contemporary, Eliot Stannard, his regular screenwriter on the nine films from *The Pleasure Garden* to *The Manxman.* For a long time Stannard, who died in 1944, was forgotten, and Hitchcock never talked about him; but his writings about the medium of cinema were there, waiting to be rediscovered, and they turned out to be a revelation—expressing ideas, from 1918 onward, that often unmistakably anticipate Hitchcock's own dicta and practice.[30] It can be argued that Hitchcock must, likewise, have learned from Graham Cutts, who did not, like Stannard, leave a legacy of articles, but who gave some interesting interviews and made some imaginative films, not only during the collaboration with Hitchcock but before and after it as well. *The*

Rat (1925), his first post-Hitchcock film, attracted a lot of attention for its innovative use of a restlessly moving camera at the expense of conventional cutting, and Cutts, on the set, spoke of this technique with an articulate enthusiasm that curiously anticipates Hitchcock's discussion of the rather more extreme nonediting strategy of *Rope* (1948). Might Hitchcock have taken note of the film and the interviews and stored the memory away, to be drawn on later?[31]

Suggestions like this, and arguments for the importance to him of men like Cutts and Stannard, are sometimes resented on Hitchcock's behalf, as if he were thus being disparaged and diminished. This is a misreading. One has constantly to revert to Jane Sloan's visionary metaphor for how Hitchcock operated: as, essentially, a *sponge*. More purposefully, more thoroughly, and more productively than anyone else of his generation, he soaked up data, both theoretical and practical, about filmmaking, digested and processed them, and used them with supreme assurance over the decades in his own practice.

In his youth working in silent cinema in Britain, he soaked up whatever was around, from his viewing and reading and from his work with, successively, Famous Players-Lasky, Cutts, and Stannard—and from many others, not least Alma Reville. A reading of the trade papers from his early years—and we know that Hitchcock did read those papers assiduously—throws up other interesting names, such as that of Henry Edwards, a British actor and director, few of whose films survive. There is no evidence that Hitchcock knew him, let alone worked with him, though they may have run across each other at the Kinema Club during the three years of its existence. But Edwards even before that had published an article in *The Bioscope* (1 July 1920) devoted entirely to a discussion of the contrast between "surprise" and "suspense" in film narrative and arguing in favor of the latter—an argument that would later become very familiar, in precisely those terms, in Hitchcock's own discourse. At another time, Edwards set out an argument in favor of minimizing intertitles; to test out his theory, he made a feature film, *Lily of the Alley* (1923), that eliminated them altogether, thus anticipating by a year the strategy of Murnau in *The Last Laugh,* which Hitchcock always named as a major influence.

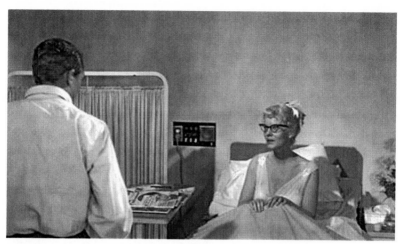

Figure 1.46. Cary Grant and Patricia Cutts in *North by Northwest* (1959; MGM). (© Loew's Incorporated)

In short, a study of Hitchcock's early years in the industry reveals not only a number of rediscovered or hitherto neglected films, or fragments of films, but a lively film culture, British as well as American, that helped in a variety of ways to shape his ideas as he progressed to becoming a director.

On Cutts and Hitchcock, there are two puzzling footnotes. First, Hitchcock claimed to have employed Cutts in the mid-1930s to do some insert shots on *The 39 Steps* (1935), feeling embarrassment, but agreeing in order to do him a much-needed favor. Anthony Slide, in his entry on Cutts in Brian McFarlane's *Encyclopedia of British Film,* says that "if it is true, it is a pathetic end to a notable career." Yet it would hardly have been the end of his career, since he went on to direct several more features. Slide describes Cutts, incidentally, as "without question, the finest of the country's directors in the 20s," thus rating him above Hitchcock.[32]

Second, Graham Cutts died in England in September 1958. Early in 1959, Hitchcock was shooting studio scenes for *North by Northwest* in Hollywood and employed Cutts's daughter, Patricia, in a tiny part. She had worked in British cinema, and briefly in Hollywood, but her film career petered out by the end of the 1950s and she returned to Britain, taking a role in the long-running TV serial *Coronation Street*. Her appearance near the end of *North by Northwest* is brief but memorable. Cary Grant, escaping from confinement in his quest to foil the enemy agents and save the heroine, leaves his hospital room via the window, inches his way along the outside ledge, and enters through another window. The woman occupant, sitting up in her bed in alarm, calls out "Stop!," takes a closer look at the man, and says "Stop" in an altogether different tone of voice (fig. 1.46). One has to wonder whether Hitchcock was even aware of the actress's identity, or if, conversely, he was extremely aware of it, and giving some sort of veiled acknowledgment to his collaborator of a third of a century ago, via another trademark *entry through a window* (as in *The Passionate Adventure*) that confronts one of the major stars of all time, briefly, with a minor actress in decline—and which thus in turn plays out a farewell from the great director at the peak of his career to the man who has just died in obscurity. With Hitchcock, you never know.

2

The Early 1930s

The beginning of the 1930s was an uncertain transitional time for Hitchcock, as for cinema generally—adjusting to the multiple challenges of the new synchronized sound format and also starting to be aware of the developing medium of television. The transition stage effectively begins in 1929, when British cinema commits itself to talkies, and to the radical and expensive changes they necessitate in production and exhibition.

In the list that follows, the eight films with an asterisk are all credited unproblematically to Hitchcock as director. The other six are films with which he was either definitely or allegedly involved, in subsidiary capacities.

1929 *The Manxman**
1929 *Blackmail**
1930 *Juno and the Paycock**
1930 *Harmony Heaven*
1930 *An Elastic Affair*
1930 Baird Television
1930 *Elstree Calling*
1930 *Murder!**
1930 *Mary**
1931 *Let's Go Bathing!*

1931 *The Skin Game**
1931 *Rich and Strange**
1932 *Number Seventeen**
1932 *Lord Camber's Ladies*

There are various "lost and found" elements here, which need to be seen in the context of the upheavals of the time as they affected British International Pictures (BIP) in particular. Hitchcock had joined the company from Gainsborough in 1927; *Number Seventeen* was the last film he directed for them before he moved to Gaumont-British, and then to a renewed collaboration with Michael Balcon, who had launched his directing career with *The Pleasure Garden* (1926).

Blackmail (1929)

Hitchcock's last all-silent film, *The Manxman*, had only limited exposure, being completed just at the point when decisions were being made to convert to dialogue production. Unlike many silent films of the late 1920s, it was not recalled to have talkie scenes added but was effectively stranded, seeming instantly out of date. Hitchcock always dismissed it as a failure, and this may have persuaded him to drop his regular screenwriter, Eliot Stannard, as being an accomplice in the failure, or simply as someone identified with a directing apprenticeship from which he was ready to move on.

In contrast, the triumph of *Blackmail* is well known. Hitchcock began shooting it as a silent adaptation of the play by Charles Bennett, but he was shrewd enough to anticipate the instruction to add dialogue to the final reels, contriving to shoot two versions of most scenes and thus to spread dialogue passages throughout the whole narrative: it was released as a 90 percent talkie, soon changed by promotional sleight of hand to a less-than-accurate 100 percent. It had a major commercial and critical success in Britain, and in the *Film Weekly* poll for the best British film of 1930 gained more than three times as many votes as any other title. (Although *Film Weekly* had close ties to BIP, the previous year's winner had been a Gainsborough film, *The Constant Nymph,* directed by Adrian Brunel and coscripted by Alma Reville.)

There were alternative versions of *Blackmail,* the main one being all-silent. Many cinemas, especially in suburbs and the provinces, were slow to convert to sound, and silent versions of certain new films were for a time supplied to them. Since *Blackmail* had been planned and shot as a silent, this was no problem; after the spectacular launch of the sound version, the silent one started unobtrusively to do the rounds. For decades subsequently, this film was effectively lost, never shown and virtually forgotten, but it did survive in the archives, and the British Film Institute (BFI) produced a viewing copy in the early 1980s. Since then, it has become reasonably well known: never as prominent as the sound version, but regularly screened with live musical accompaniment, and critically studied. So it would be redundant to go over this same ground here.

Less familiar are the cut-down versions of the film that circulated at the time. The future director Thorold Dickinson visited New York at the end of 1929 and wrote a report for the January 1930 issue of *Picturegoer* magazine on the way in which American cinema and American audiences were responding to the sound revolution. After discussion of films including *Hallelujah!* (King Vidor) and *Applause* (Rouben Mamoulian), he noted that *Blackmail* was already playing in New York but had been "shortened by the removal of the prologue." This must indicate the cutting of the whole of the first reel, the elaborate nondialogue section of nearly ten minutes documenting police procedure as a suspect is brought in from his East End home, charged, and locked up. American audiences were considered to be too impatient to wait for the first dialogue scene. This will have made for an abrupt start, and the loss of the careful symmetry of the original, in which the prologue is pointedly and precisely reprised in the extended nondialogue hunting down of another suspect, the blackmailer. As late as 2013, impatience was still evident: at a double-bill screening in Los Angeles of the silent *Blackmail* and then of the sound one, many of those in the audience walked out during the first reel of the former, in advance of the first dialogue.[1]

Dickinson reported in 1930 that the public, though interested by

Figure 2.1. U.S. advertisement for *Blackmail* (1929). *New York Times*, 6 October 1929.

the film, still seemed to find it "slow in development." Advertising exploited the sensational element more boldly than had been done in England (fig. 2.1). Elsewhere this sensational element was itself the problem: specifically, the long scene in the upstairs studio, culminating in sexual assault by the artist and then Alice's killing of him in self-defense. The Irish censor banned the film altogether, before an appeal board reluctantly let it through in a cut form; the same thing happened in Australia.[2]

Of course, in all three countries the full original version now circulates freely in DVD form, but the cut versions are in a sense "lost" ones—though easy to find again if anyone cares to do some do-it-yourself editing, chopping off the whole of the opening, or the whole of the studio scene.

Juno and the Paycock (1930)

The history of *Juno and the Paycock* is in some ways comparable to that of *Blackmail,* involving controversies and altered versions. There is no evidence of any alternative silent version, even though Hitchcock had been interested in filming Sean O'Casey's play about a Dublin family ever since he first saw and admired it in London in 1924. He had already made a silent film of Noël Coward's very talky play *Easy Virtue* (Gainsborough, 1927), so why not *Juno* likewise? However, there were delays, and instead it became an attractive subject for his first 100 percent sound feature, so dominated by dialogue that any back-up silent version would have been hardly practicable.

The film was well received at the time by critics and public in England. Its staginess and talkiness, dictated largely by the crudity of early recording technology, were no deterrent, given the strong attraction of the novelty of the speaking voice, but these qualities soon made it seem dated, and it is now little valued and rarely revived. In Ireland it was less well received even then. In more conservatively Catholic areas beyond Dublin itself, the stage play had been edited to tone down the language and to eliminate the extramarital pregnancy of the daughter of the family, Mary. The film, however, was unexpurgated, and after condemnation by priests it was seized from the projection box in Limerick and burned in the streets.[3]

Already in England, but for different reasons, the film had been cut after its initial screenings, and there is a "lost" ending, missing at least from prints that now circulate. When the film was first shown in London, the *Daily News* critic (31 December 1929) wrote, "I am glad the director has had the courage to retain the cynical ending of the drunken men." For *Kine Weekly*, however, "the return of the husband drunk comes as rather an anti-climax." When the film reached Scotland soon afterward, this had been cut: a very positive review in the *Glasgow Evening Times* (9 January 1930) noted, "Much of the humour of the 'Paycock' and 'Joxer' is lost in the film; indeed the last scene of the stage play has been entirely cut, and thus the new version ends on a tragic note." Reviews in the English papers of Sunday, 5 January, seem to indicate that the cut had already been made by then—in other words, almost immediately after the first screenings.

All surviving prints of the film known to us have the "tragic note" ending: Juno lamenting the death of her son, in front of the figure of the Virgin Mary. But there does survive, in the New York State Library at Albany, a script with the original ending, based quite closely on the play's final scene, which follows on from the lament. The New York censors required full scripts to be deposited with them to help them in their deliberations, a policy that explains the richness of the script collection held by the library. *The 39 Steps* (1935) likewise had a final scene that was scripted and shot but was cut out at an early stage, perhaps even before the first screenings; that final scene is included in the script that was submitted to New York but has been firmly crossed out. The fact that the final scene of *Juno* is *not* crossed out may well mean that it remained part of the American release version, at least initially, and perhaps that version does somewhere survive. This, anyway, is the ending in the Albany script, the fragmented nature of the prose constituting an attempt at a close transcription of the scene as played by Edward Chapman and Sidney Morgan:

JUNO: . . . . Blessed Virgin, where were you when me darlin'
     son was riddled with bullets, when me darlin' son was

riddled with bullets? Sacred heart of Jesus, take away our
hearts of stone, and give us hearts of flesh! Take away
this murthering hate, and give us thine own eternal love!

BOYLE: I'm able to go no farther . . . two polis, ay . . . what
were they doin' here I wonder . . . up to no good anyhow.
Won single solitary tanner left out of all I borreyed

JOXER: Put all . . . your troubles . . . in your oul' kit bag . . .
an' smile, smile, smile

BOYLE: The counthry'll have to steady itself . . . it's goin'
to—where'r all the chairs gone to?—steady itself. . . . Joxer
. . . chairs'll have to . . . steady themselves . . . no matter
what anyone may say . . . Irelan' sober is Irelan' free

JOXER: Chairs an' slaveree . . . that's a darlin'. . . . a darlin'
. . . motto

BOYLE: I'm tellin' you . . . Joxer . . . th' whole world . . . in a
terr . . . ible state o' chassis

Hitchcock's next film, *Murder!,* which, like *Juno,* he coscripted
with Alma, had its first showing eight months later, in August 1930.
Before that, he was linked with four other projects, each of them
somewhat mysterious.

Harmony Heaven (1930)

This early British musical, produced at BIP early in 1930, seems an
entirely phantom entry in the Hitchcock filmography. It is listed in
different editions of the François Truffaut interview book *Hitchcock*
as being directed by him in 1930, and others have followed this. However, the print credits Thomas Bentley as director, with no mention
of Hitchcock, nor have we found anything in contemporary British
trade papers, or indeed in the film itself, that hints at his involvement.[4]
Nevertheless, *Harmony Heaven* was screened in full at the Museum
of Modern Art in New York as part of the Hitchcock centenary retrospective, on 2 May 1999.

The explanation for the phantom credit seems to be that Hitchcock had been announced as director in advance, either by accident or

by design, before the schedule was adjusted. Interviewed much later by Peter Bogdanovich, he seemed genuinely bewildered by the mention of this title. The BIP management may have enjoyed playing off their bright young director against an experienced journeyman in the published schedules, partly out of genuine uncertainty at this uncertain time, partly just to keep him in his place. In 1932, they would once more play Hitchcock off against Bentley, switching Bentley at a late stage to direct the adaptation of John van Druten's play *London Wall* (renamed *After Office Hours*), which Hitchcock had been keen to make, and leaving him instead with what he saw, or at least claimed to see, as the chore of filming *Number Seventeen*. Meanwhile he was having to fulfill some more modest BIP commitments.

An Elastic Affair (1930)

The first listing of this title appears to be in Denis Gifford's thoroughly researched *British Film Catalogue,* published in 1973; other sources have followed suit, including *Film Dope* magazine, the online Film Index International, and the Internet Movie Database. Hitchcock is credited as director of a one-reel comedy showcasing Aileen Despard and Cyril Butcher, winners of a talent competition mounted, in collaboration with BIP, by the magazine *Film Weekly,* which gave extensive publicity to the competition and its aftermath. The two winners were chosen from several thousand applicants; they won £250 each plus that initial role in *An Elastic Affair* and six months of full-time work at the BIP studio, learning the trade and picking up some parts here and there.

What can we learn about the film and Hitchcock's connection with it? He was definitely involved in judging the competition, as the coverage from *Film Weekly* early in 1930 indicates (fig. 2.2). It may be that Gifford ascribed the direction of *An Elastic Affair* to Hitchcock simply on the evidence of this picture. But clearly someone at BIP did direct it, and it could perfectly well have been Hitchcock; the case of *Elstree Calling,* soon after, would show that he was available, even if perhaps reluctantly, to do bits and pieces of work around the studio in the gaps of preparing his own next big project. Moreover, he would

TESTING "F.W.'s" SCHOLARSHIP FINALISTS

Screen and microphone tests have now been made at the British International Studios at Elstree of the Finalists in "F.W.'s" Screen Scholarships. The names of the two successful competitors will be announced in our issue of January 18, and their contracts will be publicly presented to them at the London Palladium on Sunday, January 19. (Above) the Finalists and (Left) the Editor of FILM WEEKLY and Alfred Hitchcock with one of the competitors.

Figure 2.2. Talent competition publicity photos in *Film Weekly,* 4 January 1930. Winners Cyril Butcher and Aileen Despard are at the extreme right of the group; in the second photo, Despard is between the editor and Hitchcock. (Courtesy of the Cinema Museum, London)

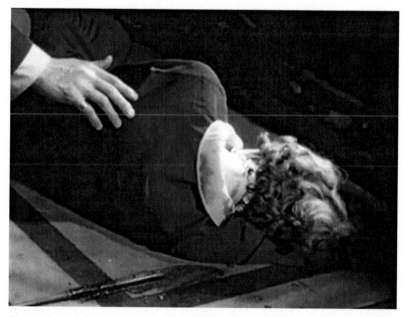

Figure 2.3. Aileen Despard as the dead Edna Druce in *Murder!* (1930; British International Pictures)—a role she retains in the German version of the film, *Mary.* (Courtesy of the BFI National Archive)

use Despard in *Murder!* in a tiny and uncredited but indispensable role: she plays the murder victim, the corpse (Edna Druce) discovered at the film's opening (fig. 2.3).

This casting was revealed on 3 May by *Film Weekly*'s regular columnist Nerina Shute, whose lines are typical of the paper's upbeat coverage of its two trainees:

Aileen Improves

AILEEN DESPARD, the FILM WEEKLY girl, becomes more attractive than ever. When she first won her acting scholarship, the only fault I could find was a certain shyness and reserve. It made her seem cold. But already she has conquered it, and the reason, I think, is that she is taking acting lessons from Madame Novello-Davies, Ivor Novello's brilliant mother. . . .

Aileen has been busy, just lately, smearing herself with jam, or blood, or something, in order to look like a corpse. She plays the part of "body" (it's the only word) in "Enter Sir John" [the working title of *Murder!* was that of the novel it was based on]. But quite shortly she and Cyril Butcher, the FILM WEEKLY boy, will appear in important parts in a picture to be made by Alexander Esway. Aileen tells me that she gets quite a lot of fan letters.

The film referred to here is Esway's *Children of Chance,* shown in late 1930. Before long, both would drift away from films altogether. Despard married a doctor and devoted herself to their family; Butcher became the long-term partner of celebrity author Beverley Nichols.

Their debut film, *An Elastic Affair,* was given some early high-profile screenings, which may have been the only ones: in London, and then in Ipswich, Butcher's hometown. On 19 January, at a charity film show at the London Palladium,

they received an enthusiastic reception from a crowded audience which contained many filmgoers and many important film personalities [Hitchcock perhaps included?].

They appeared on the screen in a short sketch entitled "An Elastic Affair," and proved that they possessed undoubted acting ability which only needs the development which their exhaustive training will give them. Owing to the fact that the London Palladium has no talkie installation the film was silent, but the audience was able to judge the quality of their voices when they spoke from the stage following the presentation of their contracts.

This report in *Film Weekly* (25 January) noted that Despard would make a second personal appearance on the day of the issue's publication, after a screening of the film in the program of the Rialto cinema in central London. She would be introduced to the audience by Donald Calthrop—another Hitchcock link, since he is prominent in three of the director's films for BIP around this time, *Blackmail*, *Murder!*, and *Number Seventeen*, as well as in the part-Hitchcock *Elstree Calling*.

There had also been publicity in the *Surrey Comet*, local paper for Despard's home in Surbiton, but there is no evidence of a local screening. However, there was compensation for this in Ipswich. For the full week of Monday, 27 January, the film was screened in support of the all-talkie *The Letter* (Jean De Limur, 1929), as advertised in the *East Anglian Daily Times* (fig. 2.4). The issue of Saturday, 25 January, had given a full report of an initial screening on the previous evening, introduced by Butcher. This is the nearest we can get—pending a rediscovery—to a sense of what the film was like:

An elegant young man, with dark, wavy hair presented himself. Just previously he had been shown in a four-minute film with Miss Aileen Despard, the successful girl candidate. Here, he exhibited an unaffected natural poise. There was restraint and grace about his movements; mobile features and penetratingly dark eyes were eloquently expressive. He knew what to do with his hands. And yet there was an indefinable air of amateurism, although it is but fair to say that this may have been suggested to the mind by the knowledge of

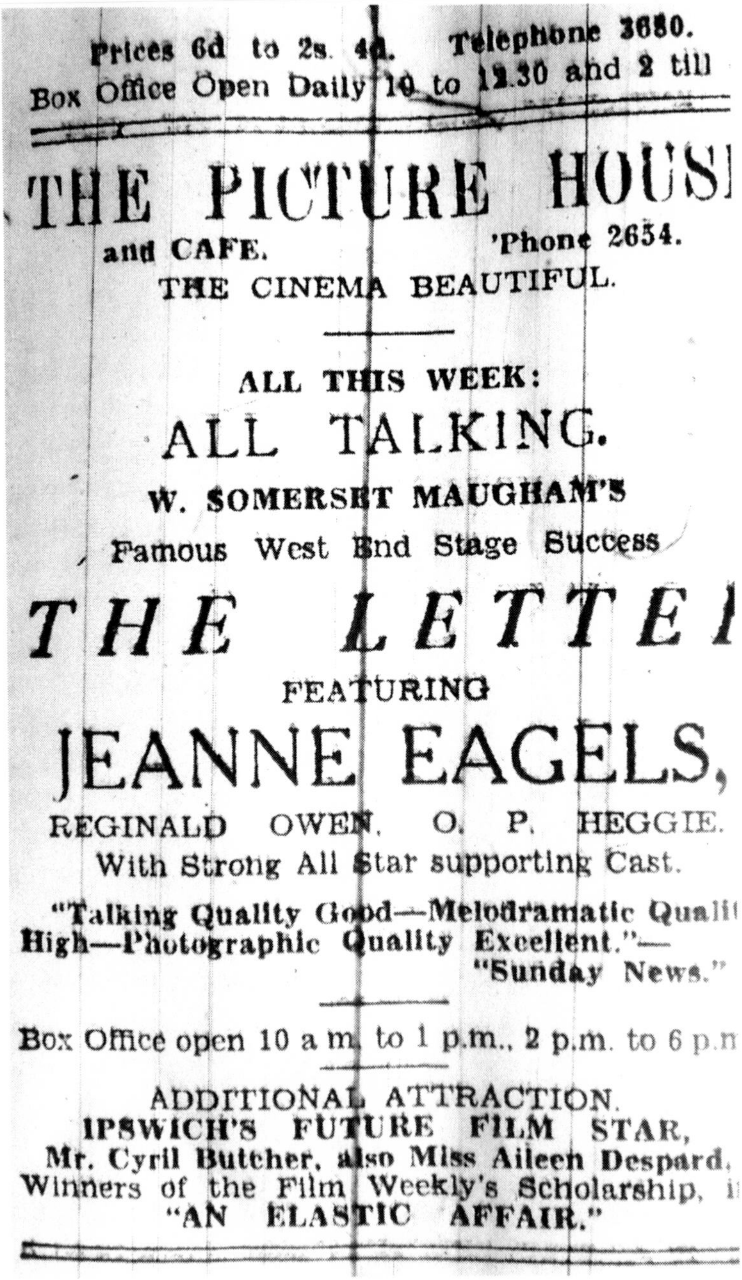

Prices 6d to 2s. 4d. Telephone 3680.
Box Office Open Daily 10 to 12.30 and 2 till

THE PICTURE HOUS

and CAFE. 'Phone 2654.
THE CINEMA BEAUTIFUL.

ALL THIS WEEK:
ALL TALKING.
W. SOMERSET MAUGHAM'S
Famous West End Stage Success

THE LETTE

FEATURING
JEANNE EAGELS,
REGINALD OWEN, O. P. HEGGIE.
With Strong All Star supporting Cast.

"Talking Quality Good—Melodramatic Quali
High—Photographic Quality Excellent."—
"Sunday News."

Box Office open 10 a.m. to 1 p.m., 2 p.m. to 6 p.n

ADDITIONAL ATTRACTION.
IPSWICH'S FUTURE FILM STAR,
Mr. Cyril Butcher, also Miss Aileen Despard,
Winners of the Film Weekly's Scholarship, i
"AN ELASTIC AFFAIR."

Figure 2.4. Advertisement showing *An Elastic Affair* (1930) billed as support film. *East Anglian Daily Times*, 27 January 1930. (Courtesy of Suffolk County Library)

Mr Butcher's comparative inexperience and youth—he is just 20 years old. Immediately he began to speak from the platform it was obvious that, as had been stated, he had been chosen from the thousands of competitors as much for his voice and elocution as for his appearance. "I only want to thank you for tolerating this picture," he began, easily, clearly and resonantly. "I hope to do something better," he confided, with assurance. And, then, as a commentary on the somewhat insipid nature of the playlet just screened, he added, explosively, "something with some—er—guts in it." (Laughter)

So the film was evidently four minutes long rather than ten, not even a full reel, and silent; unlike the London Palladium, the Ipswich Picture House could have played out a soundtrack, since it was wired for sound, as the newspaper advert confirms, and had recently shown the talkie version of *Blackmail*. Assuming that Hitchcock did direct it, it was evidently not much more elaborate than the kind of screen test that he would sometimes shoot in later years in Hollywood.

Baird Television (1930)

If *An Elastic Affair* is a seemingly lost 1930 item from BIP, we have an unexpected find from that same company and that same year. In 1959 the BFI's archive received from Associated British Pictures Corporation (ABPC), direct descendant of BIP, a mysterious piece of film featuring Seymour Hicks—the same actor who had enlisted the then unknown Hitchcock to help complete his comedy *Always Tell Your Wife* in 1923. It seems possible that the archive will have received other old bits and pieces from ABPC/BIP, as yet unidentified, and if so these could conceivably include *An Elastic Affair*. In this surviving item, Hicks introduces, or purports to introduce, the first ever television screening of a talking film, one directed by Hitchcock. He speaks straight to camera; after a time, the image abruptly improves in quality, without any change in angle (figs. 2.5 and 2.6).

Figures 2.5–2.6. TV item featuring Seymour Hicks (1930; British International Pictures). (Courtesy of the BFI National Archive)

These are his words:

Good Evening, Ladies and Gentlemen. Delighted to see you. Here you are and here I am. . . .

I'm terribly excited tonight, I hope you are; as a matter of fact you ought to be, you know, because we're all of us assisting at an epoch-making event. It's the first talking film to be televised in the history of the world. Think of that. And it is all British. Cheers from all parts of the house. It's a film, I may tell you, Ladies and Gentlemen, that's been made by British International Pictures and has been directed by our greatest producer, Mr. Alfred Hitchcock. And it's being transmitted from the Baird Television Company's studio in Long Acre, London, England. Well, Ladies and Gentlemen, I have been asked by Mr. Hitchcock—well, I was requested—well, as a matter of fact, I was *ordered* by Mr. Hitchcock—to tell you a few stories . . .

He goes on to tell some rushed and unfunny stories, still without any cutaway or change of angle. There is no lead-in to even the opening of a film, nor is the film named.

The film stock dates from 1930, the year in which the Baird Television Company, from its studio in Long Acre, made some well-publicized experimental broadcasts to audiences at the Coliseum Theatre—daily for a fortnight, starting on Monday, 28 July. It is tempting to assign it to one of those broadcasts, but there are problems. None of the reports of the two weeks of trial broadcasts includes any reference to Hicks or to Hitchcock, or to any feature film; a long film could hardly have been fitted in, though of course Hicks's words could refer to a short extract from a talkie like *Blackmail,* or to a specially shot bit of talking film. Also, there is no way that this footage of Hicks could actually have been generated from a TV camera of the time; even the initial image is of too high a quality, and the technique of telerecording the TV's camera image onto film was in any case still far in the future. It could, however, be prefilmed footage, shot in such a way as to mimic the simple TV image, transmitted on the day via telecine; TV was already able to transmit the film image by this system. So we could be witnessing prefilmed footage, *possibly* directed by Hitchcock, of Hicks introducing some kind of film *definitely* directed by Hitchcock—the new gimmick being simply that all of the film material was being transmitted via telecine from Long Acre to the Coliseum rather than being screened from the cinema's projection booth. If it was not part of the Coliseum fortnight, it could have been another form of experimental transmission, sometime in 1930, to a smaller audience at a private screening.

From the Hitchcock angle it is tantalizing not to know more about the episode—what film of his was being screened, how much input he had overall—but it does underline two significant points. One is his interest in new technologies, already evident in the radio scenes of *The Pleasure Garden* and *The Lodger* (both 1926), and to be confirmed in his early commitment to regular television production in the United States in the 1950s, in advance of any of his contemporaries. The second is his readiness at this time to get involved in a variety of tasks to oblige his employers, as in the business of the talent contest— and also the BIP feature of early 1930, *Elstree Calling*, which itself displays a fascination with the still-primitive television medium; it would almost certainly have preceded the Hicks broadcast.

Elstree Calling (1930)

The film *Elstree Calling* itself has never been lost; what has remained missing is firm evidence of what exactly Hitchcock contributed to it. It has sometimes been marketed, in the United States at least, entirely on Hitchcock's name, both at the time of its release and since. But his credit is a subsidiary one: "Sketches and other interpolated items" (fig. 2.7).

The question of what Hitchcock actually did on this production— a collection of comedy and musical items, a British equivalent of films like *Hollywood Revue of 1929*—remains one of the most obscure issues in his career. What is beyond dispute is that Adrian Brunel planned and shot most of the film but was removed from it at a late stage by the BIP management, who then called upon Hitchcock for

Figure 2.7. Opening credits for *Elstree Calling* (1930; British International Pictures). (Courtesy of the BFI National Archive)

some repair work. To interviewers, Hitchcock routinely dismissed his contribution as being brief, marginal, and (speaking to Truffaut) "of no interest whatever," giving no details and thus allowing commentators a free hand to assess where his input might be detected.[5]

The American critic James Vest goes as far as to claim, in the *Hitchcock Annual* for 2000–2001, that he is likely to have directed "well over one-fourth of the film"—using the familiar kind of argument that (a) anything of any merit or interest must surely be attributable to Hitchcock, and (b) various elements can be identified as "Hitchcockian" by linking them to work that he did before and/or after. The case he makes is ingenious, but he considers neither the documented evidence (not all of which, to be fair, was available at the time he was writing) nor the track record of others who were involved, even that of the credited director, whom we have met before. Although his career declined after 1930, Brunel can hardly be dismissed as an unambitious hack. *The Constant Nymph,* which he directed for Gainsborough in 1928, preceded *Blackmail* as British

Film of the Year in the poll of *Film Weekly* readers; one of those credited for the script was Alma Reville.

Leaving aside the extravagant additional claims made by Vest, there are three main elements in the film that critics have attributed to Hitchcock. The first is a series of brief scenes in which a "ham" (Gordon Harker) tries to pick up, on his primitive home receiver, pictures of the show that is being transmitted from Elstree in vision as well as in sound; he manages to find brief glimpses of the compère (Tommy Handley) but nothing of the show itself (fig. 2.8). His six short comic scenes add up to less than three minutes of running time and are likely to have been shot in quick succession in a single day. Hitchcock had worked with Harker on three recent BIP films (*The Ring* [1927], *The Farmer's Wife* [1928], and *Champagne* [1928]), and with Hannah Jones, who plays his wife, on two (*Champagne* and *Blackmail*); and he had already shown an interest in the mechanics of broadcast technology in both *The Pleasure Garden* and *The Lodger*. So there is a plausible case. The authorized biography by John Russell Taylor names this element as Hitchcock's one contribution, and Jane Sloan, in her comprehensive filmography, follows him.[6]

The second element is "The Wrong Flat" (the title used in publicity posters), the film's most self-contained sketch and the only section of it, apart from the framing scenes with Harker, not to have a theatrical setting (fig. 2.9). Again, screen time is brief, less than two minutes. A man enters a strange flat to shoot his wife and her lover, only to find, too late, that he has come to the wrong place. This recalls the "twist" endings of some of the short stories Hitchcock wrote for his company magazine even before he entered films, and in turn looks ahead to the many twist endings in his TV show launched in 1955, *Alfred Hitchcock Presents*.[7] "The Wrong Flat" uses familiar Hitchcock actors, Jameson Thomas from *The Farmer's Wife* and John Longden from *Blackmail*, while the uncredited woman is a look-alike of Longden's *Blackmail* fiancée, Anny Ondra. So again a case can be made. The otherwise negative review of the film in *The Sunday Times* (9 February 1930) by Sydney Carroll singled out this sketch: "The item that appealed to me most was a little thriller arranged by Mr Hitchcock."

Third is a strand in which another Hitchcock player, Donald

Figures
2.8–2.10.
Three sections
of *Elstree
Calling*
(1930; British
International
Pictures) that
are commonly
attributed to
Hitchcock: a
rare moment
of successful
TV reception;
the adulterous
couple in
"The Wrong
Flat"; Donald
Calthrop
struggling to
fit in some
Shakespeare.
(Courtesy
of the BFI
National
Archive)

Calthrop (*Blackmail,* and subsequently *Murder!* and *Number Seventeen*), has a more sustained role, as an actor determined to insert some Shakespeare into the revue (fig. 2.10). After popping up a few times and being snubbed, he eventually succeeds with a recitation of lines from *Hamlet* and *Henry V*—simultaneously performing magic tricks in order to sugar the cultural pill—and then a slapstick burlesque of *The Taming of the Shrew,* made topical by the recent Douglas Fairbanks–Mary Pickford film adaptation. As Petruchio, he is pelted with custard pies by Anna May Wong, who happened to be over from Hollywood at the time on a BIP contract. This is the one item mentioned in Brunel's 1949 autobiography, *Nice Work,* as having been reshot by Hitchcock, and Anna May Wong is the one star of the film mentioned by Hitchcock in the interview with Bogdanovich, even though he does not explicitly state that he worked with her.

So how do we decide between these bits of evidence? Brunel's testimony, both in his book and in his papers held at the BFI, seems to establish beyond reasonable doubt that the Calthrop scenes, or at least their Petruchio climax, were reshot by Hitchcock. As for "The Wrong Flat," Brunel wrote a letter to Sydney Carroll in response to his negative review, protesting that his own overall concept had been vulgarized but not disputing the attribution of this sketch to Hitchcock—might he not otherwise have made the point that he himself had directed the item singled out by Carroll for praise?[8] As for the Harker scenes, Hitchcock could himself, if he chose, have contested his biographer's attribution to him of these and nothing else—but there were other elements in the book that he chose not to correct, and he may simply have wanted to suppress the memory of the film altogether.

Hitchcock, then, could plausibly have reshot any or all of these three elements of the *Elstree Calling* revue, but it is still hard to confirm the details. He told Bogdanovich dismissively that he recalled doing only one day's work on the film, and that he was just one of a number of Elstree directors to be enlisted, but there is no evidence of any additional film (as opposed to stage) director being involved. A crucial factor is one considered neither by Vest nor by other commentators: the personal and professional relationship between the two directors, which went back many years. When Balcon, several times, called in Brunel, and later his colleague Ivor Montagu, to supply help or advice, Hitchcock was treated tactfully and kept fully informed. Now, at BIP, the roles were reversed: Hitchcock was abruptly brought in to do a repair job on Brunel's film, but neither he nor the studio informed Brunel, who was left to piece together the story of what had happened in painful retrospect. He plainly and understandably saw this as an act of betrayal by an old associate, and Hitchcock in turn must have felt guilty about going behind his back. Given his notorious hatred of confrontations, it seems entirely in character that he should have stayed silent about the whole episode both at the time and subsequently.

Seen in context, it is a complex story of two strong egos: a clash, not head-to-head but at a distance, between two innovative young men of British cinema who had begun to build a career in the 1920s. Brunel was seven years older and was active in the film business much earlier. When Hitchcock was struggling unsuccessfully in 1922 to complete *Number Thirteen,* Brunel had already gained distribution and friendly reviews for a number of comedy shorts of his own and was directing an ambitious first feature with Ivor Novello, *The Man without Desire.* He was one of the founder members in 1925 of the Film Society, which from time to time included his own short films in its program, and was busy, in addition, running a Soho company that specialized in film titling and editing. His partner in the company, Ivor Montagu, another Film Society pioneer, has an editing credit on *The Lodger* and worked on several later films with Hitchcock; Brunel was employed by Balcon at Gainsborough to supply intertitles for *The Blackguard* and *The Prude's Fall* (both Graham Cutts, 1925), as well as to attempt to salvage the latter film by re-editing. Writing to the producer of the former, Erich Pommer, in Berlin, Balcon explained: "Mr Brunel has been working for some time on the titles for the above mentioned production, first of all from the script when the picture was being finished, then with Mr Hitchcock on his return to England, and finally after the print arrived here. . . . Mr Brunel is not a title writer in the sense of the word (though he is the best man in England at this work)—he is a Film Director with an excellent reputation and is doing this work as a personal favour to me."[9] Throughout this period, Hitchcock remained on friendly terms with Brunel; a few months later he wrote him a chatty letter from Munich, mentioning that "I am very pleased to hear that the Prude's Fall has come out of your 'film hospital' a new being" (see fig. 1.23).[10]

Having so far been the junior partner, Hitchcock from that point quickly developed his career and his reputation. Brunel does not, unlike his associate Montagu, seem to have been involved in any of the five films Hitchcock went on to direct at Gainsborough; unlike Montagu, he was directing films of his own. Hitchcock then moved to BIP, starting with *The Ring,* and Brunel followed him there when invited to direct *Elstree Calling.*

Brunel's files on this film, held at the BFI, contain a lot in the way of scripts, letters, and memos. They show him buzzing with ideas about the staging of dance, music, and comedy, some of them better than others. Of particular interest is the planning of what ended up as the brief sketch "The Wrong Flat."[11] The script of 15 December 1929 includes this description: "Mr Adrian Brunel walks on and makes an announcement to the effect that Mr Alfred Hitchcock, the celebrated director, will direct a short sketch in three styles. He will be aided by Monty Banks and Jameson Thomas who will play the parts. The announcer then introduces Hitchcock to the audience and then walks out, leaving him on scene. Hitchcock starts giving instructions to Banks and Thomas and CUT TO . . . [*staging of the sketch, no details given*]." In a revised script of 30 December, this concept has been changed and much expanded. Brunel still appears in person, talking to a journalist interviewer about the differences between theater and cinema: he introduces "a little sketch as it would be done on the West End stage in the modern manner, and as it would be done by various directors on the screen." The initial script is very close to the sketch that we have in the film. After the punch line, "*Dash it!—the wrong flat,*" Brunel reappears and tells the journalist: "That's the way they produce a little sketch on the West End stage. Now to show you the extreme difference between the stage and the screen, I will produce the same sketch as Alfred Hitchcock, the famous English director, would produce it as a film." This time the setting is not a smart flat but "the staircase of a mean dwelling," and the couple is typed as Cockney.

> He: Don't forget you are my woman and if I catch you being bad with another fellow I'll knife him. Yes, I'd *knife* him swelp me [*sic*, "so help me"], knife him I would.
> She: Knife?
> He: Yes, knife!
> She: I call that a dirty way of committing a murder, besides which what about Scotland Yard?
> He: Huh, Scotland Yard? Who ever would have heard of Scotland Yard if it hadn't been for Alfred Hitchcock?

Suddenly they see something scary: "They both look out of picture and both hold scene in the well-known suspense device used by Mr Hitchcock as we cut to what they see." Sinister-looking shadows are revealed as being a trick of the light, and tension is released in laughter. But we then cut to the close-up of a heavy tread on the staircase and pull back to reveal an assassin—who, after shooting them both, exclaims, "*Blast! Damn! Dash!—the wrong landing.*"

Two more variants of the sketch follow, an early one-reel western version as directed by D. W. Griffith, and an Al Jolson version. These need not detain us, but the "Hitchcock" script is fascinating for the snapshot it gives of his status at this historical moment. The audience envisaged by Brunel will recognize two specific echoes of *Blackmail*: the repetition of the word "knife," and the Scotland Yard reference (adapted from the original line, spoken by Anny Ondra in the early scene at the café, to the effect that no one would have heard of the Yard if it weren't for Edgar Wallace). But they are also expected to associate Hitchcock—at this early stage in his career, when only two of his films, *The Lodger* and *Blackmail,* could be called Hitchcockian thrillers—with suspense and violence, as well as with the shot-reverse-shot construction.

Both the dates and the documents suggest that, like the Griffith and Jolson versions, this was never shot. Would Brunel have asked Hitchcock himself to shoot it? Had he obtained Hitchcock's agreement to appear in person, in the episode as originally scripted? No evidence on this has been found, but the script does in any case indicate an affectionate admiration for Hitchcock that would make his subsequent perceived betrayal all the more painful.

The final irony is that the version of "The Wrong Flat" that actually made it into the film corresponds to the script's account of "the way they produce a little sketch on the West End stage," as contrasted with the various cinematic versions, notably the Hitchcockian one; and this "West End stage" sketch has been widely credited to Hitchcock himself, starting with Carroll's contemporary review. Brunel was removed by BIP in early January 1930; he might by then have directed the initial sketch, though not the extravagant assortment of later versions. If he had not done so, presumably Hitchcock rapidly did it instead, leaving it as the stand-alone version that survives, and thus supporting Carroll's attribution.

Even at the end of December 1929, Brunel's script was tentative. It seems that the basic revue items had by now been shot: the bulk of the film, involving artistes like Lily Morris, Will Fyffe, Cicely Courtneidge, Jack Hulbert, Helen Burnell, and Teddy Brown. Brunel complained that his elaborate editing scheme for these items had not been honored, but his basic material remained. The more ambitious items, those that went beyond the recording of a preexisting stage act, still remained to be finalized in the December scripts: the multiversion "Wrong Flat" sketch, the Shakespeare thread, the framing sequence that plays with broadcasting technology. Not long after this, BIP management called a halt, for two reasons: wanting to get the film out quickly, and distrusting Brunel's fancy devices. As a contracted BIP director, Hitchcock was called in. Whatever by this time needed doing, he quickly did: *certainly* simplifying the Calthrop scenes, *probably* shooting the "Wrong Flat" sketch in the single basic version, and *very possibly* shooting at least some of the framing material. The on-screen credit for "Sketches and other interpolated items" certainly suggests something fairly substantial.

From early 1930, Brunel was frozen out by BIP: he was not invited to the film's première, and his offer to refine the editing for overseas versions was refused, as were his pleas for more work as director or writer. From this point, while Hitchcock's career went steadily ahead, Brunel became for the rest of the decade a director of cheap quota quickies, with not much to follow for the next two decades up to his death in 1958. There seems to have been little or no contact between the two men after *Elstree Calling*.

Our conclusion is that this is another instance of Hitchcock putting behind him an early associate in the British industry from whom he reckoned he now had nothing more to learn, and from whom he could move on: after Graham Cutts and Eliot Stannard, Adrian Brunel. He had blanked out the other two, and now he did the same with Brunel, pretending to have had nothing much to do with *Elstree Calling*, when in fact the episode had been so much more complicated.

Murder! and *Mary* (1930)

By the time *Elstree Calling* was in cinemas, Hitchcock was deep into the preparation of his own next feature film, *Murder!*, which was based on a novel and is bolder and less stagey than *Juno and the Paycock*. It too has a problematic ending; it also has a twin, *Mary*, a German version made by Hitchcock himself alongside the British one.

Mary is not exactly a lost film; it has been held in archives for a long time, but it remains little known and shown, and scarcely written about, and thus merits discussion here.[12] It is now available on a German DVD, and the BFI's screening print had English subtitles added for its inclusion in the big Hitchcock Retrospective of 2012.

Hitchcock was following a trend of the early sound period in making a bilingual production: two full separate versions, using the same story, the same sets, mainly the same camera setups, and often the same shots, but with two different casts, speaking their respective languages.[13] This multilingual trend continued sporadically for a few years, but he did not repeat the experience and always looked back on *Mary* as a failure. However, both versions of the film, like the sound and silent versions of *Blackmail*, bear his signature as director, and the relation of the two cannot fail to be of interest, both as a relic of that multilingual moment and as another instance of Hitchcock's pragmatic ingenuity—even though he was clearly not as urgently engaged by the instant remake of *Murder!* as he was by that of *Blackmail.* The pattern is set from the start: (1) establishing shots of a street at night, identical in both versions; (2) an elaborate lateral tracking shot alongside the outside of a building, as sleepers are awakened by commotion below and open the window to look down and react—*Mary* repeats the camera movement but substitutes German actors and speech; (3) variation of business, as the Markham couple (renamed Brown in *Mary*) prepares to go down and investigate. In *Murder!,* the stage-manager husband speaks indistinctly, then he puts his dentures in, and at once his words become clear; *Mary* has no equivalent. His actress wife struggles to get dressed: in *Murder!* she hops about and gets both feet stuck in the same leg of her underwear; in *Mary* she just puts on stockings. Then back to mode 2, with the discovery of the murdered Edna Druce, the tableau being restaged with the German cast, apart from one actor who is common to both (figs. 2.11 and 2.12).

These three basic strategies will run through the film: identical shots, straight restaging, and variation. The dressing scene is typical of many of the variations in being comic; Hitchcock found that much of the humor both of action and of treatment did not work in German, partly because of cultural differences, partly because of his own limitations. As he told Truffaut, "Many touches that were quite funny in the English version were not at all amusing in the German one. . . . I came to realize that I simply didn't know enough about the German idiom."[14]

Some of these "touches," like the dentures and the underwear, were changed or dropped; others were retained, with awkward results. Immediately after the murder is discovered, Mrs. Markham and the landlady bustle around making tea. Hitchcock shoots this in a single elaborate take running nearly two minutes, repeatedly moving right to left and back again as the two women move between kitchen and breakfast room, gossiping all the time. This restless staging wittily mimics, and enacts, the fussiness of the flutteringly anxious landlady, played to comic perfection by Marie Wright. But in *Mary,* she is replaced by Hermine Sterler, a genuinely great film actress but one who is very different in age, looks, and style; she brings no comedy to the

Figures 2.11–2.12. Same set up, different cast, apart from Miles Mander crouched over the body: the scene of the crime in *Murder!* and *Mary* (1930; British International Pictures). (Courtesy of the BFI National Archive)

role, and the mannered staging of the scene thus seems anomalous, quite apart from the fact that the ritual of the nice cup of tea has less meaning in German culture than in English (figs. 2.13 and 2.14).

Subsequent comedy business involving Marie Wright is lost or abbreviated, and some other humorous bits of presentation are dropped altogether, such as the celebrated shot of Markham's feet sinking into the carpet, as if into quicksand, when he goes nervously into an interview with Sir John in his lavish Mayfair rooms, and the two subjective cutaway shots representing the meals fondly imagined at different times by Markham's wife and by Sir John.

It is hardly necessary to go through the whole film scene by scene to map out the way in which these strategies are consistently applied, other than to note a recurrent error in the cursory accounts of the film that are on record, involving the lead actor, Alfred Abel. Like Hermine Sterler, he was a distinguished star of German silents; indeed, they both star in one of the masterpieces of 1920s cinema, Gerhard Lamprecht's *Menschen untereinander* (*People to Each Other,* 1926)—could this be among the German films that so impressed Hitchcock at a formative time, alongside the more famous Fritz Lang and F. W. Murnau titles? In the entry on *Mary* in his *Encyclopedia of Alfred Hitchcock* the American scholar Thomas Leitch offers this summary: "Alfred Abel, in the role of the playwright/juror/sleuth played in the English-language version by Herbert Marshall, insisted on wearing formal attire to visit Diana [Mary] Baring, the woman he had unwittingly voted to condemn, in her prison cell, and refused to endure the indignities of a comic scene in which Sir John, visiting a shabby boarding house in his search for evidence that will exonerate Diana, is beset by children who climb all over his bed."[15]

Leitch surely cannot have looked at the two films together.[16] The juxtaposed stills are another indication of their formal closeness, at least for most of their length—clearly each pair of shots was taken in quick succession, with a quick substitution of actors (figs. 2.15–2.18). They also exonerate Abel from the charge of standing unhelpfully upon his dignity. Far from dressing informally in tweeds and shabby mackintosh, as McGilligan has it, Marshall wears a formal double-breasted suit, with smart coat and neatly displayed handkerchief—

Figures 2.13–2.14. Preparing tea in *Murder!* and *Mary* (1930; British International Pictures). Marie Wright and Phyllis Konstam; Hermine Sterler and Lotte Stein. (Courtesy of the BFI National Archive)

Figures 2.15–2.16. *Murder!* and *Mary* (1930; British International Pictures). Herbert Marshall; Alfred Abel. (Courtesy of the BFI National Archive)

Figures 2.17–2.18. *Murder!* and *Mary* (1930; British International Pictures). Herbert Marshall; Alfred Abel. (Courtesy of the BFI National Archive)

this formality is a strongly marked element of his persona throughout. Abel's suit is darker but no more formal, and his bow tie is surely more of a dandy effect than a pompous one. The still from his boarding-house scene speaks for itself. The main difference is that the kitten in *Mary* does not wriggle under the bedclothes as it does in *Murder!* Perhaps Abel just did not like cats, or Hitchcock and his team were concerned to shorten the scene, as they shortened so many other passages; *Mary* runs for seventy-eight minutes, compared with the ninety-eight minutes of *Murder!*—or more than one hundred, in its fuller version.

Current DVD editions of *Murder!* supply a ninety-eight-minute narrative plus an "alternative ending," a final reel longer by two and a half minutes. The former ends—after the death of Handel Fane, the man revealed as the killer of Edna Druce—in a rather abrupt manner, with scenes 1, 2, 4, and 7 in the following list. The alternative final reel interpolates the three italicized scenes 3, 5, and 6, each of them taken in a single shot.

1. At the circus, Fane leaps to his death.
2. Shock and panic in the tent below—rapid montage.
3. *Fane's body is carried off on a stretcher. The manager gives Sir John a note left by him, and he reads it and reacts, as women weep uncontrollably in the foreground.*
4. Sir John reads Fane's note to Markham and sums up what it means.
5. *Diana walks out of prison and is met by Sir John.*
6. *In the back of a taxi, they look ahead to a partnership on- and offstage.*
7. Theater set: Diana enters stage left and is embraced by Sir John; the curtain falls.

But do the DVD editions have these versions the right way round? It seems more plausible that the longer ending is the definitive one, and that at some later point this ending was shortened for a reissue. Just to confuse things further: *Mary* ends with the first six of these seven scenes but omits the final scene in the theater, which draws together the threads so neatly (figs. 2.19 and 2.20).

Figures 2.19–2.20. The penultimate scene in the fuller version of *Murder!* and the final scene of *Mary* (1930; British International Pictures). Norah Baring and Herbert Marshall; Olga Tschechowa and Alfred Abel. (Courtesy of the BFI National Archive)

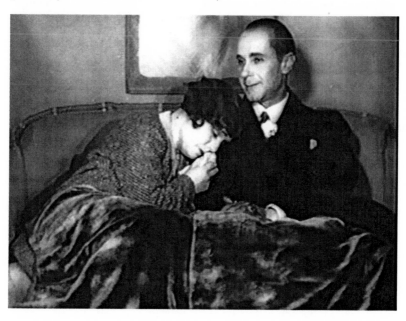

Unlike the contemporary reviews of *Juno,* those of *Murder!* do not provide clear evidence as to what ending was shown when and where. The episode simply offers another instance of the difficulty of pinning down definitive versions, and also, possibly, of Hitchcock's occasional uncertainty about how to end a film, particularly after a strong dramatic climax—how much time should be allowed for an audience to "wind down" and reflect on what has happened? See, for instance, the discussions of *Juno and the Paycock* previously and *The 39 Steps* to follow (another scene of a couple in a taxi). Later, there are the contrasting cases of *Vertigo* (1958), where a final scene between Midge and Scottie following Madeleine's death fall was cut out at the last minute, and of *Psycho* (1960), where the madness of the fruit cellar is followed by five minutes of calming-down talk from the court psychiatrist.

Pending new evidence, it seems more likely that the shorter version of *Murder!* was a later one, done independently of Hitchcock himself. What is beyond doubt is the simplification in *Mary* of the killer's motivation. In *Murder!,* the secret that Handel Fane is determined to conceal from Diana is his half-caste status, the fact that he has—in Sir John's shocked and shocking words—"black blood." Commentators have debated at length the issue of how far this constitutes a coded reference to a bisexuality—hinted at in Esme Percy's performance—that could not have been made explicit at the time. But *Mary* cuts through all such debates and subtexts. As in *Murder!,* the secret so desperately concealed from the loved woman is, ironically, one that she already knew. But here it is simpler: as Sir John explains at the end, "He had escaped from prison, and lived in constant fear of being captured again." This easy way out does seem to confirm the relatively mechanical exercise that *Mary* constituted for Hitchcock, in contrast to *Murder!* itself, and to the second version of *Blackmail*—fascinating as the details of the comparison surely remain.

Let's Go Bathing! (1931)

On 21 February 1931, the trade paper *The Cinema* carried a brief reference to a "Hitchcock talkie made 18 February at BIP Studios Elstree, largely consisting of a parade designed to show the resources of the Cotton Industry." A number of stars are mentioned, including Cicely Courtneidge—who had recently played in *Elstree Calling*, though not in any of the possible Hitchcock sections—and Evelyn Laye. This evidently refers to a short item, which survives, issued by Pathé News on 23 February. It runs just over four minutes, starts with the title "Let's go bathing!," and presents "a novel Parade organised to help the Middlesex Hospital re-building fund." A sign announces "Screen & Stage Stars Beach Parade." The item ends with Evelyn Laye telling us, in poorly synchronized close-up, that "this little film has been designed to show us some of the smart beach suits being made this year, to help British Cotton goods and to help with the rebuilding of the Middlesex Hospital."

After a few establishing shots of lido and beach, it is all studio. Cicely Courtneidge and Nelson Keys sit outside a beach hut and watch women in swimsuits getting ready to parade. Her swimsuit is an old-fashioned one, and she looks at them with envy, ashamed of her dowdiness; he looks at them with lust. This goes on for twenty-five shots, almost pure alternation: we never see either of them in the same frame with the young women. Then they join the women for a moment at the edge of the pool, and Keys falls in, after which Laye delivers the message.

It is all as crude as it sounds, in concept and execution, but there seems no reason to doubt the report that Hitchcock did shoot it—there are of course no personal credits on a Pathé News item. It is the kind of work that he could have knocked off in a morning, leaving it for an editor to string together, a very basic demonstration of the Kuleshov principle that he always relished explaining and practicing; for instance, in *Rear Window* (1954), where shots of James Stewart looking are alternated, for long stretches of film, with shots of what he is ostensibly looking at, creating, as Hitchcock put it to Truffaut, "the purest expression of a cinematic idea."[17] In that film, as at the start of *The Pleasure Garden,* there is a shock when the object of the gaze looks back (the killer at James Stewart; the dancer at the voyeur in the front stalls), and *Let's Go Bathing!* even plays with this effect as well, when one of the young women whom Nelson Keys is ogling returns his look, exciting and disconcerting him.

This tiny ephemeral item is further evidence of the status that Hitchcock seems to have accepted, with whatever degree of resentment, at BIP in this early sound period, doing various chores in the margins of his main work. Here he takes the chance to set himself a little cinematic exercise with the Kuleshov effect, like a pianist practicing scales. There could be other such ephemera waiting to be found.

Lord Camber's Ladies (Benn Levy, 1932)

Hitchcock's career at BIP, which had reached such a high point in 1929 with the success of *Blackmail*, ended in anticlimax three years later with a film that he produced but did not direct. Though his last three BIP films as director—*The Skin Game, Rich and Strange*, and especially *Number Seventeen*—are full of interest, they progressively lowered his standing with the public, with the critics, and with the company. Soon after the completion of the last of these three, it was announced that Hitchcock would take time off from directing; instead, he "will undertake supervision of a number of British International productions during the next twelve months, and will 'tutor' young film directors" (*The Bioscope*, 6 April 1932). Later that month he explained the plan himself in the pages of *Film Pictorial* (30 April), starting with praise for the work not of any British producer but of men like Irving Thalberg in Hollywood and Erich Pommer in Germany. He continued:

> If I am to do my work at Elstree as I know it should be done, I have a busy year in front of me. I have, for a start, six stories to choose, directors, stars, six individual casts. I hope in the end to be able to bring in raw material from outside the industry, and train a new generation of directors and players. I have my eye on several people at the moment, who, I expect, have never heard of my existence and would be horrified to learn that I planned to make them into the talkie directors of the future!

A week later, on 6 May, *Kine Weekly* announced the first name: "Auriol Lee, the West-End actress and stage producer, is to direct a film for British International Pictures under the supervision of Alfred Hitchcock." This never happened, though Lee would play the part of Isobel Sedbusk for him in *Suspicion* in 1941; soon after this, when she was on the point of directing the young Patricia Hitchcock in a Broadway play, she died in a car crash. Lee had worked regularly with the playwright John van Druten, someone else whom Hitchcock tried to persuade to become one of his group of new directors, again without success.[18] On 13 July 1932 another trade paper, *The Cinema*, revealed that "Alfred Hitchcock, supervisor of productions for British International, has completed arrangements for three new films. The first will be *The Case of Lady Camber*, the play by Horace Annesley Vachell. The director will be Benn Levy, whose experience in Hollywood should make him a real acquisition to British talking pictures. Hitchcock's second subject will be the Haymarket comedy *Priscilla Runs Away*, and the third, which the producer may direct himself, will be *Yellow Sands*, one of the most successful plays yet written by Mr Eden Phillpotts."[19]

In the event, only the first of these three plays was filmed, renamed *Lord Camber's Ladies* and billed as an Alfred Hitchcock Production (fig. 2.21)—the only outcome of the original ambitious scheme. After a brief run in cinemas, the film was lost and forgotten for years. Although the British archive acquired a copy in 1959, it has since been little shown or studied. It was not included in the full Retrospective of Hitchcock's films mounted by the BFI in 2012.

The first-time director, the playwright Benn Levy, provides a link back to *Blackmail*, for whose sound version he wrote the dialogue; his main Hollywood work had been for James Whale, on *Waterloo Bridge* (1931) and *The Old Dark House* (1932). His friendship with Hitchcock did not survive their second collaboration. According to the Taylor biography, "Hitch one day on set began to instruct the prop man, and Levy interrupted with 'Don't take any notice of him!' After that they hardly spoke for thirty years." Donald Spoto states that Levy found him "ill-tempered and meddlesome."[20] Hitchcock was evidently unable to resist the kind of interference, looking over the director's shoulder, that he always deeply resented and resisted on his own behalf, notably from David O. Selznick in Hollywood. By

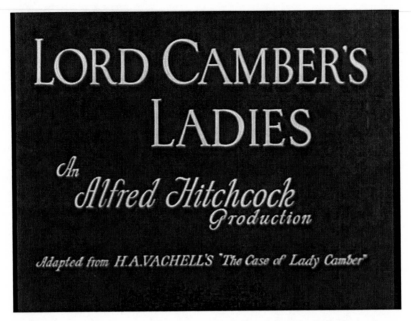

Figure 2.21. Opening credits from *Lord Camber's Ladies* (Benn Levy, 1932; British International Pictures). (Courtesy of the BFI National Archive)

the time of his TV show *Alfred Hitchcock Presents,* he would have worked out more tactful ways of handling directors.

Meanwhile, as successively with Graham Cutts, Eliot Stannard, and Adrian Brunel, Hitchcock would now coolly acquiesce in the ending of a friendly collaboration and move on, though this time the estrangement would not be permanent. In 1967 he invited Benn Levy to America to collaborate on what McGilligan persuasively describes as "the greatest film Hitchcock never made"; its title, *Frenzy,* would be appropriated a few years later for his penultimate film, made in London.[21] This first *Frenzy,* also known as *Kaleidoscope,* was inspired on the one hand by Hitchcock's obsessive interest in real-life sex-killers like Neville Heath (hanged in London in 1946), and on the other by his viewing of new European films: "I've just seen Antonioni's *Blow-Up* [1966]. These Italian directors are a century ahead of me in terms of technique! What have I been doing all this time?"[22] This new freedom of technique and of sexual explicitness

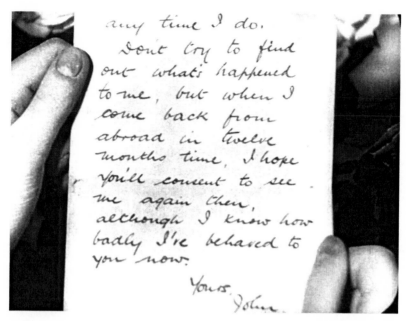

Figure 2.22. Letter insert in Hitchcock's handwriting from *Lord Cam-ber's Ladies* (Benn Levy, 1932; British International Pictures). (Courtesy of the BFI National Archive)

led Hitchcock, with the help primarily of Levy, and later of others, to develop plans for the New York sex-murderer story, sadly blocked by Universal, that were bolder than anything ultimately realized in the London *Frenzy*. His experience with Universal in some ways echoed his experience with BIP: all sweetness and light to start with, but then frustratingly restrictive.

The lost data and lost visuals from the *Frenzy/Kaleidoscope* project have by now been found and widely publicized, most recently in *Hitchcock Lost* by Dan Auiler, and we have nothing to add. But the episode does reflect back on *Lord Camber's Ladies*, a viewing of which confirms the evidence of 1929 and 1967: Levy and Hitchcock did have a genuine rapport and could surely have worked profitably together more often. The on-set row testifies to Hitchcock's involve-ment in the production, which is nicely confirmed by the fact that—as, long ago, in *Always Tell Your Wife* (1923; see fig. 1.22)—the insert of a message is given in his own handwriting (fig. 2.22).

The letter has been written by Lord Camber (Nigel Bruce, whom Hitchcock used later in Hollywood in *Rebecca* [1940] and *Suspicion* [1941]) to his girlfriend (Benita Hume, used earlier, in the celebrated telephone-switchboard scene in *Easy Virtue* in 1927). Lord Camber is engaged to be married to another woman, an actress played by Gertrude Lawrence, and is torn between the two women, Hume and Lawrence. The triangle intrigue will be echoed two decades later in *Dial M for Murder* (1954), though with the sexes reversed: there, Grace Kelly is torn between two men (husband Ray Milland, and Robert Cummings). Each film hinges on a murder plot aimed at resolving the triangle: that of Milland to murder Kelly, and that of Hume—or is it Bruce?—to murder Lawrence. What they unmistakably have in common is a sensuous moving-camera adulterous embrace, shown in close-up before a word has been spoken: between Bruce and Hume, between Cummings and Kelly. In *Lord Camber's Ladies* it is the first shot of the film; in *Dial M* it is the first time we see them together. As so often, this can be taken in different ways. Did Hitchcock dictate the initial shot? Did Levy (or his screenwriting collaborators) do so, and Hitchcock later thought back to it? Again one can take refuge, more convincingly, in the notion of an affinity, positioning Hitchcock not as a visionary among cinematic illiterates, but working among people responsive to his own ideas about the medium.

After leaving BIP, Hitchcock was under contract for nearly a year to Alexander Korda. There is scope for more research on the projects that they tried to develop, but no films resulted, and we have no evidence of lost or found material. After returning to the Gaumont/Gainsborough stable, briefly with the independent producer Tom Arnold on *Waltzes from Vienna* (1934), and then for years with his old associate Michael Balcon, Hitchcock became much more settled than he had been at BIP: the years 1933–1939 yield little in the way of lost, found, or neglected items compared with the periods on either side. But two films have lost endings—not found, but well documented. These are *The 39 Steps* (1935) and *Secret Agent* (1936).

The 39 Steps (1935)

The script for *The 39 Steps,* held at the BFI library, indicates a lost beginning as well:

INSERTS
A pattern of a series of amusement guides & books, such as a stranger would use in London

STOCK SHOTS
A pattern of a series of brightly lighted sky scenes and London amusement buildings.

The inserts are a clear echo of the immediately preceding Hitchcock/Bennett film, *The Man Who Knew Too Much* (1934), which opens with a shot of hands leafing through a series of brochures advertising Switzerland. Prints of *The 39 Steps* that include the similar opening may exist somewhere; some accounts refer to them, though it may be that these are based on the script rather than the film itself. Whether or not the scripted introduction was actually shot and assembled, it was thrown out in favor of the wonderfully economical opening that we now have, in which Hannay pays to enter the Music Hall and then finds a seat, enacting precisely what the cinema audience of 1935 had just done in order to view the film.

While the shooting script includes the cut opening, it does not include a final scene that was evidently incorporated at a late stage and was then shot and subsequently cut (either, as in *Juno,* after initial screenings, or in advance of them): Hannay and Pamela leave the Palladium in a taxi (fig. 2.23). This taxi scene was integral enough to be contained in the script routinely sent to America for approval by the New York State censorship, as a transcription of the film print, although before submission it was (unlike that of *Juno*) crossed out, with a single X over the whole page, leaving it legible. It shows Hannay and then Pamela speaking alternately (fig. 2.24).

Figure 2.23. Production still: Hannay (Robert Donat) and Pamela (Madeleine Carroll) in a taxi. The final scene cut from *The 39 Steps* (1935; Gaumont-British Pictures). (Courtesy of the BFI Stills Library)

The abbreviated ending of the film's definitive version, as Hannay and Pamela clasp hands after listening to the final words of Mr. Memory, is—like the opening—so satisfying that one can't regret the loss of the taxi scene. But we can note links with two films of the early 1920s. One of the eleven films for which Hitchcock designed the titles at Famous Players-Lasky British, *Beside the Bonnie Brier Bush* (Donald Crisp, 1921), hinged on this same element of Scots law, in which a couple are deemed to have married after making a "declaration." The same thing is highlighted in reports of *The Romany* (Martin Thornton, 1923), another lost film, scripted by Hitchcock's future collaborator Eliot Stannard and shot in Perthshire in 1922. We can picture him carefully squirreling away details like this for possible future use, even if, as here, they did not make it into the film as released.

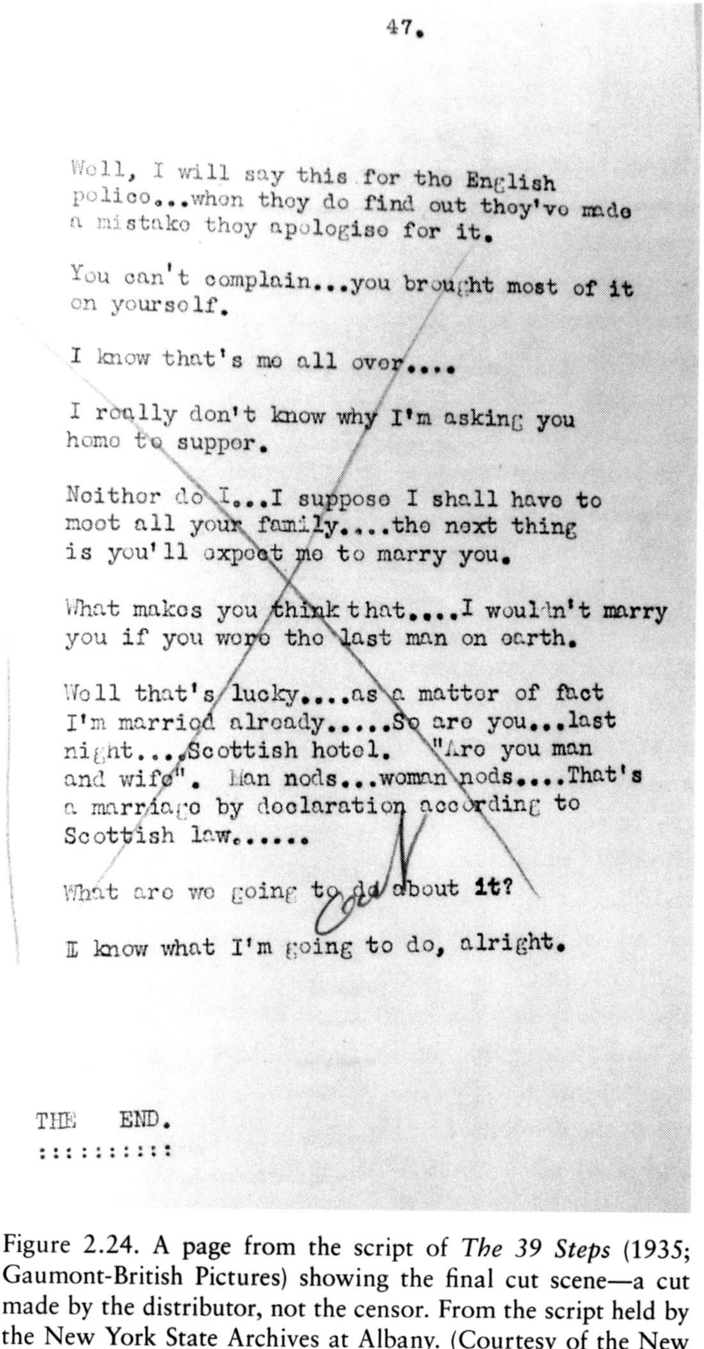

Well, I will say this for the English
police...when they do find out they've made
a mistake they apologise for it.

You can't complain...you brought most of it
on yourself.

I know that's me all over....

I really don't know why I'm asking you
home to supper.

Neither do I...I suppose I shall have to
meet all your family....the next thing
is you'll expect me to marry you.

What makes you think that....I wouldn't marry
you if you were the last man on earth.

Well that's lucky....as a matter of fact
I'm married already.....So are you...last
night...Scottish hotel. "Are you man
and wife". Man nods...woman nods....That's
a marriage by declaration according to
Scottish law......

What are we going to do about it?

I know what I'm going to do, alright.

THE   END.
::::::::::

Figure 2.24. A page from the script of *The 39 Steps* (1935;
Gaumont-British Pictures) showing the final cut scene—a cut
made by the distributor, not the censor. From the script held by
the New York State Archives at Albany. (Courtesy of the New
York State Library)

Secret Agent (1936)

Any uncertainty about the *39 Steps* ending was soon painlessly resolved. Negotiations over the rail-crash climax of the next film, *Secret Agent,* set in Europe in 1916, were much more complicated. Ivor
Montagu, who had been called in a decade earlier to help with the
completion of *The Lodger* and then with its two successors, was now
back for a time with Michael Balcon at Gaumont-British. Though not
credited on-screen, he acted as associate producer on three successive
Hitchcock films: *The 39 Steps, Secret Agent,* and *Sabotage* (1936). He
left various accounts of their work together, both in published essays
and in unpublished documents held in the Montagu collection at the
BFI; these are illuminating on the subject of the alternative versions of
the rail crash and its aftermath

One issue was how to present the crash visually. In a subsequent
letter to Balcon, Montagu reminded him that "the hand-painted colour flames that I had Len Lye paint on the rail crash, to make it
more realistic and bring the realism right into the audience, which we
had a fine barney about—to keep or not to keep—with me wanting
to, at any rate for the trade show to see how it went and you (quite
reasonably) hesitating and Hitch (equally reasonably) sitting on the
fence—'tis you yourself voluntarily decided to take it out on the eve of
the show."[23] Len Lye was an artist from New Zealand who had made
several films for John Grierson's GPO (General Post Office) Film Unit,
using dazzling forms of animation to put over mundane messages to
do with postage. Some accounts claim that his hand-painted flames
were included in initial screenings and led projectionists and audiences to panic, fearing that the film itself had caught fire, but Montagu's
account suggests that this version was never risked. According to the
author of the definitive Len Lye biography, Roger Horrocks, "Len's
footage no longer survives. When he moved to the USA in 1944, he
seems to have lost almost all of the (wild) footage from his British
period."[24]

It is interesting anyway to see Hitchcock "sitting on the fence."
This is the image of him that Montagu, a longtime friend and associate, consistently offers. On *The Lodger* in 1926, he went along

happily with all of Montagu's suggestions for reshooting and retitling. The debate about who should shoot whom at the end of *Secret Agent,* in the wreckage of the train, was again, it seems, conducted between Montagu and Balcon, with Hitchcock on the sidelines.

The American, Marvin (played by Robert Young), has now been revealed as a German agent. The British agent Ashenden (John Gielgud) and his exotic and much less fastidious colleague the General (Peter Lorre) have just caught up with him, along with Elsa (Madeleine Carroll), the future Mrs. Ashenden. Marvin is trapped in the wreckage, badly hurt. Ashenden reaches out as if to strangle him, but then draws back. There are three versions of what follows:

(1) As scripted. The General gives Marvin brandy, then shoots him dead. Ashenden and Elsa "clutch each other in horror." The General offers the brandy flask to them, and "they both turn away shudderingly." Ashenden knew Marvin had to die but couldn't kill him with his own hands, and they both have the luxury of despising the man who was ruthless enough to do it.

(2) "Alternative Ending," a half-page addendum to the script. There is no killing, but the final note of superiority over the General is maintained. Marvin dies from his wounds before the General can use his revolver. "Almost in ecstasy Ashenden shouts out 'He's beaten you—thank Christ he's beaten you!' Elsa breaks down sobbing into Ashenden's arms."

It may be that both these endings were shot, but the initial edit definitely used the first one. However, both the British censor and the production company were, like Ashenden and Elsa, unhappy with a resolution that left the General victorious and proud of it. The censor might well have accepted ending (2), but the company insisted on a third ending, which was duly shot and included in the final edit:

(3) The General walks over to Marvin, and puts down his gun in order to take a flask from his pocket and offer a

Figure 2.25. Production still for *Secret Agent* (1936; Gaumont-British Pictures), after the crash, which allows for any of the three endings. (Courtesy of the BFI Stills Library)

drink. Marvin picks up the gun and shoots him, before dying himself. The General recites his own name and titles one last time, then dies. The Ashendens embrace.

Writing to Balcon on 4 May 1936, Montagu articulated a protest on behalf—at least partly—of Hitchcock as well as himself:

The substitution of the scene has, I am aware, been demanded by the censor. Yet it remains true that the censor was deeply committed not to hold up the film, by his previous admissions, and the substitution was in fact proposed to him, having been resolved upon by the Corporation [Gaumont-British] separately from his decision. The motive underlying this decision was, I am aware, the view that public taste would demand the death of the General, and that any other ending would destroy any good impression the film might up to that point have created. As you know, both Hitch and I disagreed with this view, holding that the subsequent cheap conventionality and thematic muddle of the climax (and in retrospect of the whole story) would more than outweigh the possible popularity of the General's death. . . . In the circumstances it is not surprising that I, and, as far as I can judge, Hitch also, should feel disappointed that our own guess of audience reaction should not have received the endorsement to which, it might have been suggested, the results of our precedent collaborations had laid at least some claim.[25]

In favor of the Director's Cut ending, Montagu argues that "if Lorre does his vile murder then—at last, at the end of the film—we realise the hero and heroine as sensitive, noble, humane, with imagination enough to see what we could not see—how vile is really killing, even of the object that reason says must die—and to shrink from it." Whereas in the imposed ending: "Lorre, instead of being the thing vile with tempting outer charm that makes us forget his vileness until it suddenly unveils itself, becomes a charming thing never doing anything vile. . . . If Lorre instead is killed, then the vile thing the hero and heroine feared never happens, they are wrong, and become instead merely a couple of irresolute cissies whose shilly-shallying results in the death of their unwaveringly dutiful colleague."

But if the hero and heroine are "irresolute cissies" in the new ending, are they not just as much so in the original one? Their stance there, leaving their colleague to do the dirty but necessary work of killing, can scarcely be called "noble." Ashenden's action of moving to strangle Marvin and then freezing is common to both. It is hard to imagine Hitchcock seeing the case quite as simplistically as Montagu claimed to, and it seems significant that Montagu should perform a forward-back maneuver comparable to Ashenden's own: first confident in speaking on behalf of them ("Hitch and I disagreed with this view") and then hesitating ("I, and, as far as I can judge, Hitch"). The film has a coda that was not part of the initial script, depicting the Allied advance toward victory. The lesson is strong in either version: the elimination of the agent, Marvin, is the kind of thing that has to be done in order to win a war. Both endings enforce the necessity of being consistently hard—the new one by showing that Marvin himself has stayed hard right to the last.

Hitchcock's Cold War spy story *Topaz* (1969) likewise has three endings, all of them shot and edited, and all of them accessible on DVD. Slavoj Žižek has elegantly argued that these endings are not conflicting but complementary: "The ending we have now presupposes the other two, with the three endings forming a kind of syllogism."[26] *Secret Agent* is similar. You have to strangle or shoot Marvin (ending 1), otherwise he is likely to shoot one of your own men (ending 3); you cannot rely on him obligingly dying of his wounds before he has a chance to do so (ending 2). It is a striking early example of what Žižek terms "the implicit resonance of multiple endings" in Hitchcock.

The BFI holds a variety of *Secret Agent* footage, different prints and different sections; but no copy of the original ending—or of the Len Lye color footage—has yet been found.

3

The War Years

Like the early 1930s, the war years were a busy transitional time for Hitchcock. They throw up a rich variety of "lost and found" material, and of questions attaching to it. A six-year narrative of transition and tension forms the context for a wide range of shorter projects—lost and found—that he worked on in the margins of the early Hollywood features.

As an Englishman who arrived in Hollywood in March 1939, he soon had to endure the anxieties of being in a neutral country while his own was at war, and then, even after Pearl Harbor, of being far distant from the conflict that was more directly and dangerously affecting many of his family and former colleagues. During these years he was caught between the pulls of three powerful executives, the three most influential producers of his whole career, representing at this time respectively his past, present, and future: Michael Balcon, David O. Selznick, and Sidney Bernstein.

Michael Balcon had given him his first big chance in the 1920s at Gainsborough and had enabled him to relaunch his career in the mid-1930s at Gaumont-British. Balcon now criticized him publicly and bitterly for failing to return to England to contribute his skills and authority to the cinematic war effort. The attack came to a head in a prominent and widely publicized feature occupying a full page in the *Sunday Dispatch* newspaper on 25 August 1940, headed "DESERT-

ERS." Hitchcock was not the only one under attack (and Balcon was not the only attacker), but the main thrust was unmistakable: "Some of [these deserters] owe their careers to my interest in them. I had a plump young junior technician in my studios whom I promoted from department to department. Today, one of our most famous directors, he is in Hollywood, while we who are left behind are trying to harness films to the great national effort. . . . I do not give this man's name as I have decided not to mention any of the deserters by name."

There is no doubt that the attack hurt Hitchcock deeply. He quickly published an aggressive reply to it in the *New York World-Telegram*, on 27 August, and it took years for the two men to be reconciled. It would be facile to suggest that the attack shamed Hitchcock into doing anti-Nazi work from his American base; he was already very active. But the bitterness of the episode plainly confirmed him and his wife in their commitment to staying in Hollywood.

Balcon's attack had consigned their long and productive association firmly to the past. The present was David O. Selznick, who had put Hitchcock under contract in 1939. Their only intensive personal collaborations were on *Rebecca* (1940) at the start of the contract and *The Paradine Case* at the end of it in 1947, neither film having a war background. Selznick was a possessive and controlling employer throughout, dictating the terms of Hitchcock's various loan-outs to other producers and irritating him by the big profit he made on these deals. Selznick did not, of course, prevent Hitchcock from doing pro-British or pro-Allied films for other Hollywood producers, or from doing more modest work for the British government, though the time spent on the latter work often caused him strong irritation in turn. This is where Bernstein comes in, as agent of Hitchcock's future.

Sidney Bernstein, born within a few months of Hitchcock in 1899, had been a friend since the 1920s, when both were members of the Film Society in London and belonged to an informal progressive association of film people. He was not then involved in production, but he developed a successful career as an impresario, building up a chain of cinemas; early in the war he took up a senior position in the Films Division of the Ministry of Information (MoI). One of his main initial tasks was to ensure a screening for pro-British films in neutral America; later, his focus was on getting a range of films into Europe once Liberation became imminent. He drew Hitchcock into working for him at both these stages, and by the end of the war they had set up firm plans for an independent production company, Transatlantic. Selznick was resentfully aware that Hitchcock's main loyalty had by now been transferred to Bernstein, and that he was working on his plans for the future on Selznick time, while drawing his Selznick salary; but Selznick could hardly prevent this because of the serious war work Hitchcock and Bernstein were engaged upon. Hitchcock would duly follow his last film under the Selznick contract with two for Transatlantic: *Rope* (1948) and *Under Capricorn* (1949).

There are five main blocks of "lost and found" Hitchcock material from this period:

1. An episode in the feature film *Forever and a Day* (1943). This multi-episode epic of English history was conceived early in 1940 by representatives of the "Hollywood British" community, though it was not completed until late 1942. Hitchcock was closely involved from the start and helped to prepare his own piece of the narrative jigsaw. He was too busy to shoot it himself at the scheduled time, and his name is not on the credits, but the twelve-minute episode is aptly described by Patrick McGilligan as "quasi-Hitchcock."[1]

2. A pair of drama-documentary films produced for the MoI in London and re-edited by Hitchcock for the American market: *Men of the Lightship* (David Macdonald, 1940) and *Target for Tonight* (Harry Watt, 1941). The original British films have always remained available, but the re-edited versions were lost or ignored for decades, buried in American archives, and have not previously been scrutinized.

3. Two short French-language narratives directed by Hitchcock in Britain early in 1944, for the MoI: *Bon Voyage* and *Aventure Malgache*. These have been available for

some years now, after being for a long time blocked from public screening; new light is shed here on their production, exhibition, and long-term suppression.

4. Two "public service" short films made for American audiences, neither of which, unlike the French-language pair, carries credits: *The Fighting Generation* (late 1944), a brief appeal to buy War Bonds; and *Watchtower over Tomorrow* (early 1945), a more ambitious film urging support for the new United Nations. Hitchcock directed the first, but not the second, though he was originally scheduled to; at the very least he helped to plan the structure, and like the *Forever and a Day* episode it could be seen as "quasi-Hitchcock." Serving such immediate topical purposes, both films were long forgotten, but both survive and are well documented.

5. A film about the Nazi concentration camps. In the summer of 1945, Hitchcock worked intensively in London on the process of assembling and shaping actuality material. At the time, the film was aborted, but versions of it have been shown, and it remains the focus of a lot of research.

Forever and a Day (1943)

One of the seven credited directors of *Forever and a Day* is Victor Saville, a longtime associate of Hitchcock's from the Gainsborough and Gaumont days who had moved to Hollywood at around the same time as he did. On 17 September 1941 Saville wrote to Sidney Bernstein, who had been visiting America from England on behalf of the MoI: "I heard from Hitch that you had arrived back safely. I am in the middle of directing my sequence of the picture. Hitch follows with Cary Grant and Ida Lupino."[2]

This indicates that Grant and Hitchcock must have come close to making their episode. In the event both were too busy: adjustments to *Suspicion* (1941) had dragged on, and Hitchcock was having to work fast on preparing his next project, *Saboteur* (1942). Grant was replaced by Brian Aherne, and Hitchcock by René Clair, who became

Figures 3.1–3.2. Ida Lupino and Brian Aherne (in the part originally intended for Cary Grant) in *Forever and a Day* (1943; RKO Radio Pictures). (Courtesy of the BFI National Archive)

the only non-British director among the seven (he was currently active in Hollywood, had worked in Britain in the 1930s, and saw himself as an honorary member of the Hollywood-British community). Hitchcock had developed a detailed script with Charles Bennett (one of twenty-one credited writers overall) and Alma (uncredited); Clair, coming in at short notice, seems to have respected the script, and the result, which runs for only twelve minutes, has a distinct Hitchcock feel to it.

It starts with a protracted scene based on his familiar motif of *scopophilia,* the urgent desire to gaze. Ida Lupino's character, a maid in the London house on which the story is centered, longs to watch Queen Victoria's Diamond Jubilee procession, but she only manages to look through low railings and has even that view blocked by a man's legs. Neither she nor the audience ever gets a proper look, as he does, at the parade, but a cross-class romance develops; the man (Brian Aherne) is a distant cousin of the titled family of the house, set on emigrating to America (figs. 3.1 and 3.2). Having begun with the mechanics of the gaze, the episode ends in similarly Hitchcockian style with suspense and crosscutting. Aherne is outside, about to drive away in his 1897 motor car, while Lupino is upstairs doing tasks for the family. Just in time, she breaks off and joins him in a happy ending. To the question from the startled butler (Eric Blore) as she dashes past him, "Where do you think you're going?," her answer is "America," the last word spoken; the last shot shows her leaping onto the car as it draws away from the house. The two characters thus anticipate in terms of 1897, and re-create in terms of the early 1940s, the journey taken by Ida Lupino and Brian Aherne, and by Charles Bennett, Alma Reville, and Alfred Hitchcock, from interwar British cinema to work in Hollywood. It is the most compact and forceful section of an uneven film, and the most effective in expressing an upbeat Anglo-American spirit.

British Films Re-edited

Forever and a Day was very Hollywood, and its production turned out to be very protracted: it was not shown until 1943. Meanwhile,

Hitchcock had responded to a request by Sidney Bernstein, his old associate back in London, to do an urgent job of re-editing two early British propaganda films in order to make them more acceptable to American audiences: *Men of the Lightship* and *Target for Tonight,* produced for the MoI in 1940 and 1941, respectively. The original versions have stayed in circulation and are now widely available on DVD; the Hitchcock re-edits survive in American archives but have not previously been scrutinized. The changes he made to *Target for Tonight* are minor, but the changes to *Men of the Lightship* are much more radical: it acquired a new title, *Men of Lightship "61,"* and its running time was cut down by one-third, from twenty-four minutes to sixteen. Hitchcock clearly devoted serious time and care to this reworking, as our analysis demonstrates.

A crucial aim of the MoI Films Division, from the start of the war in Europe, had been to get its output widely shown in still-neutral America in order to increase public sympathy for the British cause. This needed careful calculation if it was to overcome two major obstacles: political resistance to anti-isolationist propaganda, and resistance on the part of the popular audience to British cinema. Early short films such as *London Can Take It* (1940), stitched together from vivid actuality footage of the effects of the aerial Blitz of late 1940, made an impact in America, but the MoI was also by then financing more ambitious longer films of a drama-documentary type, *Men of the Lightship* and *Target for Tonight* being pre-eminent among them.[3] These dramatize respectively an actual event (the destruction in January 1940 of a North Sea lightship by Nazi bombing) and a "typical" one (a late-1940 Royal Air Force [RAF] bombing raid over Germany, undertaken as if in revenge for that kind of outrage). In the course of their narratives, the films celebrate the understated heroism of the crews of lightship and aircraft. With a single exception, the cast are servicemen enacting their real-life roles.

Both films had immediate success with British critics and audiences. A report of March 1943 showed that they had become the two most profitable of all government-sponsored releases up to that point.[4]

Men of the Lightship / Men of Lightship "61"
(David Macdonald, 1940/1941)

A review on 3 August 1940 in the political weekly the *New States-man* testified that "the effect of *Men of the Lightship* on an ordinary audience enjoying an average programme was electric."[5] The reviewer may well, in fact, have seen the film in the same program as Hitch-cock's own first Hollywood production, *Rebecca,* on its initial run in the West End of London, since that was one of the several high-profile supporting slots negotiated by the MoI (fig. 3.3).

Despite the spectacular impact the film made in Britain, Bern-stein was quickly deflated by finding that the companies he invited to distribute it in America, RKO and Fox, were reluctant to do so, "chiefly because the commentary and voices were unsuitable for those markets."[6] There was also a feeling that its pace was too slow. This was certainly the view of John Grierson, founding father of the British documentary movement, who was now running the new National Film Board of Canada and coordinating its own propaganda efforts. Looking back over the initial months of MoI production, he wrote to Bernstein from Ottawa on 11 February 1941 that "in general the films are slow, roundabout and far more concerned with sympathy than action. Sympathy you can take for granted. It is the direct ac-tivist style that will create confidence and participation. . . . I don't like to call it dullness, but certainly there is a lack of narrative lift." He cited *Men of the Lightship* as an example of this slowness, and Bernstein, in forwarding the letter at once to colleagues, endorsed his comments. But by this time, Hitchcock was at work on speeding up this particular film, and he may already have finished the job.

After the refusal by RKO and Fox, Bernstein had taken rapid ac-tion. As he recalled later in a lengthy summarizing memo to the MoI administrator E. St. J. Bamford of 3 April 1941: "We therefore tele-graphed Hitchcock and asked him if he would undertake re-editing and re-dubbing the voices. He agreed, and I discussed the suggestion with you, when it was arranged that I should cable Hitchcock and ask him the cost of this work. Hitchcock replied: 'Will take care of all costs myself for the time being.' "[7]

GAUMONT, Haymarket.   11.35 to 11.15.
Laurence Olivier, Joan Fontaine in
REBECCA (a) .
MEN OF THE LIGHTSHIP (u).
Programmes comm. 11.50. 2.35. 5.25. 8.20.   Whi. 6655.

Figure 3.3. Advertisement for *Rebecca* (1940) and *Men of the Lightship*
(David Macdonald, 1940) in the Entertainment columns of *The Times*,
29 July 1940.

As soon as Hitchcock's involvement became known, the MoI had
been attacked, predictably, by Michael Balcon, who had evidently offered without success to have the editing work done free of charge at
his own base, Ealing Studios. He wrote on 20 November to the Head
of Films Division, Jack Beddington, that "it is particularly galling to
people over here to have work of this nature tampered with by people
so far removed from actualities. . . . Anti-Hitchcock feeling is very
strong." But of course it made good sense for the re-editing to be done
by someone who was much closer to the realities of the American
market than Ealing was. Hitchcock was ideally positioned between
the two countries and the two cultures, between American audiences
and the aesthetics of British documentary production.

A memo from Bernstein to Bamford on 27 January 1941 suggests
that he had by then made good progress: "Alfred Hitchcock phoned
me from Hollywood on Friday night (2 a.m. actually) to say that
Hutchinson of Twentieth Century Fox Films had agreed to release
Hitchcock's re-edited version of this film throughout the United States
and Latin America, on a commercial basis." It is clear, anyway, that
by the start of April 1941 *Men of Lightship "61"* had entered U.S.
distribution, giving it a chance to do its bit in encouraging pro-British
sentiment—many months before the Pearl Harbor attack of 7 December tipped the United States into joining the war. Bernstein's long
memo of 3 April summarized the position thus: "The film has now
been successfully cut and the voices re-dubbed, and Robert Sherwood

has done the commentary. . . . Cdr Jarratt saw the film in America, and thinks it is excellent and that it will be a great success."[8]

There is evidence of a screening in Connecticut as early as March 1941: a newspaper advertisement for *Footsteps in the Dark* (Lloyd Bacon), with Errol Flynn, includes the words, just below: "ADDED, MEN OF LIGHTSHIP '61.' Filmed in England—Proceeds to Allied Relief." There is similar evidence of screenings in Wisconsin in April and in Florida and Texas in May, and we can surely assume that these records represent just the tip of an iceberg of nationwide screenings.

Hitchcock's work on the re-edit had thus achieved Bernstein's objective, and we can now examine the changes he made.

The film "reconstructs" (the term used on the original credits) the shocking bomb attack by German planes on a lightship off the east coast of England, early in 1940. This is the basic narrative.

We are introduced to the crew of Lightship 61 and its skipper as they anticipate a period of shore leave; official arrangements are confirmed for a relief boat, *Argos,* to take over. From on board the lightship a floating mine is spotted, and a combined operation between crew members and a passing naval ship succeeds in blowing it up. Later, two planes approach, but it is assumed that, even if they are German, they will respect the neutrality of a lightship, as in the First World War. However, the planes dive-bomb the lightship repeatedly, attacking with bombs and machine-gun fire. The skipper is wounded; the lifeboat is lowered. Meanwhile, the dispatch of the *Argos* has had to be delayed. The lifeboat is filled, the lightship sinks, the planes depart, and the men row away. Eventually, the *Argos* arrives at the location, but finds nothing. By now the men are exhausted and cannot continue their heroic efforts. The boat and the bodies are washed up on the east coast.

The most immediately noticeable change in the U.S. version of the film is the provision of a different voice-over commentary at the start and the end. But the film itself has been quite radically reworked, in ways that are summarized in table 3.1. For ease of reference, this comparative table divides the original film into numbered sections, juxtaposing its narrative with details of the Hitchcock re-edit. Hitchcock's strategy has been variously to *delete* whole scenes, to *compress*

Table 3.1. Summary of Changes to *Men of the Lightship* for U.S. Version

	Men of the Lightship	*Men of Lightship "61"*
1	Newspaper headlines from early 1940: Nazi bombing of the East Dudgeon lightship	
2	Credit titles	Adjusted credits, cleaner type
3	Introductory images, with voice-over foreword	Changed text and different voice
4	Conversation on deck: turn off fog signal, relief period coming soon	Adjusted dialogue
5	Below, getting up; establish characters and their keen anticipation of relief; Lofty takes tea to the skipper	Part retained; part cut; part compressed and moved to later (7a)
6	Voice-over orients us. Trinity House: confirm plan for relief by another boat, *Argos*	No voice-over
7	Voice-over orients us. *Argos:* making preparations for relief	No voice-over
7a		Moved from earlier (5). Below deck: Lofty takes tea to the skipper
8	Lightship 61: crew climb mast, deal with the light mechanism	DELETED
9	Various other activities, work and relaxation; meanwhile we see a floating mine nearby	DELETED the anticipatory shots of the mine
10	Toss coin to decide who is to throw out slops; Lofty loses, wind blows contents of pail back in his face—and then he sees the mine	DELETED all until the sighting of the mine
11	Quick response to mine; crew set out on lifeboat to deal with it; distress signal is fired	Some shots trimmed
12	A passing ship takes note and moves close; a squad of its men fire rifles to explode the mine, cheered by the men from 61	Recut and tightened to cover complex action more quickly
13	More singing and relaxation below deck; Lofty exits	Compressed
14	Couple on deck observe two planes approaching; Lofty joins them; no sense yet of danger	
15	The planes are German and launch a fierce attack; the skipper is wounded	Minor transposition of shots
15a		Two attacks are brought forward (from 18)
16	Trinity House: crisis elsewhere, so Argos is diverted—relief of 61 will be delayed	
17	*Argos:* message received and acted on	Adjusted dialogue
18	Five new attacks by German planes	Two attacks moved forward (15a); the three remaining attacks have minor transposition of shots
19	Attacks continue; crew get into lifeboat and are fired on there	
20	Images of the inside of the abandoned lightship	
21	Crew watch the lightship sink as the planes fly off	
22	*Argos* is baffled by not being able to find Lightship 61	DELETED
23	Crew keep rowing; days pass; getting weaker	
24	"Wish I was in the pub"; we see and hear women in the pub	DELETED all the pub material
25	Exhaustion—one man breaks down; land is sighted, but it's too late	
26	Boat washes up in the surf: final voice-over	Changed text and different voice

scenes, and to *transpose* scenes; to *transpose* shots and to *trim* shots; to *eliminate* voice-over commentary from the body of the film; and to *redub* some lines of dialogue. The overall effect is to reduce the running time by one-third, from twenty-four minutes to sixteen, and to provide a more streamlined and linear narrative, one calculated to appeal more effectively to an American audience.

It is essential to note at the start that this is emphatically not a case of a dull film being "saved," of a staid documentary being invigorated by commercial know-how. *Men of the Lightship* had brought together British personnel from the feature industry as well as from documentary. Editing was done by one of the great professionals of documentary, Stewart McAllister, known above all for his collaborations with Humphrey Jennings; on *Listen to Britain* (1942), they even share a joint final credit, analogous to the celebrated joint Michael Powell–Emeric Pressburger one, for "Direction and Editing." In 1983, most unusually for an editor, McAllister had a book devoted to him, written by Dai Vaughan—himself a working film editor as well as a distinguished critic—and including a full eight pages that analyze the subtleties of his work on *Men of the Lightship*.[9] The film's producer, Alberto Cavalcanti, was about to move to Ealing Studios to work for Michael Balcon on features as well as documentaries, while the main previous experience both of its director, David Macdonald, and of its writer, Hugh Gray, had been in 1930s feature production. Moreover, Gray was an old and valued friend of Hitchcock's: they were classmates at school, and in the 1960s Hitchcock would personally finance him for a year of research and writing in Paris.[10]

It is frustrating not to be able to find any evidence of communication between Gray and Hitchcock over this particular film—Gray was by then serving in Europe, and time was short—but Hitchcock must surely at least have noted his name on the credits and respected the professionalism of the film's structure, centered on one familiar kind of belligerent threat, the floating mine, efficiently dealt with, followed by a second, the air attack, that could not have been foreseen or repulsed. The script is also adroit, if predictable, in the way it sketches in something of the personalities of the crew members, alternating between their scenes and the action scenes, and between Lightship

Table 3.2. Comparison of Opening Commentary in *Men of the Lightship* and *Men of Lightship "61"*

Men of the Lightship	Men of Lightship "61"
Year in, year out, all round our coasts, the beam of the lightship shines through the night, and its siren pierces the fogbanks. Light and fog signals reach vessels of all nations equally, and for three centuries lightships and lighthouses were considered international. Three hundred years of warfare left them untouched, from the day when Louis XIV told his navy, "I am at war with England, but not with humanity." From that day, until the 29th of January 1940 . . .	To men who sail the seven seas, the lightship has always been a symbol of humanity—a symbol as sacred as the Red Cross. The lightship has done its job in peace or war—giving warning of danger to sailors of all nations. It has been a guiding beacon for friend and foe alike. Night and day for hundreds of years, off the perilous coast of England, the East Dudgeon lightship has ridden the foggy, stormy waters of the North Sea, sending its friendly signals to ships and men. During the First World War of 1914 to 1918 never once was this exposed, undefended lightship threatened by enemy action. But 1940 has brought into the North Sea a new kind of war—a new kind of enemy.

61 itself and the wider operation of which it is part, involving scenes at the control center at Trinity House and on board the sister ship *Argos*. It is no surprise that the film was a major success in Britain, nor that Bernstein and his MoI colleagues should have been so keen for American audiences to see it—to be outraged by the Nazi atrocity and impressed by the quiet heroism of its victims.

As already noted, the immediate problem identified by American distributors, and at once addressed by Bernstein and Hitchcock, was a verbal one: the commentary and the accents. Hitchcock quickly gained approval for his suggestion that he should work with the playwright Robert Sherwood to supply a new foreword and afterword. In both versions, the foreword (section 3) does a necessary job of concise factual and dramatic orientation. Comparing the two, one sees how the text has been made simpler and less insular for a non-British audience (table 3.2).

The insular "our coasts" becomes "the seven seas." Three centuries, three hundred years, Louis XIV, the specific January date: these historical details are replaced by a single, instantly graspable reference point, the 1914–1918 war, and the universal symbol of the

Red Cross. Meanwhile the North Sea (twice), East Dudgeon, and the date of 1940 are set up as pragmatic coordinates for the action that follows.

Neither version identifies the speaking voice, either on the credits or in publicity, but a GPO (General Post Office) Film Unit memo of 13 July 1940 authorized a payment of £5 for this commentary work to the actor Robert Newton, who had recently played the romantic lead in Hitchcock's last film before leaving for America, *Jamaica Inn* (1939).[11] Once one has this piece of archival evidence, the voice on *Men of the Lightship* does indeed become recognizable as his. The accent is lucid and unpompous, and does not in itself seem to require changing, but Hitchcock obviously needed someone close at hand to speak the new lines by Sherwood. He initially planned to use Robert Montgomery, and may have done so, though the voice on the re-edit is not as distinctive as Newton's is on the original.[12]

The other half of the Sherwood commentary (section 26) will be given in its chronological place at the end. Meanwhile, Hitchcock has had to address the issue of dialogue. It is sometimes said that—as implied in the Bernstein memo of 3 April 1941—he did a wholesale "re-dubbing" both of this film and of *Target for Tonight;* but if he considered the idea, he must have rejected it very quickly. For better or worse, these are modest, often self-deprecating, Englishmen: imposing American voices on them, or even Hollywood-English voices via actors like Ronald Colman or Nigel Bruce, would be anomalous. Instead, Hitchcock eliminated some of the dialogue altogether and unobtrusively redubbed certain lines to amend the words rather than the accents.

This process begins at once, in scene 4, the establishing scene on deck. Two men are waiting to go on leave but are worried that the fog may come back and prevent the relief ship taking over. The older says to the younger: "Might come back for a week, and you getting married next Tuesday and all." The redub makes it less oblique: "Might come back for a week, and mess up your wedding next Tuesday." The change is made easier by the fact that the words are spoken, in both versions, against an image of the sea. This part of the original film's dialogue had itself been separately recorded: an informative 1944 article in a British journal notes that "dialogue was post-synchronised for the exteriors; quality is good but synchronism variable."[13]

In other exterior scenes, Hitchcock makes similar small adjustments, again in the interests of clarity. In scene 17, for instance, the sister ship, *Argos,* gets a message to postpone its scheduled relief of Lightship 61—which is now, as we know but the Trinity House depot does not, under attack from Nazi planes—in order to deal with a crisis elsewhere. The radio operator who takes the message reports to his captain: "Spot of bother from the depot, sir." The redub simplifies this: "Here's word from the depot, sir."

In one scene (the start of section 12) Hitchcock subtly adjusts the dialogue's content. Spotting a floating mine, the lightship crew fire a distress signal. Cut to the other boat, which is within sight and earshot. One officer asks, "What was that?," and gets the reply, "Sounded to me like another ruddy mine, sir." The line is neat: "another" mine emphasizes that these are dangerous waters, and there is irony in the fact that this detonation is not in fact a mine but a call to help dispose of one. But Hitchcock's redub—aided again by the fact that the speaker is facing away from the camera—flattens this out, preferring to go straight to the point: "What was that?" "Sounded like a distress signal."

This process of simplification is Hitchcock's basic strategy, not only on the verbal level but, more radically, in the editing, in both macro and micro terms—adjustments to the overall narrative and, often, to the shot-by-shot construction. Nowhere is this more striking than in the episode (section 10) of the floating mine itself, whose sighting triggers the distress signal. In the original, we see the mine, in two ominous cutaway shots, before it is spotted by any of the crew. It is a small but effective instance of editing for suspense, as so often expounded and practiced by Hitchcock himself (the bomb under the table, which we see but the characters don't). In his book on McAllister, Dai Vaughan makes much of the very precise editing of the sequence, not simply the crosscutting itself ("to create anticipatory tension by intercutting is a familiar enough device") but a further range of associations created around the cuts.[14] Hitchcock again flattens out the complexities, and there is an obvious irony in the way he

Figures 3.4–3.5. *Men of the Lightship* (David Macdonald, 1940; Crown Film Unit). Lofty spots the mine. (Courtesy of the BFI National Archive)

thus eliminates the most Hitchcockian element in the whole of the original film, the moment of anticipatory tension. Instead, we see the mine for the first time when it is spotted from the rail of the ship by Lofty, the crew member who has been most strongly established as a distinct character (figs. 3.4 and 3.5).

Whether or not he was aware if it, Hitchcock was thus reverting to the terms of the script written by his old friend Hugh Gray. But in the lead-up to this key moment (scenes 5 to 10), he has made big changes to Gray's structure, as table 3.1 indicates. This re-edit has two functions: to cut through quickly to the action, and, in so doing, to shorten drastically the affectionate presentation of the crew members, and of the very English understated humor of their dialogue. Even if wholesale redubbing was not a realistic option, this humorous dialogue could at least be cut back.

The main focus of the humor is Lofty—named thus, of course, because he is short in stature, just as his pet tortoise is named Lightning. Originally, the crew were played by professional actors; producer Cavalcanti found the results "totally unconvincing," and on his orders they were replaced by authentic seamen, with the one exception of Lofty, who was played by the experienced character actor Leonard Sharp.[15] Sharp fits in perfectly well, and Hitchcock respects and retains his role in taking tea to the skipper (fig. 3.6) and, soon after, spotting the floating mine. But he cuts out the comedy that leads up to that (his misjudgment of the wind direction, so that the slops get blown back in his face), and he not only shortens the below-deck business but breaks it up into two parts. We thus get a quick sketch of the crew and of their humanity (starting in scene 4 with the reference to the imminent wedding) and their humor, but without the danger, for an American audience, of their outstaying their welcome.

Comparison between the two films at this point underlines the sheer care and detail of Hitchcock's work on the re-edit. The lengthy section 5 in the original ends with a sequence of fifteen shots: Lofty prepares to take tea to the skipper, then finds his way through the ship and delivers it. Hitchcock (a) postpones this until after the contextual scenes at Trinity House and on board the *Argos,* and (b) shortens it, using only shots 1–4 and 8–15. The postponement compensates, as

Figure 3.6. *Men of the Lightship* (David Macdonald, 1940; Crown Film Unit). An iconic British teacup moment that Hitchcock took care to preserve in his re-edit. (Courtesy of the BFI National Archive)

it were, for the loss of the buildup to the mine-spotting, so that this doesn't come too abruptly, while the shortening simply accelerates the momentum: the original has fifteen shots in seventy-eight seconds; the re-edit, without any breach of smooth continuity, has six shots in forty-two seconds. Lofty leaves with the tea then brings it to the skipper, omitting all of the strictly dispensable shots en route.

Two subsequent scenes, the two main action scenes of the film, demonstrate similar care in the re-editing. Section 12 involves elaborate coordinated maneuvers between the lifeboat in which crew members set out to pull the mine away from the lightship, and the naval ship that then obliges them by detonating it harmlessly with a rifle barrage. Here, Hitchcock streamlines the action not so much by deleting shots as by shortening them. His version has twenty-four shots, against twenty-seven in the original, but the running time is cut by more than half: from two minutes sixteen seconds (average shot length [ASL] 5 seconds) to one minute five seconds (ASL 2.7). There is no radical change here, simply a skillful speeding up, without any sacrifice of lucidity in the presentation of a complex piece of teamwork.

The threat averted is followed by one that is unresistible, forming the central action, and indeed the raison d'être, of the film: sections 15, 18, and 19, the air attack on the defenseless lightship. There is no temptation here to speed up the cutting rate: the original is powerfully shot and edited, based on vivid alternation between the viewpoints of attackers and of victims—a fluency made possible by the cooperation of the British Air Ministry, who were happy, once they had been convinced of the film's potential propaganda value, to put a variety of planes and pilots at the Film Unit's disposal.[16] The planes attack repeatedly; we cut away to the Trinity House controller—who is frustratingly, at this moment, postponing the dispatch of the relief ship *Argos*—and then to the *Argos* itself as it receives the order; then back to the aerial bombardment that culminates in the survivors abandoning ship. Hitchcock's main alteration here is to "front-load" the action, giving us much more of the attack and its devastating effects *before* the cutaway to Trinity House and *Argos*. Once again this seems to make sense as a way of engaging the American audience, hitting them as hard as possible before risking the drop in tension.

Though the tempo of the attacks themselves is not changed, close analysis shows that Hitchcock, here as elsewhere, made a number of small, unobtrusive, trims and transpositions. Anyone who has done archival research on the production of some of his later films will be familiar with "Mr. Hitchcock's Cutting Notes": documents that transcribe his reactions to seeing a provisional cut of a reel of film. Instructions range from the use of a different take, to the loss or insertion of a reaction shot, right down to the shaving even of two or three frames here and there. Documents of that kind survive from Hitchcock's fine-tuning, in 1944, of *Bon Voyage* and *Aventure Malgache,* and it seems likely that he operated in the same way in watching and rewatching *Men of the Lightship.* In section 11, the mechanics of firing the distress signal from the lightship are depicted in an awkwardly protracted shot of ten seconds; the awkwardness is rather eloquent, showing the physical difficulty of the process and adding some tension, as we wait for ignition. Hitchcock prefers to cut out the waiting, making it a four-second shot: no sooner do we grasp what we are being shown, than it fires. Both versions are effective in their different contexts, aimed at different audiences. Of his many small adjustments to the air attacks, one is especially neat. A crew member, one who has not been foregrounded in the scenes below deck, observes the planes going over, and, a few shots later, flinches back inside a doorway. Hitchcock cuts the second shot and reserves it for later, for use at another dramatic moment. Again, it is hardly a necessary change, but one that demonstrates his drive to fine-tune the film as carefully as if it were one of his own.

After the attacks and the sinking of the ship, the lifeboat scenes (section 19 onward) are left virtually intact; they are given more concentration by the deletion of two scenes that take us elsewhere. The sister ship *Argos* provides a clear strand in the narrative of *Men of the Lightship:* it is ready to take over from Lightship 61 (section 7), it is diverted to other duties (section 17), and then it arrives at the location, baffled to find nothing there (section 22). Hitchcock sacrifices this third appearance, just as he eliminates the human touch of the cutaway to loved ones at home (section 24). He keeps the line "Wish I

Figures 3.7–3.10. *Men of the Lightship* (David Macdonald, 1940; Crown Film Unit). The skipper is shot; the image itself is riddled with bullets as he thinks of his wife. Stewart McAllister and Alberto Cavalcanti created a typically bold rapid montage, which Hitchcock respected and retained. (Courtesy of the BFI National Archive)

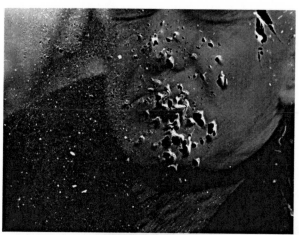

was in the pub," but he deletes the brief scene of the cheerful women drinking there. Like the third appearance of the *Argos,* this answers an earlier scene: when the skipper of the lightship is wounded by bullets from the Nazi plane (section 15), a rapid subjective montage includes a shot of the woman we now see in the pub, presumably his wife (figs. 3.7–3.10). But Hitchcock's strategy for the final scenes is to focus on the exhausted crew, allowing no distraction from them until the death of the last of the men when in sight of land.

Hitchcock could easily have cut out the earlier view of the wife as well, along with the rapid montage of which it formed part, "a fusillade of little shots" affectionately analyzed by Dai Vaughan: it also features brief glimpses, likewise only a few frames each, of the skipper's canary.[17] That montage, a tour de force by Stewart McAllister, is not in Hugh Gray's script, and it jars unashamedly with the more sober documentary mode of the rest of the film. Leaving it in could be seen as a mark of respect by Hitchcock to McAllister, to the team of which he was part, to British documentary, and to the wartime work that Bernstein and his colleagues were starting to do with such success.[18] If he had not approached the re-editing work with this basic respect for the original, he could hardly have done the job so effectively. Indeed, it is tempting to go further. The scratching of the image itself, as the skipper is shot, is the kind of bold effect that Len Lye had been enlisted to create for the rail crash in *Secret Agent* (1936) using "hand-painted colour flames," but which Michael Balcon had vetoed (see chapter 2).[19] The brief image of the wife is the kind of swift subjective cut-in that Hitchcock had used more than once in *Murder!* (1930), along with other bits of formal experimentation such as the synchronized chanting of the jury members; but after *Number Seventeen* in 1932 he had increasingly phased out such obtrusive devices in favor of more-integrated narratives. Now, under the tighter control of Hollywood, he may have felt a certain envy of the freedom to experiment that had been part of the remit of British documentary in the 1930s, and that continued to be given to men like McAllister, and Len Lye too, in wartime.

By the time of the second view of the wife—the one cut out by Hitchcock—we are close to the end, and the final voice-over com-

Table 3.3. Comparison of Closing Commentary in *Men of the Lightship* and *Men of Lightship "61"*	
Men of the Lightship	*Men of Lightship "61"*
On January the 31st, a new light vessel is towed out to the East Dudgeon station. [Images of drifting wreckage, no words]	On January the 31st, a new light vessel is towed out to the East Dudgeon station. *As dawn arose on the morning of February the 1st, there was still no news of the ill-fated Lightship Number 61 or its crew. It was not until several days later that a resident of an east coast resort brought in the news that*
The men of the East Dudgeon light died of cold and hunger and wounds on the sands of the east coast. Their story is only one episode in a war of unparalleled horror. The Nazis must be stopped. We must— we can—we will—stop them.	the men of the East Dudgeon *Lightship Number 61* died of cold, hunger, and wounds on the sands of *England's* east coast. *This* story is only one episode in a war of unparalleled horror. *Many men go down to the sea in ships, but surely no men ever died a braver death than these defenseless heroes of Britain's lightship service.*

Note: Text in italics indicates new commentary.

mentary in the re-edit is much closer to the original than it was at the start (table 3.3). The rewording is more expansive and more explicit, taking care to give a brief explanation of when and how the bodies were found: a minor early illustration, perhaps, of Hitchcock's sense of a distinction between British and American audiences, the latter liking to have points more clearly spelled out. The defiant first-person rhetoric of the final two sentences obviously had to be changed, but Sherwood still ends on a powerful note.

Target for Tonight (Harry Watt, 1941)

Hitchcock's task in re-editing *Target for Tonight* was far simpler. The whole point of the film was that, instead of celebrating resistance, as in films like *London Can Take It* and *Lightship* itself, it showed Britain on the attack—mounting a successful bombing raid on German targets. In the course of little more than forty-five minutes, the film traces the planning of the raid, the detailed preparation, the dispatch of aircraft, the long flight to the targets, the dropping of bombs, and the suspenseful return to base—despite strikes by the enemy—of the crew on which the film has focused.

Prime Minister Winston Churchill relished repeated viewings. The American journalist Quentin Reynolds reported how, along with two American diplomats, Harry Hopkins and Averell Harriman, he was invited by Churchill to a screening at his weekend base, Chequers, in late July 1941: " 'We're going to see a film *Target for Tonight,* the story of our bomber planes. I have seen it twice, but I want to see it again.' . . . Churchill smoked furiously, and was as tense as any film fan when things looked bad for the RAF bomber planes over Germany. He smiled when the bombs hit their Nazi targets, and he drew a deep breath of relief when the planes returned safely home."[20] As this suggests, the film was just the kind of hard-hitting story to appeal to American viewers in that period—and indeed after, when America had joined the war. It had a winning topical combination of distinctive British virtues with tense filmic narrative. To quote the review from *Time* magazine (3 November 1941): "*Target for Tonight* (Crown Film Unit; Warner) could never have been made in Hollywood. It is too real. It had to be made exactly where it was: on the flying fields of England, over the grim, green, greasy waters of the Channel; high in the Flak-lit night over Germany. . . . This exquisite documentary film, restrained, intelligent, free from feeble flag-waving and dramatic pretense, is eloquent with superb photography and suspense. It is far & away the best picture that has come out of World War II." All Hitchcock had needed to do was to allow these qualities to come through more rapidly—repeating a pattern that went back as far as *Blackmail* (1929), whose introductory reel had been excised for American audiences (see chapter 2).

The one significant difference between the British and American versions of the film is that in the latter we get to the action more quickly. A total of five shots and fifty-two seconds are lost in the buildup, during which photographic images of German targets are dropped by parachute, collected, and processed, ready to be acted upon. Here and there in the narrative, swear words are toned down, in deference to American censorship—"Hell of a party" becomes "Heck of a party," "By god" becomes "By gosh"—but it is not clear, so far at least, whether Hitchcock or someone else made those adjust-ments. Conceivably there exists somewhere a third version of the film, redubbed (as some sources have assumed) with American accents, but this would hardly fit the terms of the admiring *Time* review, nor is it easy to imagine Hitchcock undertaking it; all we have found in American archives is the modest re-edit. After his more radical work on the *Lightship* film, Hitchcock had surely recognized that this film needed only a minor trim.

What, finally, can we take away from this hitherto obscure episode in Hitchcock's career? His re-editing of the two films provides further evidence, if any were needed, against the attacks on him that were launched at the time by Balcon and others: far from being a deserter, Hitchcock was, from an early stage, operating vigorously in Holly-wood in the British interest, not only through *Foreign Correspondent* (1940), the high-profile anti-isolationist feature film with which he followed *Rebecca,* but also, soon after, through this unobtrusive and uncredited, but committed and craftsmanlike, work for the MoI. But that "deserters" battle was won a long time ago. Of greater interest now, as touched on earlier, is the incentive that the episode gives to rethink Hitchcock's relationship to the British documentary move-ment, and to its founding father John Grierson, who was by now in Canada but had been instrumental in the 1930s in taking on both Cavalcanti (producer of *Men of the Lightship*) and Harry Watt (direc-tor of *Target for Tonight*) as key members of his team.

This issue is discussed in our final chapter, in the context of the extensive tribute to Grierson that Hitchcock filmed for Scottish Television in 1969. Meanwhile, he contributed, in the margins of his feature-film schedule, to a further range of documentary or drama-documentary projects between 1941 and the end of the war.

Bon Voyage and *Aventure Malgache* (1944)

"Lost World War II Classics of Espionage, Suspense and Murder!" This is the tagline for a current DVD release of *Aventure Malgache* and *Bon Voyage,* the two short French-language dramas that Hitchcock directed for the MoI in England early in 1944. Strictly speaking, they were never lost; but they were little seen at the time and were then buried for decades, and in the case of *Aventure Malgache,* actively suppressed. After they became available nearly half a century later, a number of scholars linked them astutely to their political context and to aspects of Hitchcock's work before and after; but the full story remains to be told, and we can at least fill in parts of it.[21]

Sidney Bernstein had liaised closely with Hitchcock over the re-editing of *Men of the Lightship* and *Target for Tonight,* and the two men saw plenty of each other when MoI business brought Bernstein in person to America; there were lunches and dinners, and he was a guest at the Hitchcock home. When Bernstein's remit switched to Europe, and to planning films ahead of invasion and liberation, it was not surprising that he turned again to Hitchcock, who may well, as Selznick feared, already have become tempted by the idea of a longer-term partnership. Although John Russell Taylor suggests that Hitchcock stayed on in England for most of 1944, the records show that this was a short and intensive visit, from early December 1943 to late February, covering planning, preparation, shooting, and initial editing of the two films.[22]

Angus Macphail, an old associate of Hitchcock's from the 1920s onward, had been released from Ealing to work as a script editor for the MoI. He sent advance bulletins to him in America, reassuring him that he would have unrestricted input of his own into the films: "I've already warned Sidney of the dubious value of confronting A. Hitchcock with a completed script." This first letter, dated 29 October 1943, sets out six stories that are under consideration, one of them already recognizable: "Another deals with an R.A.F. pilot who has bailed out over France, been contacted and protected by the French resistance, who have organised his return to England. Reporting to the British and French Intelligence on his return, he states that everybody was very friendly, but that he didn't see any signs of any resistance organisation whatever. . . . We see his journey across France and appreciate that it is the very perfection of the organisation which has caused him to form this impression."[23] By 22 November this subject has acquired a title, *Bon Voyage,* and V. S. Pritchett is working on the script, but the story is essentially the same as before, the story that the film itself will tell—with one crucial exception. There is no hint yet of the twist that will be central to the film, by which the pilot's comrade, Godowski, whom he trusts and admires, is revealed, in the retelling of the story by the intelligence officer, to be a Nazi agent: he has used the naïve pilot to carry a crucial letter to a spy in London and, along the way, to help him identify and eliminate members of the Resistance. It is possible that this twist was now in the process of being developed by Pritchett, a prolific writer known especially for his short stories; Hitchcock admired him enough to call him in two decades later to contribute to the scripting of *The Birds* (1963). *Bon Voyage* carries no personal credits other than Hitchcock's own and that of John Blythe, who plays the pilot, but the minutes of a meeting at his base, Claridge's hotel, on 28 December show that he was by then working on the final script with Macphail and Major J. O. C. Orton (another experienced screenwriter for British films).

In contrast, *Aventure Malgache* is not mentioned ahead of Hitchcock's arrival. Although embarked upon later, it seems to have been scripted and shot first, and its reception, when completed, was much less positive. It is considered separately later.

Macphail had taken care in his letter of 29 October to give Hitchcock this advance warning: "Sidney wants me to make very clear to you the limitations of the scheme. The pictures will not be costly; far from it. Production facilities, as you can guess, are not exactly facile. The time factor is important, so they'll have to be made pretty fast. In fact, it'll need all your ingenuity to give these two-reelers a first-class rating. This certainly isn't meant to scare you off the project; Sidney merely feels that it would be unfair to let you arrive under the impression that we are operating on an M.G.M. basis." Welwyn Studios in Hertfordshire, "where your old associate Robert Clark is in charge," was indeed very different from MGM. The association with Clark dated back to Hitchcock's time at Elstree with British International Pictures (BIP), either side of 1930; the successor company to BIP, the Associated British Pictures Corporation, was forced to move all of its production to the much smaller Welwyn when Elstree was requisitioned for war purposes. The company's wartime output was much inferior in ambition, achievement, and production values to what was being done at studios like Ealing and Pinewood. With *Bon Voyage,* Hitchcock was having to work rapidly and cheaply, and to create atmospheric French settings out of minimal resources.

A strategy becomes apparent as soon as the film goes into flashback from the scene of the pilot's initial debriefing in London to the start of his narrative. No location inserts, no process shots, no elaborate sets, but tight framing, which enhances the sense of oppressive confinement, dodging in the shadows. It is the same kind of minimalist approach that Hitchcock relished explaining to his biographer John Russell Taylor on the set of his last film, *Family Plot* (1976).[24] You can put over basic information and atmosphere out of the simplest of components, the key question always being "What are we selling in this shot?" The pilot and his escort are given instructions about their onward travel, and the next shot locates us with the simplicity of a diagram, making it instantly clear what is being "sold": barn, bicycles, the arrival of two men (fig. 3.11). The later scene on a train, where the men make contact with another Resistance member who enables them to escape, recalls the economy of the train scenes in *The Lady Vanishes* (1938), which was shot on another tiny set, at Islington. Their contact turns out to be a young woman, Jeanne (Janique Joelle), who succeeds in hustling them off the train and away from surveillance—and who from this point becomes the film's emotional center (fig. 3.12).

Janique Joelle, the last surviving member of the cast, has vivid memories of working with Hitchcock; she was interviewed by Alain Kerzoncuf at her home in London in July 2010. Janique had had some experience on the stage, but not in films. She came to England early in the war, toured with Entertainment National Service Association (ENSA) in 1943, and then acquired an agent. She recalled:

> One day he phoned me and said: "Janique, Alfred Hitchcock is at Welwyn Studio, filming." So I said, "All right, I'll go there." Then . . . this is funny. I was supposed to have an audition. When I opened the door, where I was directed to go, facing me were two young men that I knew very well from

Figure 3.11. Visual economy in *Bon Voyage* (1944; Phoenix Films). (Courtesy of the Imperial War Museum film archive)

Figure 3.12. Janique Joelle in *Bon Voyage* (1944; Phoenix Films). (Courtesy of the Imperial War Museum film archive)

a show I'd done. So we talked, and I forgot completely about Alfred Hitchcock. But this was an enormous room, and at the end of that room Hitchcock was filming. After I'd been there about three-quarters of an hour, nothing had happened, so I said to those two young men, "Now we've had enough talk, I'd better go." And they said, "But, you haven't seen Hitchcock." I said, "If he wanted to see me, I've been here long enough." In those days, you see, I never knew the value of Hitchcock at all. So I thought I'd go. And I went!

So I got home at night around eight o'clock, and my agent phoned and he said, "What did you do?" I said I waited for so long, he didn't want to see me, that's that." So he said, "But he wants you on the set tomorrow morning!" I said, "How can he want me on the set? He didn't see me!" He said, "He must have, because that's what he said. He wants you on the set in the morning . . . this man has been seeing twenty-odd girls!" It was an extraordinary situation. He cast me straight away, without having talked to me! I think it was simply my gestures, while I was talking to those friends, that appealed to him, so he said, "That's that. She'll be all right."

Well, it was quite impressive, somebody wanting me. I didn't know Hitchcock at all, but to me, the fact that some chap wanted me to do something, I thought, "It's fantastic!" So I got there, and the first thing I had to do—and you see it in the film—is to go in the train where I'm pushing people out of the door. There's this compartment with the two men and they need to escape from the spies.

And I fell. Bang! I came out of the train door. I only had one short scene, I'm already down on the floor . . . and I split open my knee quite badly. So, "bye-bye." I came home and thought, "Well, that's it." And then my agent said, "What are you doing?" and I said, "I can't go. I've got a bandage on my knee now. A doctor said I should give it two days to recover. So Hitchcock will find somebody else." My agent phoned him and then told me, "No, he doesn't want anybody else. He'll wait." So I said, "Well, if he wants to wait, very good." At

Figure 3.13. A memento from Hitchcock to Janique Joelle in 1944. (Courtesy of Janique Joelle)

Figure 3.14. Janique Joelle with Alain Kerzoncuf, 2010. (Courtesy of Janique Joelle)

the time he didn't mean all that much to me, because I didn't know him. I didn't know he was such an important man. He was a big man, and very funny too.

He was very kind to me. At Welwyn, it is only a few hundred yards from the station to the doors of the studio. But Hitchcock was there on that second day, with somebody else, waiting for me to come out of that train! He's only seen me a few hours doing this funny scene, flopping on the floor.

And there he was! So I thought, "Wow, that's very nice." So
we started that day with something different. My next scene
was, if I remember rightly, I'm bandaging somebody. Some
young man [in fact, the Nazi agent, Godowski]. Now this
scene starts with my father . . . and I knew him in ENSA, a
Belgian actor who used to play on a musical saw, as a solo
act. I knew him quite well. And of course, I wanted to laugh,
before he came in.

He must have been around sixty. The scene began, he
came in, I said hello to him, he talked to me about the Ger-
mans, he said there was one Gestapo man in the area, and
then there was a close-up for an important line, when I said,
"C'est étonnant . . . généralement ils travaillent par deux . . ."
Hitchcock said, "Cut!," so I said, "Oh, what have I done?"
Now I would probably have spoken more respectfully, but at
the time to me he was nobody special, so I said, "Oh, what
have I done?," and he said, "No, I want that again." Oh. So I
did it again, and he said, "Now I've got to tell you something
. . ." And by then, you see, there were about twenty crew men
around, on lights and what not, and he said, "You know,
that face . . . you know . . . not pretty-pretty . . . but that face
will make a lot of films." So I thought, "That's it. At least
something is good." So we got on with that. And of course
after that I see the boy who's leaving for England. So I'm
nearly in tears to see him say good-bye, and he says we must
meet again.

And when he's gone, then I move to the telephone, and
the other chap, who was a German in the story, arrives, and
he's aware what I'm doing. . . . That is a grim scene when he
ends by shooting me. And I went, "Oh!," and I went down
on my knees.

They were my own costumes. That jumper in the scene
where I'm killed was mine, something I knitted myself.

As Macphail had advised, no MGM-style wardrobe department was
at Hitchcock's disposal. The scene of this character's death, killed

by Godowski as she telephones (figs. 3.15–3.17), is the film's climax, beautifully played, and given the kind of meticulous care in tempo and composition that Hitchcock brings to high-intensity moments of death and suffering in feature films before and after.

The film ends with three quick episodes: (1) Godowski using the same telephone to report to his superior and to arrange to visit him that evening; (2) the revelation that this man, on the other end of the phone, is surrounded by Resistance workers and guns, so that we know Godowski will be walking into a trap; and (3) the return to the pilot in London, now sadder and wiser.

There is no doubt that Hitchcock undertook this film with full professional commitment, as the intensity of the death scene indicates, and as other evidence confirms. Manny Yospa, then a junior camera assistant at Welwyn, recalls that Hitchcock storyboarded both films in detail: "He drew every composition—and he was very keen on pace. Because I remember he had his stopwatch and there was a sort of conversation [in *Aventure Malgache*] between two French people and he timed it and said, 'We want it a bit quicker.' Until he got the speed he wanted."[25] In both respects he was following his habitual feature-film practice, as he did also in postproduction, giving extensive "Dubbing and Cutting Notes" after seeing an initial cut, and taking care to check the results. For *Bon Voyage*, these notes covered three close-typed pages, sixteen numbered instructions to his editor Alan Osbiston for the fine-tuning of points of visual rhythm and of soundtrack. Interviewed by Colin Belfrage for his oral history book *All Is Grist*, Osbiston looked back on the experience of working on the two films: "[They were] half-hour fictional thrillers with a heavy propaganda base, and they were bloody good films. I edited both of them, and we got on terribly well together. I learned a lot of tricks from him, elementary stuff really, but all good suspense pointers. When the films were finished I had to go to New York to show them to him. By then he was working, with Ben Hecht, on a film for Cary Grant and Ingrid Bergman, *Notorious* [1946]."[26]

In his cutting notes, Hitchcock had agonized over one specific editing point:

Figures 3.15–
3.17. *Bon
Voyage* (1944;
Phoenix Films).
The Resistance
fighter (Janique
Joelle) is
killed by the
Nazi agent
Godowski as
she telephones.
(Courtesy of the
Imperial War
Museum film
archive)

I feel I am faced in this item with one of the greatest decisions of my whole career. It is whether to include two cows in the Cow Barn scene [fig. 3.11] or to cut them off. When one considers the trouble gone to by the Welwyn authorities to secure two cows as a piece of atmosphere, and when one considers the nauseating job that the prop man had to clear up after them, I really don't know what to do. For the moment I am torn between the Prop man and Robert Clark, who would turn in his prospective grave at the wilful waste of hiring two cows. It is matters like these and problems of this nature that appear to beset the British film industry today. Anyway, enough of all this. I have come to an irrevocable decision—cut out the cows. On second thoughts on hearing a groan from Miss Hopkin at this decision, I pass the buck to Mr Bernstein again, who shall make the decision.

We can take it that Miss Hopkin was taking dictation from Hitchcock and that her response was heard, not imagined. Despite the groan, the final decision was to cut the cows, typically putting what he and Bernstein saw as the interests of the finished film above any other considerations.

McGilligan's biography reveals that Hitchcock watched *Bon Voyage* again in 1958, even toying with the idea of expanding it into a feature, and a link can in fact be made to the film that was then in preparation. Toward the end of *North by Northwest* (1959), at the Mount Rushmore café, Eve draws a gun and appears to shoot Thornhill dead, in front of Vandamm and Leonard, aiming to dispel any suspicion on their part that she might be allied to him and to the U.S. government rather than to them and their side. Later Leonard realizes, and explains to Vandamm: "It's an old Gestapo trick: shoot one of your own people, to prove that you're not one of them. They just freshened it up a bit with blank cartridges." This echoes *Bon Voyage*, where the pilot is puzzled by Godowski's action in killing a Nazi agent after their rendezvous in a café, and asks his London interrogator, "But if Godowski was a spy, why would he kill a fellow spy?"

The officer duly explains. Hitchcock—along with his screenwriter, Ernest Lehman, if he too saw the film in 1958—was surely drawing on this to resolve that notoriously tricky plot point in the long process of scripting *North by Northwest*.[27]

Before it could be shown publicly to its intended French audience, *Bon Voyage* ran into difficulties for diplomatic reasons. There were negative reports on it, as well as on *Aventure Malgache*, from French officials in London, who queried some of the accents and other details and expressed a preference for something authentically French and appropriately epic. With predictable caution, some British officials were swayed by this; Sir Timothy Eden from the War Office, brother of the future prime minister Anthony Eden, was one of those who went on record as favoring suppression. But Bernstein hit back strongly. This was a modest British tribute to the Resistance that was not in competition with any future French epic—why not let a French audience decide? And in October 1944, the manager of a Paris cinema reported on a sneak preview:

> We ran this film as a supporting item at the Radio Cité Bastille cinema.
>
> The public, who had no advance notice of the film, gave it a very good reception.
>
> The Englishman who plays the man on the run gained immediate sympathy, for his youth and his pleasant personality.
>
> The members of the Resistance created suspense as the audience tried to work out who was going to come to the help of the two men. This was especially so in the scene on the train, where the pair made use of a password to identify themselves.
>
> When the officer of the Deuxième Bureau in London told the narrative of the Gestapo intrigue, the audience waited eagerly for the end of the story—and did not hold back on its feelings of outrage.
>
> Finally, when Holberg [*sic*] is held prisoner by the Resistance in his hotel room, the audience applauded, and did so again when the word The End came up on the screen.

To sum up, this short supporting film made a very positive impact on an ordinary local audience.[28]

Janique herself caught the film at another Paris cinema, probably during 1945. She recalled: "The first time I saw *Bon Voyage* was out of the blue, when I went to Paris with my sister. I said 'Let's go to the Champs-Elysées,' and then, after walking about a bit, 'Let's see a film.' I forget now what the main film was, but when I bought our tickets the woman cried out, 'Oooh, c'est la vedette [the star].' I thought she was mad, but then she said, '*Bon Voyage, Bon Voyage.*' "

This was very possibly at the Cinéma des Champs-Elysées, during the week of 21–27 September 1945, where its screening as a support film was publicized. Truffaut told Hitchcock that he recalled seeing it in Paris in late 1944; he may have confused the year, or he may have been present at the 1944 preview referred to previously.[29] Either way, his memory confirms that the film did make an impact. In 1945, it formed part of a purposeful schedule of films released throughout Liberated Europe by the Films Division of the MoI. Copies of dozens of British films were made available via the relevant embassies: features and documentaries and a few "specials." Among these specials, available on request from the embassies in Belgium and France, was *Bon Voyage*.[30] An article by D.R. in *Le Film Français* for October 1945 gives an account of this MoI initiative and indicates that more than twenty French distributors are taking advantage of it. After running through a number of popular titles, it ends by singling out two films that are sure to be particularly attractive to French audiences, *Bon Voyage* being one of them.

Its sister film, *Aventure Malgache,* however, is nowhere in the list. Hitchcock told Truffaut firmly that this was not released;[31] the criticism levelled at it after the first previews was harder to resist, and it is not hard to see why. But it is of comparable interest to *Bon Voyage* both as a document of its time and as an ingenious Hitchcock exercise.

It was not included in Macphail's advance list of topics for Hitchcock to consider, but seems to have been developed as a result of Hitchcock's talking at Claridge's hotel to a variety of Frenchmen in

exile and realizing the extent of their divisions, which invited dramatization. One of these men was a lawyer, Jules Clermont (also known
as Paul Clarus), who was now acting with the Molière Players in London and had been prominent in the recent struggle of the Resistance
in Madagascar against strong Vichyite opposition. His story had clear
appeal as a vivid topical one, and preparations to film it were rapid.
Notes from the conference held in Hitchcock's suite at Claridge's on
28th December 1943 indicate that this scenario was already finished;
its authenticity was to be strengthened by enlisting Jacques Brunius
as consultant and the actor Claude Dauphin to finalize the dialogue;
"meanwhile, Mr Calder-Marshall will proceed immediately to obtain
written consent to the story from the official departments, not forget-
ting the French."[32] Clermont would reenact his own role, under the
name of Clarus, as well as helping to supply dialogue. Since the script
of *Bon Voyage* was not yet complete, *Aventure Malgache* may have
been shot first.

Ironically, the very intensity of its French focus would work
against the film. In contrast to *Bon Voyage,* which deploys a naïve
Briton, ruthless Nazis, and heroic French Resistance workers, in
Aventure Malgache Clarus and his allies have to struggle vigorously
against fellow countrymen, led by the crooked police chief Michel
and the feebly collaborationist governor. As in *Bon Voyage,* the most
intense scene involves a woman and a telephone, but the emphasis is
very different, symptomatic of the factors that made the film unacceptable to its intended audience. Men are being smuggled off the
island of Madagascar in order to join the Free French. Clarus has
given in to the plea of one of them, Pierre, to be allowed to go first
to say good-bye to his fiancée. In a simple unbroken two-shot lasting
two minutes, Pierre (at left of frame) explains why he has to leave her;
she urges him desperately to stay, without success. He exits, and the
camera then moves slightly to the right to foreground the telephone,
which after a moment she uses to inform the police.

In style, the scene is typical of *Aventure Malgache.* In contrast to
the close-ups and cutting of the main flashback part of *Bon Voyage,*
it consists mainly of *plans-séquences,* long takes of anything up to
two and a half minutes, often setting antagonists within the same

frame: an alternative way of handling the challenge of limited time and studio resources, appropriate to this story and its succession of encounters and arguments. In these two shorts, then, Hitchcock was making skilled and rigorous use of the two contrasting filmic strategies that he would push to an extreme soon after: the tight editing-based style of *Notorious,* and the long-take style of *Rope.*

Although it failed in its immediate purpose, *Aventure Malgache* has all the more historical value as a contemporary record of conflicts that a straightforward propaganda film could not have acknowledged. According to the initial title, the film would show "that in the furthest parts of the French Empire, across the seas, the same spirit has inspired its citizens." But it proceeds to show that not all citizens were thus inspired. And in 1947 this particular French colony would be the site of a major uprising, ahead of the achievement of independence in 1960. Another of Hitchcock's long takes has Clarus, after his arrest, pretending to be ready to be submissive at his trial—he expresses his true intentions only after the lawyer's exit. Between the two men, a black soldier looks on impassively throughout, like a portent of the future (fig. 3.18).

The awkward topicality of the story counted against the film in a further way, and continued to do so for decades. Since it was based on real people, there was a fear of libel actions, as well as of offending the sensibilities of the French, who had successfully opposed the initial release. Archival documents vividly illuminate the complexities of the case and the factors that led to the film's long suppression; they add up to an absorbing contextualizing narrative to set alongside the narrative of the film itself.

The film's central figure, Clermont/Clarus, can be tracked through the files of Special Operations Executive (SOE), to whom he was attached for a time under the code name DZ 91.[33] The files contain an undated cutting from the *Evening Standard:*

> Maitre Jules Clermand [*sic*], Paul Clarus as he is known at the Theatre Molière here, tells how he was once a "radio station" all on his own.
>
> He was being sent back from Madagascar to Vichy France

Figure 3.18. *Aventure Malgache* (1944; Phoenix Films). Jules Clermont *(right)* as Clarus. (Courtesy of the Imperial War Museum film archive)

as a Gaullist prisoner when British warships raided the convoy. He was freed, taken on board a destroyer, and broadcast from the ship in the Indian Ocean as "Madagascar Freedom Radio."

M. Clermand was a lawyer in Madagascar for many years. His start in life was on the stage, then a legal appointment took him to Madagascar. Now in his early fifties he has gone back to his first love.

An internal memo of 2 February 1942 gives more details:

The new one-man [radio] post (*Madagascar Libre*) averaged 45 minutes each night. Mr. Clermont is extremely versatile: he speaks in French, Malgache and the trade Creole patois used by Indian and Chinese merchants in Madagascar. His personality is powerful and somewhat disreputable. He never minces words and both his idioms and his anecdotes are frequently vulgar without being coarse. He exalts in his freedom to listen to world radios and to comment freely on the news they give. He is robustly confident in an Allied victory.

This voice has aroused intense interest and amusement among listeners in Mauritius who consider his performance to be witty and admirably suited to the mentality of the average French Functionnaire [sic] or merchant in Madagascar.

Just before the second Madagascar operation, the station was closed down for reasons of security and for the same reason our Mission pressed us to allow them to send him to the U.K. as they did not want him in Mauritius or South Africa during the operation. We agreed that he should come with the idea that he should be transferred to P.W.E. [Political Warfare Executive] for work with their new Propaganda Mission in West Africa which was then being organised.

M. Clermont's arrival coincided with the North African operation, and P.W.E.'s plans for subversive propaganda had to be changed.

Since the end of October, Clermont's services have been offered to P.W.E., O.S.S., O.W.I., J. and H. Sections and to A.M.V., but none of them have been able to offer him employment.

While he has been in London he has done a little work for the London Transcription Service and the B.B.C. and also briefed General Legentilhomme and various other officials at Fighting French Headquarters on conditions in Madagascar.

The next memo is dated 16 March 1943 and helps to explain the difficulty of finding more sustained work for him:

Clermont tells me he has been trying to discover why the Fighting French refused to employ him, and from a friend who works at the Fighting French headquarters he has come to the following conclusions:

(a) Because of his Broadcasts from "Madagascar Libre,"

where his line was—"do not join the British, do not join the Americans, do not join de Gaulle—remain French and independent—denounce Vichy and the Axis and rally to the United Nations." Therefore the Fighting French argue his broadcasts were anti-Gaullist.

(b) Some of de Gaulle's influential advisers are strongly against recruiting any Frenchmen who have previously worked for or had close connections with the British.

(c) There is some suspicion that the British authorities might retain an interest in Clermont and use him as an agent inside Fighting French headquarters.

(d) There has apparently been an indication from Madagascar that it would be unwise for Clermont to return there. His very outspoken broadcasts upset too many people who have now "turned their coats" and are working with the Administration, and they would make things very unpleasant for him.

Aventure Malgache would of course focus very precisely on these "turncoats" and could be guaranteed to upset them. There is no evidence in the files as to whether Bernstein or Macphail or anyone else connected with Films Division was aware of the full complexity of the issues, or of the way they were being monitored by SOE. Talking to Truffaut, Hitchcock described the way the film—unmentioned, as we have seen, in the correspondence that preceded his arrival—was developed directly out of the work on *Bon Voyage:* "The Free French forces supplied me with technical advisers. For instance, Claude Dauphin helped us with the dialogue. We used to work on the screenplay in my room at Claridge's, and there was a whole group of French officers, including a certain Commander or Colonel Forestier who never agreed to anything the others suggested. We realized that the Free French were very divided against one another, and these inner conflicts became the subject of the next film, *Aventure Malgache*."[34]

Clermont/Clarus may have been part of these initial arguments, and he was certainly soon involved, in his double capacity as actor and activist, in planning this second script. Bearing in mind his frustrations since arriving in London, as summarized in the SOE document from 1942—"Clermont's services have been offered to P.W.E., O.S.S., O.W.I., J. and H. Sections and to A.M.V., but none of them have been able to offer him employment"—he must have jumped at the chance to work with Hitchcock in dramatizing and acting out his own story.

A fellow member of the Molière company, Elma Soiron, has recalled the routine at Claridge's.[35] Being bilingual, she took on the role of interpreter, translating and performing various roles in the story scene by scene, though she would not in the event appear in either film. Arriving in this grand establishment, "with gilt everywhere," made an unforgettable impression on her. After knocking at the door of the room to which she had been directed, she was greeted by a "small, rather stout man." She asked this charming character if she could speak to Mr. Hitchcock, whereupon he replied, "But I am Mr. Hitchcock!" With Soiron as intermediary, Clermont presented the story, in the presence of two others whose names are not recorded, possibly Angus Macphail and a colleague such as J. O. C. Orton or even V. S. Pritchett. After an "excellent lunch" at Claridge's restaurant, work resumed until the evening, during which time Soiron, as the only woman present, felt obliged to serve the tea when it was brought in on a trolley.

Like *Bon Voyage,* with its focus on John Blythe, *Aventure Malgache* foregrounds only one actor, Clermont/Clarus himself, but it builds the Molière Players into the story. The opening titles refer to a troupe of French actors working in Britain for the benefit of French exiles and also of Francophile Britons; the story is recounted by one of these actors (Clermont/Clarus) to another (Paul Bonifas) as they prepare to perform a stage version of the same narrative. The film's initial image, after the title, briefly shows a poster for the Molière Players before panning left to the Green Room.

The company was founded in 1943 by the Free French actors, under the direction of Bonifas. Membership overlapped with that of the Belgian theater company of London. Three of the *Malgache* cast were featured in a show put on at the Institute Belge in London on 4 April: Bonifas himself, Clermont/Clarus, and André Frère. All three are there again—along with Paulette Preney and the witness from

Figure 3.19. Théâtre
Molière poster, 1943.
(Courtesy of Henri
Dominique Bonifas
private collection)

Claridge's, Elma Soiron—in the Molière company's show on 12 December, staged at a prominent West End theater and well publicized (fig. 3.19).

It seems very plausible that on that occasion Alfred Hitchcock would have been in the audience, as he had arrived in London nine days earlier, on 3 December, and was already intensively involved in preparing the two films. Clermont/Clarus was integral to the deal already, since the story was his own, but the performance could have

Figure 3.20. Paul
Bonifas in uniform
as a lieutenant in the
Free French forces.
(Courtesy of Henri
Dominique Bonifas
private collection)

Figure 3.21. Paul Bonifas as Michel in *Aventure Malgache* (1944; Phoenix Films). (Courtesy of the Imperial War Museum film archive)

acted as an audition for the others, notably Paulette Preney, cast in the important role of the fiancée who makes the phone call. Bonifas would hardly have needed an audition, since he led the company and already had film experience in Britain as well as France.[36]

The care taken over casting, as well as story and scripting, confirms just what a solid and serious Anglo-French collaboration the film constituted—too solid and serious for its own good, both in the short term and for decades after, since it would not be made freely available for half a century.

After the war ended, the MoI was wound up, and some of its responsibilities, including film ones, passed to the Central Office of Information (COI). This letter between two of the COI officials, identified only as Mr B and Mr H, is dated 28 February 1957:

I should be glad of your advice on the request via the F.O. [Foreign Office] for a Monsieur Clermont to borrow a 35mm print of *Aventure Malgache* (Madagascar Adventure).

We have a print (French version), but I am not sure if we should release it.

Mons. Jules François Clermont was a French lawyer who practised in Madagascar, was imprisoned by supporters of the Vichy government, escaped and worked for the British through "Madagascar Libre" broadcasts from Mauritius. Later, he came to London with Paul Bonifas' Moliere Theatre.

Clermont was offered £50 for full rights in the story and for his collaboration with a third party in turning the story into a script. Crown's copyright appears to have been restricted to the use of the story as the basis of a propaganda short film in French and other languages "without restriction either as to the manner in which the film is to be exploited or the territories in which it is to be distributed." M.O.I. were to have the right of commercial exploitation.

International Contracts Ltd. [a subsidiary of Associated British Picture Corporation Ltd. of Welwyn], under a contract negotiated by Mr. Sydney [sic] Bernstein, undertook to make the film for a fixed price of £5,000. Alfred Hitchcock was director.

From the very beginning the idea failed to win the support of French Section and representatives of the French Resistance here in London, but the film was completed. When it was shown to the film officer and his staff in Paris, however, he advised against its release and the project was abandoned.

In the light of this, do you think we could be justified in lending our print to Clermont?

This is followed by a handwritten answer: "NO."

This obstacle to the screening of *Aventure Malgache* even at film festivals (such as Oberhausen, Brussels, and London) officially applied until 3 September 1993, when the film was at last presented in a public screening at the Everyman Cinema in Hampstead, under the auspices of the British Film Institute (BFI).

What can explain such a relentless campaign against a short film? Here is a later COI memo from 7 October 1963, the Foreign Office again being involved:

> *Aventure Malgache:* this is the title of a Hitchcock film in our Copyright made towards the end of the war. It was recently requested by the Belgian Film Archive for a Hitchcock season.
>
> Because of its subject matter, I viewed the film with Miss C. of Foreign Office and we were both doubtful of the wisdom of releasing it because of the potentially libellous material it contains. It was then seen by Mr. O., Assistant Head of Western Department, F.O., who agreed with our view and is referring the matter to Foreign Office Legal Adviser for a ruling. . . .
>
> B.F.I. hold the preservation print of the film and have been told not to release it pending further instructions. A 16mm copy has been made for C.O.I. use and is in our vaults.

This extremely rigid attitude remained unshaken, and in August 1979 prevented the screening of the film at a Hitchcock retrospective at the

National Film Theatre in London, organized by David Meeker on behalf of the BFI.

Initially authorized to show the BFI print of *Aventure Malgache* on 22 August, Meeker was later informed at short notice that this was no longer possible, for the reasons just cited. Despite attempted scare tactics (such as threatening media exposure) and other arguments, the officials could not be persuaded. This is how Meeker recalls the experience:

> Throughout the 1960s and the 1970s a major (and by far the most interesting) part of my work at the B.F.I. was to supply the National Film Theatre with the 2,000 or so films that it required each year. That is, locating acceptable copies, tracking down copyright claimants and negotiating accordingly for our screenings. Several times during that period we wanted to screen this short as part of one of our programmes but permission from the copyright holder was always refused. The various UK Government authorities set up before and during World War II to produce propaganda were all merged into one entity called the Central Office of Information (C.O.I.) and this organisation still exists today to take care of the many thousands of films in its care, and still produces all our Government-sponsored material for cinemas, television and, particularly, for overseas promotions. Back in the days when I was in contact with them they were an extremely bureaucratic office and, I always suspected, simply repeated their standard mantra to all enquiries about the film *ad nauseam* without ever taking the trouble to pass such enquiries up to their superiors. When pressed, they always argued that the film contained "operational secrets" that must be protected for the security of the country. This was plainly nonsense but I could never get them to re-examine someone's original decision even 20 or 30 years after the war. . . .
>
> Obviously, all those reactionary bureaucrats at the C.O.I. have long since departed and someone (probably a younger cine-literate person) eventually took the trouble to refer to the

original production contracts or to simply ask his superiors to review the situation which by the 1990s had obviously become scandalously absurd. The film then became generally available for screenings, video, etc. I recall taking a print to Berlin as part of a talk that I was asked to give to film students as they'd never had a chance to see it before.

Incidentally, the B.F.I. being a charitable organisation, free of censorship and strictly non-commercial (in those days) and with a strong educational leaning, it was very rare indeed for anyone to refuse us permission to screen their work—unless for strictly commercial reasons. For example, we never had the slightest problems in screening Nazi material that was totally banned elsewhere. This one short film was virtually unique in that way.[37]

Unlike Janique Joelle, who saw *Bon Voyage* in Paris at the end of the war, none of the actors in *Aventure Malgache* is thus likely to have seen the result of their work—Clermont/Clarus may have been shown it on completion, but even he, as we have seen, was refused a viewing in 1957—nor would they have had the satisfaction of knowing that others were seeing it. But the film survives, and we can honor their work here. *Aventure Malgache,* and to a lesser extent *Bon Voyage,* remained genuinely lost from view for several decades, until the continued passage of time exerted its healing power.

American Public-Service Films

All of the wartime items so far considered are British-centered: Hitchcock worked on British material in Hollywood and then went back to work in a British studio. Later in the war, though, he did two pieces of public service work, uncredited, on films with a purely American focus.

The Fighting Generation (1944)

The short film *The Fighting Generation,* sometimes referred to as a "trailer," was widely shown in American cinemas in late 1944 to promote the sale of War Bonds. Its ephemeral status, and the lack of any production credits, led to its being forgotten for decades, but a print has been held at the Academy Film Archive in Los Angeles since 1945, and extensive documentation survives in the David O. Selznick Collection in the Harry Ransom Center, University of Texas at Austin. It was shot by Hitchcock at the Selznick studios in a single day, Monday, 9 October 1944.

Set in a hospital, the film runs just one minute fifty-two seconds. A young nurse's aide, played by Jennifer Jones, recites a monologue written by Stephen Longstreet. During the opening credits, she leans over an injured man lying in bed, after which she turns to face the camera in close-up to recite her message (figs. 3.22–3.24):

> He's asleep now. His name is Johnny. Private First Class, badly wounded on Saipan. As a nurse's aide, I see many cases like this. Most of them are strangers to me. But Johnny, well, we were kids together. Johnny took me to my first high school dance, and knowing Johnny, I feel I know all the boys here. You see, they're my generation, part of my world, my fun, my hopes. Someday all the boys and girls will come back home. No, not all of them. But those that do, you can help bring them back sooner by buying a share of their faith in victory. By buying a War Bond. You know, they used to talk about the lost generation. The forgotten generation. Of generations without hope. But not Johnny's generation. Please be like Johnny. He didn't think he'd have to fight so many battles. But he went right on, giving a little extra courage. So let's all of us do a little something extra too. And buy that Bond beyond the one we've planned for. Surely that isn't too much to do for a fighting generation.

Jennifer Jones had won the Best Actress Academy Award for *The Song of Bernadette* (Henry King, 1943) and had already worn a nurse's uniform in Selznick's epic home-front production *Since You Went Away*, directed by John Cromwell and shown with great success in mid-1944. The latter film includes a formal scene in which Jones

Figures 3.22–3.23. The opening credits of *The Fighting Generation* (1944; Vanguard Films). (Courtesy of the David O. Selznick Collection, Harry Ransom Center, University of Texas at Austin, and Academy Film Archive, Los Angeles)

Figure 3.24. Jennifer Jones speaking to the camera in *The Fighting Generation* (1944; Vanguard Films). (Courtesy of the David O. Selznick Collection, Harry Ransom Center, University of Texas at Austin, and Academy Film Archive, Los Angeles)

and other young nurses take an oath on graduation; she succeeds in making us empathize with the emotions of all these young women, helped undoubtedly by her own training—noted in the *Fighting Generation* credit—as a nurse's aide only months earlier.

The studio call sheet for *A Fighting Generation* indicates that other actors were scheduled to appear, including Rhonda Fleming, soon to play a role for Hitchcock and Selznick in *Spellbound* (1945); Longstreet's initial treatment had included several scenes and several participants. In the event, Jones carries the film alone, partly no doubt because Selznick was keen to showcase the young protégée who would become his wife five years later. His concern for her and his dominance of the project are evident in the message sent on 23 October 1944 to the Director of Motion Pictures, War Finance Division:

> We have just finished editing and scoring of Bond short. I think I can honestly say that it looks superb. It runs one hundred seventy feet and I think it will do a great deal of good for the nurses' aides as well as for the War Bond program. I assume that you will give the orders for the necessary footage, in accordance with our conversation. In as much as the short is a solo by Miss Jones, it could be very damaging to her career if the laboratory work destroyed the photographic quality which we were able to achieve—thanks to the commander [Gregg] Toland who photographed it. In view of this and the extraordinary pains to which we went to make this short, directed by Alfred Hitchcock, of first class quality in every respect and up to the standard of our very best pictures, I should sincerely appreciate if you would give instructions that the laboratory work is to be done with care, consistent with first class productions instead of with usual laboratory work which trailers receive. This is one favor that I ask on behalf of Miss Jones and ourselves and I shall be grateful for your assistance and for confirmation from you.

Selznick's request was granted, and some 12,000 high-quality prints of the short were produced, and screened throughout the country.

Even prisoners at the San Quentin State Prison were shown the film, as reported by Ezra Goodman in *American Cinematographer* (August 1945), "in order to keep the inmates posted on the latest developments of war."

It would be hard to claim that this very simple film in any way bears Hitchcock's signature. All the records show that the project was shaped by Selznick, who selected the actress, the director, and the cameraman and specified the style of the end credit in an internal memo: "Make up End card, and show to DOS before photographing, using *Rebecca* type of lettering—simple and dignified." The lettering is indeed identical with that of *Rebecca*. But in one minor detail, the music, Selznick did not get his way. He suggested using a track from a scene in Paramount's *So Proudly We Hail* (Mark Sandrich, 1943), where a boy dies and his mother talks about him; the idea had to be abandoned, and instead we hear "The Battle Hymn of the Republic," possibly taken from the soundtrack of Selznick's pre-*Rebecca* production *Gone with the Wind* (1939).

An official of the Treasury Department in Washington wrote to Selznick on 22 November 1944: "On Behalf of the War Finance Division of the United States Treasury Department and on my behalf, I want you to know how much we appreciate your production of the Sixth War Loan Trailer starring Jennifer Jones. It was a fine contribution to our campaign. A great story was told in a few feet of film. When that story is magnified by the screens of 16,000 theaters, I know we will find that it has resulted in tremendous Bond sales."

Like Jones, Hitchcock was not paid extra for the work; unlike her, he was not named. Did he simply wish to do Selznick a good turn? Did Selznick put pressure on him? Or did he wish to placate him for his planned absence at the end of the year? On 11 October, only two days after the shooting of *A Fighting Generation*, Selznick cabled his assistant Jenia Reissar to complain about the way in which Sidney Bernstein had summoned Hitchcock back to England: "I am surprised by the discourtesy of seeking out Hitchcock for a second trip to England without so much as even contacting us, which is something that would not be done with an American producer by even the United States government—STOP—I should also like it to be said that I hope that one of the motives behind bringing Mr. Hitchcock back to England is not a desire to negotiate a private deal with him for the future." Selznick had good reason, of course, to be suspicious, since Bernstein was operating in his dual capacity of public service official (for the Ministry of Information) and of entrepreneur—steadily taking over as Hitchcock's preferred partner in what became Transatlantic Pictures.

It is also possible that in taking on the War Bonds film Hitchcock might—like Jones herself—have wished to be seen to atone for earlier reluctance to support this cause. On 15 June 1942, a staff member had written to Selznick noting that "with the exception of Alfred Hitchcock, Alan Marshal, K.T. Stevens, and Phyllis Walker [aka Jennifer Jones], everyone on the D.O.S.P. payroll has authorized a deduction, either weekly or monthly, for the purchase of U.S. War Savings Bonds. Whitney Bolton has agreed to call on Hitchcock and impress upon him the importance of subscribing." On 3 July, the same colleague told Selznick that "Hitch's last proposal to Whitney Bolton was that he would invest 5% of his salary in Bonds if Myron [David's brother and Hitchcock's agent] would invest 5% of his 10% commission in Bonds. This is a typically ridiculous Hitchcock proposal—Myron personally is already purchasing a considerable amount weekly."

On the one hand, Hitchcock is seen here as uncharitable. On the other, he was always ready to do low-paid or unpaid work for good causes on both sides of the Atlantic—as is evident, repeatedly, in what follows.

Watchtower over Tomorrow (1945)

A long-forgotten topical short film from 1945, urging the importance of the drive to set up a United Nations organization, *Watchtower over Tomorrow* was the subject of an enterprising piece of archival exploration by Sidney Gottlieb ("The Unknown Hitchcock: *Watchtower over Tomorrow*") as long ago as 1996, for the *Hitchcock Annual*—one of the earliest pieces of research of this kind on Hitchcock that we know, done very much in the same spirit as this book. He

located surviving prints and plenty of documentation, and we draw
heavily upon his work.

Watchtower over Tomorrow is presented by "The American Motion Picture Industry": there are no personal credits for filmmakers or
cast. Though Hitchcock was certainly involved, he is not named in the
brief notice of the completed film in Variety on 4 April 1945, which
lists Ben Hecht and Karl Lamb as writers, and John Cromwell and
Harold Kress as directors. Cromwell had recently, like Hitchcock,
worked for David O. Selznick, directing his patriotic home-front epic
Since You Went Away; since then he had remade The Enchanted Cottage (1945), which had so enchanted Hitchcock when made as a silent
by John S. Robertson. Kress was an experienced editor—never for
Hitchcock—whose few director credits lay in the future; his credit
here may acknowledge the prominence of the film's montage sequences, illustrating themes both of peace and of war.

Variety in addition credits five actors: Lionel Stander, Grant
Mitchell, Jonathan Hale, Miles Mander, and George Zucco. Mander, who had worked with Hitchcock three times in England (on The
Prude's Fall [1925], The Pleasure Garden [1926], and Murder!/Mary
[1930]), is not visible, at least not in surviving prints, but an important role is played at the end by Martin Kosleck, as sinister as he had
been in Hitchcock's Foreign Correspondent five years earlier (figs.
3.25 and 3.26).

Though unmentioned in the Variety notice, Hitchcock took part
in the planning and preparation, and he may simply have been too
busy at the time to see it through as director, as had happened early
in the war in the case of Forever and a Day. As noted previously,
that film was planned in early 1940 as a patriotic effort by the Hollywood British, but it was not finished until late 1942, a year after
America joined the war, by which time it had clearly missed its moment. Watchtower was more urgently topical and was turned around
much faster—less than four months from initial proposal to finished
film. Hitchcock's input, even if curtailed, was serious.

The film is fronted by the secretary of state, Edward Stettinius Jr.,
who speaks a two-minute introduction to camera, with a portrait of
President Franklin D. Roosevelt visible behind him. Stettinius lasted

Figures 3.25–3.26. Undermining world peace: Martin Kosleck in *Foreign Correspondent* (1940; Walter Wanger Productions) and in *Watchtower over Tomorrow* (1945; U.S. War Activities Committee). (Courtesy of the BFI National Archive / Library of Congress)

only seven months in the post: he took over from Cordell Hull in late
November 1944, after having already worked hard to promote the
United Nations vision, and in July 1945 he became America's first
delegate to the UN itself. His short tenure was dominated by twin
concerns: the UN, and the importance of mobilizing public opinion
behind it. The official historian of his time in office outlines the sheer
volume of leaflets, speeches, and radio programs that were deployed:
"There could be little question that Stettinius was the inspiration behind this public information program. On December 15, 1944, after
he had become Secretary, he commented on the importance of having
the American public discuss and understand the proposals: 'It is only
through public discussion, knowledge and understanding that the
peace to come can rest upon firm foundations of popular support and
participation—and thus be truly a people's peace.' "[38] A high-profile
film could clearly make a strong contribution to this drive.

The decision to commission a script was made in early December, after which, in the words of Michael Leigh, writing in 1976:
"The public affairs people contacted Alfred Hitchcock, who agreed
to direct the film, and Ben Hecht, the playwright, then under contract
to Twentieth Century Fox, who undertook to write the script. Hitchcock and Hecht arrived in Washington on December 26 and sat up
most of the night roughing out a script. The next day Hecht read the
script to an august meeting in the Department of State, including the
secretary. 'Everybody thought [the script] was an excellent job,' Stettinius noted."[39] Gottlieb supplements that account with material from
the MGM archives as well as the Stettinius papers, showing how the
verbal part of the script evolved through successive versions. Hecht
and Hitchcock were established collaborators, by now planning *Notorious* together after completing *Spellbound*. In a note on the initial
draft of 26 December, Hecht indicates that the visuals in support of
the words—envisaged then as a sustained narration by Stettinius—
"will be thought up by the master, Mr Hitchcock." So far, so good.

Leigh states that "Hitchcock made the rest of the film in Hollywood,"[40] which seems to be just an assumption: he was evidently
unaware of the conflicting data given in *Variety,* and there seems in
fact to be no evidence that Hitchcock, busy with other things, stayed

with the project beyond early January 1945. On 13 January, to quote
Gottlieb's research on the Stettinius papers: "A memo from Wilder
Foote indicates that Francis Russell, the director of the office of Public
Affairs, was sent to oversee the production because, as Foote notes, 'I
fear there is too much chance of the film's going wrong on important
policy points, especially with the combined imaginations of Messrs
Hecht and Hitchcock at work.' "

Foote was a loyal associate of Stettinius's: he later accompanied
him to the Yalta conference as press attaché and subsequently dedicated his career to the UN and its ideals. His memo indicates a tension that may already have been irritating the two filmmakers. Foote
also records that the formal introduction to the film by Stettinius had
been shot on the previous day, 12 January, not by Hitchcock but by
Elia Kazan.

Hecht's reference to the film in his 1954 autobiography indeed
expresses frustration: "[The film's] purpose was to make the citizenry
who gaped at it in the movie theaters fall in love with the wonders of
the United Nations. What these wonders were no one in the [State]
Department seemed to know. I finally put some scraps of information together, larded them with rhetoric and war episodes and sent the
script on to Hollywood for production. I came away from a week's
toil in the Department stunned by my own naiveté."[41] Only the initial
script of 26 December has his name on it: later ones all bear the names
of Karl Lamb and George B. Seitz Jr. But Hecht was still given a shared
script credit in *Variety,* presumably as the one whose initial concept
had given the film a basic drive and shape that it retained throughout
the subsequent negotiations. Even if Hitchcock left the film as early
as Hecht did, after a week's toil, his own initial concept may likewise
have helped to shape the way the visual and dramatic side of the film
was handled—giving him a role comparable to the one he took on
the concentration camps film in London a few months later, that of a
"treatment adviser" who exerted an influence even if he did not personally handle any scenes. At least up to a point, it can then be counted
as "quasi-Hitchcock." Gottlieb's detailed account of the film argues
that certain formal elements can plausibly be seen as Hitchcockian
and could thus have been directed or at least conceived by him.

Two details can be linked to his work soon after on the camps film. On that, he was insistent on developing a pattern of contrast between the horror of the camps themselves and the peaceful rural scenes that surrounded them. In *Watchtower* there is a comparable strong contrast between apocalyptic war scenes—both real recent ones and fictional futuristic ones—and scenes of peace. In Gottlieb's words, "A montage of scenes of fighting superimposed over a spinning globe gives way to its opposite, a montage of scenes of men working and children playing ('happy and unafraid')." As with the camps film, one can note that the structure is fairly predictable but could plausibly have been insisted on from the start by Hitchcock as a foundational element.

Another piece of his advice on the camps project, appropriate to other kinds of scene, was to use, wherever possible, long unbroken shots of atrocity footage that linked together different elements and thereby ensured against any suspicion of fabrication. *Watchtower,* in its one emotional moment of personal grief, uses camera movement in the same kind of spirit, as if pointedly to refuse conventional emotive montage. To quote Gottlieb once again: "The camera cuts to a domestic setting and pans from a child and his dog playing on the floor to a framed picture of a soldier and then to a father and mother reading a letter and crying. . . . One can perhaps recognize Hitchcock's hand in it: he of course always liked to tell stories and give background information pictorially rather than verbally, and he often used a panning action rather than straight cuts to go from one element to another, as in the opening of *Rear Window,* for example." The strategy could perhaps have been sketched out by Hitchcock in the initial brainstorming sessions and retained—or even shot by him, if he did return at some point to the project. He would certainly not have been averse to the inclusion of the dog alongside the young boy.

Gottlieb cites other shots, some of them evocative of D. W. Griffith, in whose work the young Hitchcock was steeped; he had paid tribute to him in a 1930 article as "A Columbus of the Screen." These shots include the ending: "The final title, 'The End,' appears over a cloudy sky with light shining diagonally across the frame. These concluding images are commonplace and even predictable, but perhaps we may sense another subtle overlapping of the Hitchcock

with the Griffith touch as the ending echoes the visionary and apocalyptic finale of such films as *Birth of a Nation* [1915] and *Intoler-
ance* [1916]." "Perhaps we may sense . . ." Gottlieb is right to be
cautious, but it seems in the end less important to establish exactly
what Hitchcock did or did not do than to recognize the significance
within his career of the fact of his work on this minor and ephemeral
film. There is continuity on the one hand with the camps project,
and on the other hand with the feature film that he and Hecht were
preparing at this time, *Notorious*. All three are concerned, in different ways, with the dangers of a revived fascist aggression. The camps
film seeks to help the process of damning and exorcising the crimes
of Nazism. *Notorious* identifies the survival of Nazi plotters in South
America and dramatizes their defeat. *Watchtower over Tomorrow*
ends with its own dramatization, set years in the future: What if a nation again threatens world peace? We see the delegate of "Nation X"
defying the UN and walking truculently out; a range of sanctions is
quickly put in place to isolate the offender. Gottlieb sees the delegate
as "vaguely Oriental," but, as shown here, he is played by a then
very familiar German actor, Martin Kosleck, a refugee from Nazism
who had played Joseph Goebbels on film no fewer than five times.
To imagine Russia or China as a potential threat would have been a
step too far, and diplomatically impossible at this time. Joseph Stalin
and Chiang Kai-shek have formed part of a montage representing
the "peace-loving nations," and three prominent Soviet politicians,
Anastase Mikoyan, Vistchelsav Molotov, and Andre Gromyko, are
all visible within the upbeat footage of the coming together of the
nations in 1945. It will be many years before Hitchcock engages with
Cold War tensions.

   The importance of *Watchtower* is that Hitchcock, along with
Hecht, took it on so willingly and threw himself into it, as he had
done when asked by Bernstein in 1940 to do the re-editing work.
We can end by looking further back, and further forward. The impromptu speech by Hannay at the Scottish political meeting in *The
39 Steps* (1935): Is this not a United Nations vision? Hannay asks: "A
world where no nation plots against nation, where no neighbor plots
against neighbor, where everybody gets a fair deal and a sporting

chance; a world from which suspicion, cruelty, and fear have been forever banished. Is that the world you want?" Of course the implied answer, endorsed loudly by Hannay's Scottish audience, is—as to *Watchtower* a decade later—"Yes, it is."

North by Northwest in 1959 hinges on a killing carried out at the UN headquarters in New York. The place is used primarily as a dramatic location, but it is striking that prominence is given to an Indian woman receptionist and to a group of visiting Africans—the fact that they are posing in the background at the critical moment enables the photographer to swivel round and get the crucial picture of Roger O. Thornhill (Cary Grant) as the apparent assassin. Almost subliminally we are given a sense of progressive internationalism, at a high point in UN history under the greatest of all its secretaries, the Swede Dag Hammarskjöld.

A little-known sequel is this. In 1964 the UN teamed up with the Xerox Corporation to plan a series of six one-hour films to promote its ideals. Again Hitchcock was sounded out, and again he responded with a quick affirmative answer in principle, even though he was busy at the time with promoting *Marnie* and preparing some possible successor films. Strong pressure came from Adlai Stevenson, a leading UN supporter dating back to the Stettinius years: he had been the Democratic candidate for the presidency in 1951 and again in 1955, defeated both times by Dwight D. Eisenhower. He sent telegrams to Hitchcock in May 1964 and again in December, urging the importance of his involvement. But by then Richard Condon had delivered a script, provisionally entitled *Dead Run,* which neither Hitchcock nor anyone else liked; Hitchcock backed out, and the whole project seems to have stalled. Others lined up for the series had included Otto Preminger, Fred Zinnemann, and Joseph L. Mankiewicz. Even if it had no outcome, the episode confirms that *Watchtower over Tomorrow* was for Hitchcock far from being an aberrant project.[42]

Memory of the Camps

Sidney Bernstein's major preoccupation in 1945 was with using the actuality footage of the Nazi concentration camps, shot by docu-

mentary and newsreel cameramen in the immediate aftermath of the
war's ending, as a basis for the most eloquent and effective film, or
films, that could possibly be made. Indisputable evidence had to be assembled of the reality of the camps for showing urgently to audiences
both in Germany and elsewhere.

This presented severe challenges, practical and aesthetic and, in
the longer term, political. How to obtain all the required footage,
some of it from American and Russian sources, as well as sufficient
editing equipment and personnel when these were in high demand
already? How to convey the full horror of the camps, avoiding any
suspicion of cinematic fakery, without making the result unbearable
to watch? And would the project of confronting the German people
so harshly with the record of what had been done in their name be
consistent with official policy as it evolved in the postwar months?

In the event, the last issue was to be decisive, and before long the
drive to show the film was blocked—a big frustration for Bernstein,
who was so committed to it, and who had brought in Hitchcock once
again to help. He worked intensively on it for a matter of weeks, in
London in June and July 1945.

For nearly four decades the film, and Hitchcock's involvement,
remained in obscurity. Writing of Hitchcock's 1944 visit to England
in the authorized biography published in 1978, John Russell Taylor
states that "as work drew to an end on the two [French-language]
shorts there was some desultory discussion of his staying on to make
a new feature in England, on the subject of prison camps. But nothing definite came of it."[43] It is just conceivable that there was some
speculative advance discussion at that early point between Bernstein
and Hitchcock, but the book says nothing further about the film, or
of the intensive 1945 work on it; it seems more likely that this was
a simple confusion between the two dates. As often, one wonders
why Hitchcock, who collaborated on the book and saw the draft,
did not put the record straight. Perhaps he just could not be bothered. The second biographer, Donald Spoto, does not mention the
episode at all. Soon after the publication of Spoto's book in 1983,
however, the film, and Hitchcock's association with it, became a big
news story. The trigger for this was the biography of Bernstein by

Caroline Moorehead, published early in 1984, which she trailed in an article in *The Times* at the end of 1983 (12 December), starting with this paragraph: "The five 'missing Hitchcocks' recently being shown at the London Film Festival are not the only films of his to have disappeared mysteriously: five reels of a documentary about German concentration camps, compiled by Alfred Hitchcock in the summer of 1945 and lasting just under an hour, are filed away in the archives of the Imperial War Museum. They have never been shown." (The initial reference is to the five Hollywood films, controlled by the Hitchcock estate, that had been kept out of circulation for several years: *Rope* [1948], *Rear Window* [1954], *The Trouble with Harry* [1955], *The Man Who Knew Too Much* [1956], and *Vertigo* [1958]).

On British TV, Channel 4 News picked up the story and ran a short extract from the film on 20 December, again calling it a "missing Hitchcock." In May 1985 the American Public Broadcasting Channel screened the five reels under the Imperial War Museum's (IWM) title *Memory of the Camps,* with the actor Trevor Howard reading the scripted commentary. This is now available both on DVD and on YouTube in various versions, most of which bill it as a "Hitchcock documentary." In September 1985 the British ITV network broadcast a seventy-minute program made by Bernstein's own company, Granada Television: *A Painful Reminder,* subtitled *Evidence for all Mankind.* It combined three strands: (1) substantial extracts from the film, with commentary by another speaker, John Graham, much less mannered than Howard and surely closer to how the words would have been spoken in 1945; (2) protracted and harrowing testimony from three survivors of the camps; and (3) an account of the production and eventual suppression of the film, including interviews with Bernstein himself and with one of the editors, Peter Tanner (the other editor, Stewart McAllister, had died in 1962).

In parallel with this, two scholars had been investigating the long-buried film. Dai Vaughan's book on McAllister has already been referred to in the context of *Men of the Lightship.* Published in 1983, it predates all the publicity over the "missing Hitchcock" and its discovery. Vaughan had done his own research on the camps film, at the IWM and in the government archives, and his work is invaluable in giving an account from the pragmatic point of view of an editor, skeptical about the extent of Hitchcock's possible creative involvement. In the Spring 1984 issue of *Sight and Sound,* Elizabeth Sussex, on the back of the rediscovery, gave an authoritative overview of the whole episode, based both on official documents and on interviews, notably with Bernstein and Tanner. The third of the Hitchcock biographies (by Patrick McGilligan, published in 2003) at last inserted the episode into the narrative of his wartime activities. Kay Gladstone of the IWM, who interviewed both Bernstein and Tanner for the museum's oral history archive, has since offered a full and authoritative summary of the film and its history.[44]

The "missing Hitchcock" is thus far from being missing, or undocumented; but how far is it Hitchcock? We can address the question under two related heads: First, how much actual input can we deduce that he had into the assembly of the film? And second, in what ways can it be related to his work as a whole?

Before Hitchcock came to England in June 1945, Bernstein had been busily assembling footage, and the two editors had been working on it. To quote from the *Painful Reminder* soundtrack: "The problem that Bernstein then faced was to shape the material into a coherent film. He invited journalists Colin Wills and Richard Crossman to write the commentary and treatment. Then a famous Hollywood director joined them. [Bernstein:] 'Alfred Hitchcock was an eminent director, and I thought he, a brilliant man, would have some ideas, how we could tie it all together. And he had.' " It is a measure of the unsensational seriousness of this production that its seventy minutes go by, on the commercial network, without an advertising break, and that it refrains from showing an image of Hitchcock.

Both Bernstein and Tanner went extensively on record around this time, giving careful and always consistent testimony to the Granada film, to the IWM oral history program, to Moorehead, and to Sussex. They combine to confirm these five points:

1. Hitchcock visited none of the locations but worked from his suite in Claridge's hotel, as well as, possibly, making visits to the Ministry of Information's projection theater

in Malet Street. He viewed a wide range of footage, talked to one of the editors, Tanner, and to the writers, Crossman and Wills, and helped to "shape the subject cinematically."

2. He was concerned above all to guarantee the authenticity of the footage as a true record. To quote Tanner (speaking in *A Painful Reminder*):

> Hitchcock's main contribution to the film was to try to make it as authentic as possible. It was most important that everybody, particularly the Germans themselves, should believe that this was true, that this horror had happened, that people had suffered to that extent. And I can remember him strolling up and down in the suite in Claridge's and saying, "How can we make that convincing?" We tried to make shots as long as possible, used panning shots so that there was no possibility of trickery—and going from respected dignitaries or high churchmen straight [without cutting] to the bodies, corpses, so it couldn't be suggested that we were faking the film.

3. At the same time, Hitchcock recognized the value of cutting in other contexts. Tanner again: "One of the suggestions was a montage of possessions of the people who had died . . . and they were pathetic things, wedding rings, children's toys, handbags, brooches, all that sort of thing." This is realized in a powerful sequence contained in *A Painful Reminder,* though not, for whatever reason, in *Memory of the Camps;* it is accompanied by what sounds as if it must be an extract from the commentary scripted in 1945. Without human presence, we see vast piles of shoes, human hair, dentures, combs and brushes, and spectacles, and among these the turning of the pages of a photograph album; the commentary states, "All these things belonged to men and women and children like ourselves, quite ordinary people from all parts of the world."

4. He promoted another form of montage: "Hitchcock's other main contribution was to insist on the use of shots of charming German countryside as a contrast to the horrors of the camps." This works with particular power at the start, as we gradually lead in to the reality of the camps via pleasant rural scenes with grazing cows, and later through a sequence set in the idyllic mountain resort of Ebensee. It is possible, of course, that the film would have developed this contrast without advice from Hitchcock.

5. Bernstein recalled:

> His idea was to show [on the map] the area surrounding each camp, show how people had led a normal life outside, whether it was boy meets girl or whether they were harvesting, or on the lakes, completely ignoring what was happening with a range of one to five miles. He wanted to know whether the Germans surrounding the camps knew about it. Hitch did this, drawing circles, one mile from the camp, two miles from the camp, ten miles from the camp, twenty miles from the camp, what population in each of these areas, did they know about it, and so on, which would be part— would have been part of the film, showing it to them at the end, saying now *you lived there* . . ."

This last idea never had a chance to be realized, since there was never a completed film that could be shown to these neighboring people. All that follows on from Bernstein's testimony here is a sequence of local people being brought in to see the local camp and the stark evidence of what happened there—like a trailer for Hitchcock's plan for what could have happened on a much bigger scale, via exposure to the film itself.

The IWM's assessment of the right credit for Hitchcock was the modest one of treatment adviser, and this is what appears on the credits of *Memory of the Camps*. He evidently collaborated not only with Tanner and with Bernstein but with the two writers: Colin Wills, an

Australian journalist who soon returned home, and Richard Crossman, incorrectly spelled Grossman on the PBS credits and misleadingly
labelled simply as a journalist in *A Painful Memory*. Although he had
been assistant editor of the political weekly *The New Statesman* since
1938, Crossman was on the staff of the Psychological Warfare Division of SHAEF (Supreme Headquarters Allied Expeditionary Force)
and soon became a Labour MP, later a cabinet minister; indeed, he
was elected to Parliament for the first time while actually working on
the camps film. This distraction may help to explain why Crossman
(who died in 1974 and seems to have had no great interest in cinema)
left nothing in his records about his brief spell collaborating with
Hitchcock.

The second question we posed was this: In what ways can the
camps project be related to Hitchcock's work as a whole? Was it more
than a job of work taken on briefly to oblige a past and future associate?

Although the first two biographers, Taylor (1978) and Spoto
(1983), overlooked the project altogether, it had been cited as early
as 1965 by Robin Wood, a critic with no claim to being a historian,
in his seminal book *Hitchcock's Films*. The context may at first sight
be surprising:

> *Psycho* is one of the key works of our age. Its themes are of
> course not new . . . but the intensity and horror of their treat-
> ment and the fact that they are here grounded in sex belong
> to the age that has witnessed on the one hand the discoveries
> of Freudian psychology and on the other the Nazi concentra-
> tion camps. I do not think I am callous in citing the camps
> in relation to a work of popular entertainment. Hitchcock
> himself in fact accepted a commission to make a compilation
> film of captured Nazi material about the camps. The project
> reached the rough-cut stage, and was abandoned there, for
> reasons I have not been able to discover: the rough-cut now
> lies inaccessibly, along with vast quantities of similar mate-
> rial, in the vaults of the Imperial War Museum. But one can-
> not contemplate the camps without confronting two aspects

of their horror: the utter helplessness and innocence of the
victims, and the fact that human beings, whose potentiali-
ties all of us in some measure share, were their tormentors
and butchers. We can no longer be under the slightest illusion
about human nature, and about the abysses around us and
within us; and *Psycho* is founded on, precisely, these twin
horrors.[45]

Although "captured Nazi material" turned out to be a minor compo-
nent of the film, compared with footage shot by Allied cameramen in
1945, Wood's point about the seriousness of Hitchcock's engagement
with the horror of the camps surely holds. Well, he would hardly have
been human if he had not been affected. But we can look both back
and forward from 1945 to find strong thematic links.

"I learned in the war that civilisation anywhere is a very thin
crust." These are the words of a Great War veteran in John Buchan's
novel *Huntingtower,* published in 1922.[46] Four years later, at the
start of his directing career, Hitchcock planned a film of the novel
and went to Scotland to scout locations, though in the event the film
was made by George Pearson. Peter Wollen has used the line about
the *thin crust* of civilization to illustrate the strong affinity between
Buchan and Hitchcock, as embodied not only in the film of *The 39
Steps* but in the work of both men overall, even though Hitchcock's
repeated attempts to set up films of other Buchan novels always ended
in frustration. Horror and violence can strike at any time, even from
beneath an apparently placid and civilized surface. Buchan died in
1940, but he had already extended that same metaphor of the *thin
crust* from the horrors of the Great War to what lay ahead. Writing
in 1937 about the Roman emperor Augustus, he said: "We can trace
a resemblance between the conditions of his time and those of today.
Once again the crust of civilization has worn thin, and beneath can
be heard the muttering of primeval fires."[47] In 1946 we find the same
metaphor being applied specifically to the Nazi camps: "Dachau was
the most recent, and perhaps the most violent, of a long series of expe-
riences which all seemed to illustrate that European civilisation is not
a stable and settled way of life, but a thin crust, constantly threatened

by the volcanic violence of vast and un-understood forces just below the surface."[48] Those are the words of Richard Crossman, who had visited the camps before working on the commentary for Bernstein's film. Primeval fires, volcanic violence: fire and its aftermath is unsurprisingly a dominant image in *Memory of the Camps*. We might even speculate that, in their work together, Hitchcock could have invoked Buchan, and that Crossman picked up the *thin crust* metaphor from him.

No director of the 1930s had shown himself more alert than Hitchcock to the threat of Nazism and the volcanic violence it was ready to unleash, even though he was working, from 1934 onward, in the genre of the popular suspense thriller; indeed, the genre enabled him to dramatize the threat all the more vividly. *The Man Who Knew Too Much* (1934), based unofficially upon Buchan; the official adaptation that followed in *The 39 Steps* (1935); the updating of Joseph Conrad's novel *The Secret Agent* in *Sabotage* (1936)—all these films are centered on the actions of ruthless politically motivated killers at loose in London, agents of a European power that cannot be named for the linked reasons of diplomacy and censorship but which clearly represent the menace of German aggression after the rise to power of Hitler in 1933.

The Lady Vanishes in 1938 becomes more urgent with its anti-appeasement narrative, and with the figure of Dr. Hardt (fig. 3.27), who beneath his civilized exterior is ready to abuse his calling in a way that anticipates the callous experimenters of the camps, one of whom will be foregrounded in the Bernstein film: Doctor Klein, condemned to death at Nuremberg. As *The Lady Vanishes* progresses, Dr. Hardt believes the bandaged patient is still the Englishwoman Miss Froy, even though we know that the hero and heroine have by now effected a substitution; he is ready to carry out the operation whose course he has clinically spelled out to them a few minutes earlier: "She will be taken off the train at Morsken in about three minutes. She will be removed to the hospital there and operated on. Unfortunately, the operation will not be successful. . . . The operation will be performed by me."

Hitchcock's second Hollywood film, *Foreign Correspondent* (1940), though made while the United States was still neutral, and still unable to name its villains as German, nonetheless presents a stark picture of Nazi brutality through the torture, with bright lights

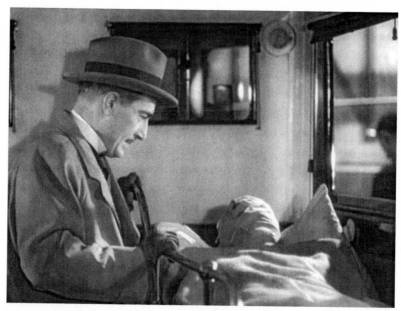

Figure 3.27. Paul Lukas as Dr. Hardt in *The Lady Vanishes* (1938; Gainsborough Pictures). (Courtesy of the BFI National Archive)

and physical abuse, of the aged statesman Van Meer.[49] Made after Pearl Harbor, *Saboteur* (1942) and *Lifeboat* (1944) dramatize the anti-Nazi struggle from the American side. In the latter, the Nazi captain adrift with the American survivors was so disturbingly powerful as to attract criticism to the film for loading things too much in his favor. Perhaps only after the revelation of the camps would critics like those realize the full potency of the evil that the Allies had had to fight to overcome.

After his experience of the camps footage, Hitchcock went on in his next two films to play out, rather neatly, the observation of Robin Wood, quoted previously, in relation to *Psycho*: digging deep first into Freud, with *Spellbound* (1945), and then into the tenacity of Nazi evil, with *Notorious* (1946). And when, with the Selznick contract over, he and Bernstein got the chance to launch their own company, Transatlantic, their first project was *Rope* (1948), the drama of two privileged youths who kill for kicks and for power. Patrick Hamilton's young men in his play of 1929 were already like an anticipation of

Hitler Youth and of concentration camp officers: Brandon, the amoral leader; Philip (as renamed for the film), the half-reluctant acolyte too weak to do other than acquiesce. Hitchcock and Bernstein and their writers update the story to the present, naming Hitler and linking Brandon implicitly to him.

We might even make something of the way Hitchcock carries over into *Rope* the strategy that he had articulated so strongly in his advice to Tanner on the camps film: use long takes where you can find them, to stop the possibility of any attempt by the perpetrators to avoid guilt for what is shown. Avoiding cuts for several minutes, until the end of a reel makes one unavoidable, Hitchcock's camera in *Rope* tracks its offenders relentlessly until their guilt is uncovered.

To summarize: although the camps film may not exactly qualify as a "Hitchcock documentary," it is an important "lost and found" episode. His work on it fits very suggestively into the narrative of his career. He brought a lot to it, and was marked by it, as he could hardly fail to be.

And there is one tantalizing footnote. One of the distinguished group of people whom Bernstein enlisted to work on the film was the scientist Solly Zuckerman. He is credited rather curiously on *Memory of the Camps* as Proposed Scientific Adviser, but the records show that he did give some actual advice, not exclusively scientific: a note from him survives headed "M.O.I. Concentration Camp Picture," dated 17 May 1945, indicating that he had seen some footage and listing a variety of intelligent points for consideration. Forty years later he claimed to have no memory of the project, but he must have met and been impressed by Hitchcock, since he acted on behalf of his Oxford friend the historian Hugh Trevor-Roper in trying to interest him and Bernstein in making a film of Trevor-Roper's book *The Last Days of Hitler,* which caused a sensation when published in 1947 and has never been out of print since. Writing to Zuckerman on 19 June 1946, in advance of finalizing the book, Trevor-Roper adds an excited postscript: "Remember you're writing to Hitchcock!" On 5 July Zuckerman reports that he has written, and on 5 November he reports a meeting with Bernstein that still seems to hold out a possibility.[50] And there, at least for now, the trail goes dead.

4

After the War

Hitchcock's career from the end of the war is much better known than his career up to 1945, and it has been much more fully worked over.

In the 1950s he achieved a spectacular increase in fame and visibility, primarily through the TV series bearing his name, which ran for a decade from October 1955: 266 shows in all. It belongs to the time when TV's dramatic output was moving rapidly beyond the initial stage of liveness and ephemerality, through two major technical developments: the recording of studio transmissions onto film via the process of *kinescoping* (the American term) or *telerecording* (British term), and the move to actually shooting on film rather than electronically, which made for better visual quality and for easier marketing and syndication. The Hitchcock show was all film from the start. The full run survives and is now comprehensively packaged on DVD. In parallel with the run of the TV show, Hitchcock took a more prominent role in the trailers for his cinema films; these too survive and are easy to find on DVD and online, along with transcriptions and comment.

Other factors were now working, in the postwar years, in favor of preservation. The international film archive movement was well established, and the value of studying film art and film history was starting to gain wider acceptance, first outside and then within academia. Hitchcock was attaining ever-growing celebrity status, critically as well as publicly, first in France and then elsewhere: the early 1960s saw the major retrospective at the Museum of Modern Art in New York, linked to an interview book by Peter Bogdanovich, *The Cinema of Alfred Hitchcock*, followed by the landmark publication of *Hitchcock's Films* by Robin Wood, and the bigger interview book, *Hitchcock*, by François Truffaut. Nothing involving Hitchcock is now going to be consigned unthinkingly to oblivion in the manner of films such as *Number Thirteen* (begun in 1922), *The Mountain Eagle* (1926), and *An Elastic Affair* (1930).

In addition to the TV show and the trailers, other once-elusive items from the 1960s have become quite easily accessible. Among these are screen tests for Hitchcock's protégée "Tippi" Hedren; the test material for the unmade project *Frenzy/Kaleidoscope* (see chapter 2); and, at the end of the decade, the alternative endings of *Topaz* (1969). Prominent in the category not of "lost and found" but of "never made" is the plan to film J. M. Barrie's play *Mary Rose*. The script by Jay Presson Allen, written after her script for *Marnie* (1964), survives, and Joseph McBride has published the result of extensive research on the play and on Hitchcock's career-long desire to film it.[1] All of these items are securely on record.

Nevertheless, a few lesser-known items remain, and we end by focusing on four of these from the decade 1959–1969: two pieces of "public service" work, and two more-personal testimonies. All of them are evidence of Hitchcock's continuing readiness to respond to requests on behalf of a variety of worthy causes. The public service pair—*Tactic* in 1959, in aid of the American Cancer Society, and the appeal in 1966 for the Will Rogers hospital charity—recall his work in the mid-1940s for the War Bonds appeal and for the United Nations ideal.

Tactic (1959)

Broadcast on 2 May 1959 by NBC in collaboration with the Educational Television and Radio Center, *Tactic* formed part of a campaign by the American Cancer Society to break down the taboo on public discussion of cancer, and to spur people into being tested and, when necessary, treated. The presenter introduces "a program to find ways in which America's great creative people can help us in the fight against cancer." The first two of these creative people are Alfred Hitchcock, who stages a short drama with two actors, and the choreographer Hanya Holm, working with two dancers.

The thirty-eight-minute broadcast begins with a lucid account of the facts and the problems from a cancer specialist, Dr. Charles Cameron. He then hands over to Hitchcock, whose section lasts for just under twelve minutes: he talks about fear and about how it may affect cancer patients, and then he sets up the scene with his actors and lets it run, intervening twice in the course of it in order to adjust details. The program then moves on, without a pause, to Holm and the dancers.

This seems to be the only extended footage we have of Hitchcock actually at work on set as a director. As such it is of course fascinating, but there are two anomalous points to note.

First, this is not film but live, or as-live, television. The whole program from start to finish has clearly been kinescoped, either in advance of transmission or during it, producing a film record of what was shot in one go by multiple bulky studio cameras—these are occasionally seen within shot as Hitchcock steps in to brief an actor or an operator. Certain slips and stumbles over words at various points in the program are left in. So we are not witnessing Hitchcock's habitual shot-by-shot filming, creating material to be put together by an editor; the editing process is here instantaneous. It is true that this has something in common with the way he had shot some scenes, with more than one camera, for early sound pictures, but even then there was greater visual precision and scope for retakes and for fine-tuning at the editing stage. This section of *Tactic* is hardly, then, a typical scene of Hitchcock directing.

The other anomaly is that Hitchcock was himself walking through a prewritten script. In the words of George Lefferts, credited on the program as cowriter and coproducer:

Mr Hitchcock flew to New York at his own expense and did the show for no fee because, he told me, his mother had died of breast cancer. The sketch which I wrote and directed at Hitchcock's request was a "supposed improvisation" (actually I scripted all the lines) in which Hitchcock explained to two actors, William Shatner and Diana Van der Vlis, how to improvise a scene in which Shatner plays a young doctor telling a young woman that she has breast cancer. So, in effect it was presented as an improvisation within an improvisation, but everything was actually scripted. As soon as the show was over Hitchcock flew back to L.A. to do a movie, I don't remember which one.[2]

At this date in early May 1959, the movie work would have been either postproduction on *North by Northwest* (1959) or preproduction on *Psycho* (1960).

None of this negates the value of the *Tactic* material. As James Allardice had already been doing for years in scripting Hitchcock's on-camera introductions to the TV show, Lefferts wrote skillfully for him, and obviously Hitchcock would never have consented to words or actions that he did not feel comfortable with. So let us look now at what is on the screen.

After the doctor's initial lecture, the presenter takes over: "Underlying all of the attitudes Dr. Cameron describes is a single common denominator, fear. With us on today's panel we have one of the world's most distinguished experts on fear, film director Alfred Hitchcock. Now Mr. Hitchcock, like our other panelists you were given the facts on the enormous waste in human life that results from unrealistic attitudes towards cancer. . . . As a director, as a filmmaker who has earned his living from terror, suspense, and fear, were you able to apply your own special talents to exposing and correcting these attitudes?" Hitchcock responds:

> First let me clear up one important point. In my opinion it is not fear that stops people doing what they should about cancer, it's the *avoidance* of fear. Fear is a perfectly normal response to a real threat. The best combat soldiers are those who know they are afraid and can handle their own emotions. I think that dread and horror and terror are all based on our attempt to avoid the experience of fear.

In *Rope,* for example, we have a rather charming scene in which a cocktail party is being held by two young men who have just strangled their companion. Drinks are being served from an antique chest, his temporary coffin. By all odds, these two murderers ought to be in a state of panic. The reality is that they are in danger of being placed inside another kind of furniture, that quaint piece of Chippendale with wiring by Thomas Edison, known as The Chair. But are they reacting with fear? Hardly. They're cold as custard. What might be normal fear now gives way to a feeling of horror. Now if I were to play the same scene with both young men in a crying sweat, there would be very little picture. In fact, both murderers would have realized their plight and boarded the nearest train for Outer Mongolia before the first reel was shot. And *Rope* would have been another travelogue.

The digression on *Rope* is hardly very illuminating in this context, and it may have been put in by the writer—or by Hitchcock himself—primarily in order to play upon his jokey/macabre public image. He is soon brought back to the point, though there is another flippant aside to come in the penultimate line:

At first I thought I might make a film about someone who suspects he has cancer and proceeds to torture himself in an attempt to avoid his own fear. Then I thought, I have to help put across an important idea. I have a limited time to develop the idea, and a limited time to demonstrate it. So instead of making a film I decided to stage an impromptu drama. . . . Several weeks ago, I told the NBC property department that I would need one door, one desk, two chairs, a paper-knife—and a partridge in a pear tree. I also requested a young woman and a young man.

He introduces them: the Broadway actors Diana Van der Vlis and William Shatner (later famous for *Star Trek*). To her: "You are a young woman of twenty-four, very attractive, a fashion model; you are engaged to be married, you are vain about your appearance. Admiration is a form of nutrition for you"—a good Hitchcock line, using the food concept metaphorically. Shatner is to play a doctor giving bad news about cancer for the first time. The real-life medical expert, Dr. Cameron, specifies the scenario from offscreen: "Well, for the purpose of our drama, let us say that she recently discovered a lump in her breast. It was removed four days ago and found to be malignant. She requires immediate surgery."

At this Hitchcock—plainly without any time lapse—announces, "Now I'll step aside to direct the cameras. Now Miss Van der Vlis, would you please knock on the door and enter."

The scene proceeds, shot by two cameras; a third one interposes a shot with Hitchcock observing in the foreground (fig. 4.1).

> Doctor: It means we have to operate to remove the breast.
> Patient: But that's ridiculous, there must be some other way.

At this point Hitchcock intervenes, speaking first to her, then to one of the cameramen: "Now I think we have an opportunity for some pictorial comment here. Diana, you have just been handed the most startling news of your life. You have cancer. Now anyone who has faced this moment knows that this is a serious, frightening time. Play this as if you are tongue-tied for a moment. Charlie, take a tight close-up of her face—we want to see her reaction to this news. Start the action again, Doctor." The dramatic tight close-up is duly cut in and makes its point. The doctor continues, talking her round into overcoming her fear, carefully spelling out the message of Dr. Cameron's initial address:

> He: Today we're curing, permanently curing, more than three out of four patients whose breast cancer has been diagnosed sufficiently early—thousands of women have had that operation. And today they're capable of loving, of receiving, of laughing, exercising, enjoying . . . even bearing children—are you going to say that the only thing in life that has any meaning for you is to have your body admired by millions of people who don't even know you?

Figure 4.1. Hitchcock on set in *Tactic* (1959; NBC Public Service). (Courtesy of the Library of Congress)

She: My fiancé knows me.

He: If he's going to marry you for your body alone, it's time you found out, isn't it? You're going to get old and lose it, you know—I'm sorry, I've no right to advise you on your personal life.

Hitchcock now moves forward to make his second intervention: "Doctor, just a moment, Doctor, I'd like to do something here, a little subconscious act which will carry out the symbolism of the letter opener. As you talk, pick it up and toy with it. Go on, please."

From this point, the knife is visible in the shots taken by Charlie's camera from behind the doctor, looking toward the woman and "carrying out the symbolism," so to speak, of the surgeon's knife that she will face the next day (fig. 4.2). The studio lights even make it glint menacingly (to an extent not fully captured in the still image repro-

Figure 4.2. The symbolism of the surgeon's knife in *Tactic* (1959; NBC Public Service). (Courtesy of the Library of Congress)

duced here), recalling the glinting of the scissors that Hitchcock took so much care over in *Dial M for Murder* (1954). Whether the angle and the light effect were thought up by him or Lefferts or Charlie or some combination, they provide a certain frisson within an exercise that is otherwise inevitably rather academic, and could even be seen as undermining the sponsor's message that there is nothing to be afraid of.

But the doctor succeeds in reconciling her to the operation, and Hitchcock rounds it off: "Thank you very much. I'd like to thank Mr. William Shatner and Miss Diana Van der Vlis for a pair of very nice performances."

The Will Rogers Appeal (1966)

Will Rogers died in a plane crash in 1935 at the age of fifty-five. He was a folksy performer active in many media, including cinema, for which he made three memorable films with John Ford in the early

Figure 4.3. Hitchcock's Will Rogers appeal (1966). (Courtesy of the Will Rogers Institute)

1930s. After his death, a hospital charity was set up in his name for the treatment of tuberculosis, later expanded into a wider-ranging Will Rogers Institute. Though he had obviously never worked with Rogers, Hitchcock was one of a succession of celebrities, mainly actors, who fronted the annual appeal for funds (fig. 4.3); others included John Wayne, Cary Grant, and Greer Garson.

Hitchcock's appeal was shown in cinemas in summer 1966. Late in 2012, it was brought out of the archives and shown, in an abbreviated version, as prelude to the American première of the biopic *Hitchcock,* directed by Sacha Gervasi and starring Anthony Hopkins and Helen Mirren. Since then, it has become viewable online, but again in the same short version. We quote the complete text below.

The material cut from current versions is given in italics. Asterisks indicate the point at which, in each version, intercut footage of the hospital and the research begins and ends: a montage of twenty-five shots in one minute in the full version, cut down in the 2012 version to nine shots in twenty-five seconds. In both versions, Hitchcock's narration continues throughout.

He is shown on a film set. A voice calls out, "Action—OK Mr. Hitchcock." As he speaks, the camera moves in slowly. After we come back to him from the intercut footage, it slowly pulls out again, but not as wide—it does not include the female assistant who was initially seen in a chair at the right of frame.

Just a moment. There may be some of you who have never acted in pictures before, and so perhaps I should explain the scene we are about to shoot. When I say "roll 'em," a most unfortunate phrase, you are to put your hand in your pocket or purse, take out your wallet, and peel off a bill, like this. Then hold on to it for the next shot. It you don't have a bill handy, coins will do. Naturally, being actors, your first question will be: What is my motivation? While the ladies are putting on their makeup I shall explain.* You are doing this as your part in building medical research. For your own benefit in the world's war against lung diseases. They are diseases that kill a man a minute throughout the world. *The individual workers in our industry have supported the research and healing work of the Will Rogers Hospital and O'Donnell research laboratories for more than a third of a century. But the job has grown so enormous that we are in urgent need of your help. After ten years of research the Will Rogers laboratories have created an anti-TB vaccine. From this can come great health blessings for all of you.* Will Rogers is helping build up the force of doctors demanded by our country's growing population.* That is your motivation. Obviously it is more than adequate, as I noticed one method actor in the rear of the theater is about to give us the shirt off his back. We appreciate it very much, sir, but unfortunately there are rules about taking one's clothes off in a movie theater. Now to review quickly, when the houselights go up, reach for that bill or coin, clutch it tightly until the Will Rogers volunteers send containers through your row. Then drop in your contribution and pass the box to your neighbor. Remember this is for medical research in diseases of breathing . . . for the benefit of all mankind, for someone you love. Perhaps even for yourself, someday. Very well, Jack, roll 'em.

The film ends with the caption "I never met a man I didn't like—Will Rogers" (a famous Rogers line) superimposed on the image of a bust of him.

It is most unlikely that Hitchcock had anything to do with the shooting and editing of the intercut sequence, any more than he designed the drama for *Tactic*. But he clearly took care, aided perhaps by a writer such as James Allardice, to put a distinctive imprint on the address that frames it, through the joke about actors needing to know their motivation, always a sore point with him, and the whole playful pretense of interacting with the imagined audience, dramatized by gestures in their direction and the direct address to the man said to be taking off his shirt.

The next and final two items supply an appropriate ending to this survey, since they both offer fresh links back across the decades to the early stages of Hitchcock's career in Britain. For two contrasting projects, respectively amateur and professional, he was approached out of the blue and agreed unhesitatingly to cooperate, as he had done so often before.

The Westcliff Film (1963)

The Cine Club in Westcliff, not far from where Hitchcock was born and raised in the same county of Essex, organized a Hitchcock evening in 1962, including a screening of *Psycho*. When they invited him to provide a message to be read out to members at a follow-up event the following year, he volunteered instead to send a message on film, shot at Universal Studios (fig. 4.4). The film was duly shot—in color

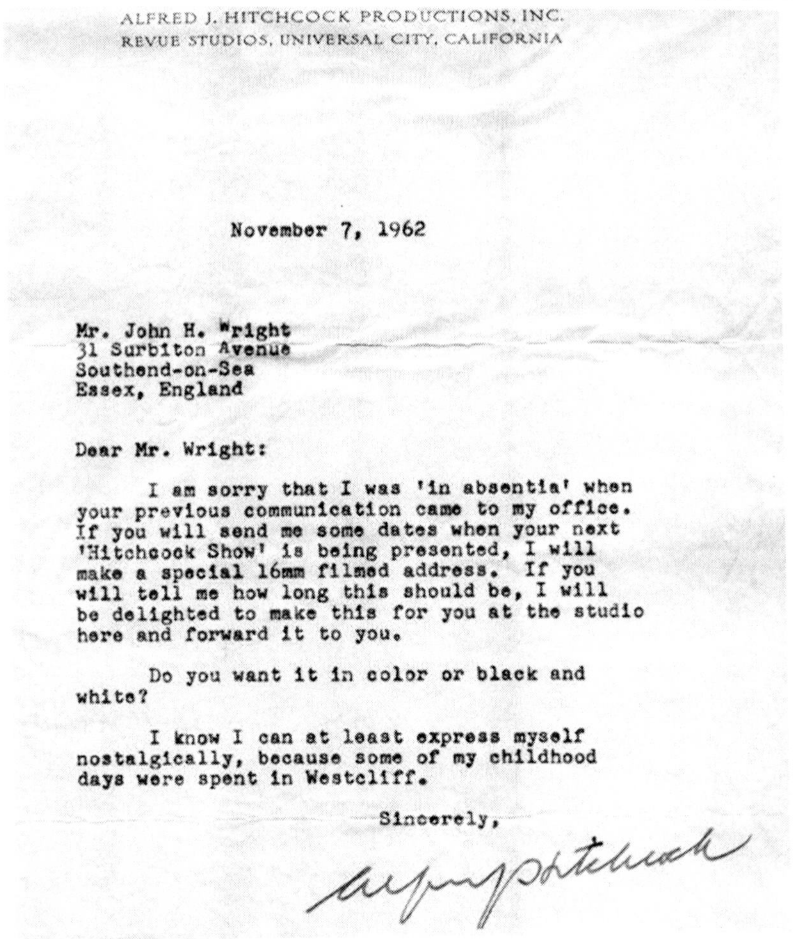

ALFRED J. HITCHCOCK PRODUCTIONS, INC.
REVUE STUDIOS, UNIVERSAL CITY, CALIFORNIA

November 7, 1962

Mr. John H. Wright
31 Surbiton Avenue
Southend-on-Sea
Essex, England

Dear Mr. Wright:

I am sorry that I was 'in absentia' when
your previous communication came to my office.
If you will send me some dates when your next
'Hitchcock Show' is being presented, I will
make a special 16mm filmed address. If you
will tell me how long this should be, I will
be delighted to make this for you at the studio
here and forward it to you.

Do you want it in color or black and
white?

I know I can at least express myself
nostalgically, because some of my childhood
days were spent in Westcliff.

Sincerely,

Alfred Hitchcock

Figure 4.4. A letter from Hitchcock to the Westcliff Cine Club, 1962.
(Courtesy of the Westcliff Cine Club)

on 16mm film—and sent, and was shown at Westcliff on 19 June
1963. The British Film Institute (BFI) has restored the film footage
and made it available for viewing in the Institute's London and re-
gional Mediatheque installations, but it has not yet been more widely
shown, which is why we include it here. We are grateful to the Cine
Club and to its officials for supplying documentation along with the
film itself, and for allowing us to use it.

There is a brief tour of studio sets, but the film consists mainly of

Hitchcock's address to camera (figs. 4.5 and 4.6), the bulk of which merits transcribing here for its strongly nostalgic autobiographical quality. His account of scripting sessions in the mid-1930s tallies with testimony given elsewhere by collaborators Ivor Montagu and Charles Bennett.

Good evening, ladies and gentlemen. I suppose some of you are wondering why I should be addressing such a particular film society as that of Westcliff-on-Sea. When I was asked if I would do so, it was probably inspired by a touch of nostalgia. You see, I was born in Leytonstone, Essex, some years ago. Please don't speculate—I am younger than I look. So of course, as a child, my visits were made to this part of the Thames estuary. I think we came by what used to be known as the London Tilbury and Southend railway. I have a vague recollection of coming sometimes by the Great Eastern railway and getting off at a place called Prittlewell. In fact I believe I had some relatives living near there. Now of course, I always felt as I grew older that Westcliff seemed to be much more elegant than Southend-on-Sea. Was this the beginning of my class consciousness? I'm not sure.

I've been intrigued that round the coast of England there has always been, and perhaps it isn't so today, complementary resorts adjacent to the more famous ones. And I say, we have Westcliff adjacent to Southend, we have Hove adjacent to Brighton, we have Frinton adjacent to Clacton, Boscombe adjacent to Bournemouth, St. Leonards-on-Sea adjacent to Hastings, Cliftonville for Margate, and so on. Anyway, I suppose it's no different from one's theory that in every city in the world there is an east and a west end. And for some inexplicable, or perhaps it is an astrological, reason, that everyone wants to gravitate from east to west. Especially those of course who live in such a charming place as Westcliff, which you realize is west of Southend. So you see, we don't know where we are. So that brings us to the final point why Westcliff is west of Southend, which in turn is east of London. I

THE WESTCLIFF
CINE CLUB
VISITS
MR. HITCHCOCK
IN HOLLYWOOD

Figures 4.5–4.6. The Westcliff Cine Club film (1963). (Courtesy of the East Anglian Film Archive)

read in the piece, I think it was in *The London Times*, I get it by airmail, the other day. It was a big article about giants in the cinema, and I found myself the only Anglo-Saxon among a group of Italian and French directors. I almost wanted to

send a letter to *The Times,* saying the inspiration to become
a giant of the cinema was inspired by a dreary November day
at Burnham-on-Crouch.

I have always had a fascination for seaside resorts looking
their worst in the winter, and I can remember writing the
script for a new film with my two scenario writers. I would
get bored sitting in the room in which we were working and
I would say, "Let's go to some dreary place, we might get
some fresh ideas." Whether my assistant writers would be
so inspired as I was, I didn't care, so long as I could get a
kick out of the dreary waste of the Thames estuary in the
winter. So we would get in a car and drive down where I felt
the country was flattest and most attrac . . . , unattractive,
I nearly said attractive, I mean unattractive. One day I was
looking at the map of the Thames estuary, in fact looking
for some inspiration, when I saw on the south side of the
Thames a little place called Allhallows-on-Sea. I said to the
writers, let's go down there. So we drove past Gravesend and
arrived at the place. I don't know what it's like today. I think
this was around 1934 or -5, and all we found was a railway
hotel and a few houses. I imagine the railway people had felt
this would be a good place to start a new resort, but for some
reason or other it didn't take. Too dreary, I suppose—I found
it attractively dreary and good enough for one idea to put in
the script. I can't remember what it was now.

I must tell you one final item about my search for the
dreary. It was a November morning and I said to my colleagues, why don't we take one of the river taxis after lunch
and go down the river. I had remembered at the time that
they operated from a pier at Chelsea. My secretary got on
the phone and made all arrangements. We had some . . . I
think we had lunch somewhere in the West End and were
told that the riverboat would go from Westminster Pier. We
took a taxi and then walked down the slope to the pier. A
man was waiting at the bottom for us. "Are you the party
for the boat?" "Yes," I replied. "This way." He led us round

onto Westminster Pier, and there waiting for us was a large river steamer with funnel and rows and rows of seats. I got very alarmed and made some remark about this seemed a bit large for our purpose, but then confirmed that the price which had previously been given to me, two pounds ten, to go as far as Greenwich and back. So off we went. It was a very drizzly dark afternoon; it must have been later than November, probably December, because it was almost dark around three o'clock. So we spread ourselves over the three hundred seats and tried to discuss the script on which we were working—actually, I can even remember the film we were working on, I think it was *The 39 Steps,* which I made with Robert Donat and Madeleine Carroll. Unfortunately that afternoon was too dreary to provide any inspiration, and we ended up down below where they had a tea bar open with an attendant, and if I can remember it all right, the milk was condensed, horrible. . . .

Please keep going to the movies, especially mine because I need the money for my starving wife and child. Incidentally, I've just finished making a movie of Daphne du Maurier's short story "The Birds." When you see this, I'd like you, students of the visual in cinema, to note the vast amount of technical work involved. I would say that this picture, purely from a technical point of view, of getting birds to attack, was to me one of the most difficult things I have attempted in movie making. So much so that I'm never going to make another picture called *The Birds.* Well, I'd better away now and thank you for having me here this evening. I must run to catch the last London Tilbury and Southend railway train to, is it Fenchurch Street?

Hitchcock on Grierson (1969)

There can be no doubt that the Westcliff script is all in Hitchcock's own words. The other big rediscovery from the 1960s, a half-hour program called *Hitchcock on Grierson* broadcast by Scottish

Television (STV) in 1969, is different in that he was reading out in Hollywood, on the set of his current production, *Topaz,* a script written for him in Scotland. But this was by now a familiar and well-developed tactic. His style was familiar enough to enable other skilled operators to write for him, the prime example being James Allardice, who wrote the introductions to his TV shows—and also the work done by George Lefferts for him on *Tactic.* If Hitchcock did not like what was written for him, he rejected or changed it. In 1967, he had quickly agreed to write a foreword to a reissue of the novel on which *The Lady Vanishes* (1938) was based, and he had asked, as often, for a complete draft to be written for him; the result was a long and digressive piece about the book's author, Ethel Lina White, written by her nephew. Understandably, Hitchcock decided against signing this and instead put together a much shorter piece based on quotes from the interview with François Truffaut for his book *Hitchcock.*[3] This bears out the approach taken by Sidney Gottlieb in the introduction to his collection *Hitchcock on Hitchcock.* He argues that even when others wrote articles or scripts for him, "it is safe to assume that Hitchcock in one way or another guided, supervised, reviewed, and/or approved the final copy before it went to press. What may or may not have been his own exact words originally became authorized (by him and then by his readers) as his words."[4]

If the words did not feel right, as in the case of the *Lady Vanishes* item, he declined to authorize them. Conversely, we can take his words about John Grierson as a sincerely authorized tribute (fig. 4.7).

Scottish Television had written to Hitchcock in December 1968, asking him to present this tribute to Grierson, and quickly secured an unconditional agreement. Copies were then forwarded of the script written for him by Jack Gerson, a Scot with extensive experience as a writer for television (soon afterward, he would write several episodes of the celebrated police series *Z Cars,* which ran on BBC TV between 1962 and 1978). Hitchcock did some editing of the script when it arrived, making a number of judicious cuts of lines he was not happy with, mostly ones that referred to his own career.[5] Page one of the script asked him to say, "But this is a film not about me—those pae-

Figures 4.7–4.8. *Hitchcock on Grierson* (1969). (Courtesy of Scottish Television)

ans of praise must await another evening—but about John Grierson." He simply cut out the eight words in the middle, between the dashes, and a few other passages like them. But he spoke the rest as if he meant it, and clearly he did. By endorsing his links with, and respect for, an alternative path to the one he followed, he encourages us to rethink his relation to documentary film, and more widely to his roots in British cinema.

It is tempting to place Hitchcock's work and documentary in simple opposition. Talking to him about *The Wrong Man* (1956), Truffaut argued that "your style, which has found its perfection in the fiction area, happens to be in total conflict with the aesthetics of the documentary."[6] Writing in an article in 1930, John Grierson had famously characterized Hitchcock's early films as "unimportant," urging him to "give us a film of the Potteries or Manchester or Middlesborough [three industrial areas], with the personals in their proper place and the life of a community instead of a benighted lady at stake."[7] Hitchcock declined the invitation and followed his own path, as did

Grierson himself, then at the start of a successful decade promoting government-sponsored documentary film in Britain and beyond.

And yet the two paths, and the two conceptions of cinema, can be seen as complementary and overlapping as much as oppositional. In that same article, Grierson called Hitchcock "the sharpest observer and the finest master of detail in all England"; this was a view endorsed in 1949, on the basis of the films of the 1930s, by another critic with documentary affiliations, Lindsay Anderson. Tom Ryall, in his book *Alfred Hitchcock and the British Cinema,* quotes Anderson as praising "the authenticity of the 'everyday locales' and the 'authentic minor characters, maids, policemen, shopkeepers, and commercial travellers' populating the films." Ryall continues: "We have already drawn attention to the semi-documentary opening sequences of *The Lodger* [1926], *The Ring* [1927], *The Manxman* [1929] and *Blackmail* [1929], but many of the later thrillers also contain social vignettes and cameos which impressed critics with a disposition towards 'documentary modes.' "[8]

Writing in between Anderson and Ryall, in 1974, Raymond
Durgnat argued that the opening sequence of *Blackmail,* in which the
police go to collect a suspect, "corresponds in every way to the canons
of 'semi-fictional' or 'reconstructed' documentary which the thriving
school of pre-Grierson documentary makers had used from the war
years onward and which the Grierson school was to adopt for such
films as *North Sea* [1938] and *San Demetrio London* [1943] (with,
as usual, no acknowledgment that the commercial cinema had been
there ten years before)."[9]

Grierson, Anderson, Ryall, Durgnat: this is an impressive range of
witnesses, bridging the fields of production and criticism. Durgnat's
reference to the war years of 1914–1918 is salutary in reminding us
that documentary, both as a word and as a mode of filmmaking, long
predates Grierson's alleged invention of the term in 1927. As near
contemporaries, born in 1898 and 1899 respectively, Grierson and
Hitchcock were both formed in the British film culture of the interwar
years and drew, in their different ways, upon overseas influences from
Hollywood and beyond in order to shape a fresh and distinctive path
for the native product. Both were involved with the Film Society, established in London in 1925, and both were particularly struck by the
impact, at the end of the decade, of the new Soviet films and theories:
Grierson adapted Sergei Eisenstein's *Battleship Potemkin* (1925) for
its Film Society screening in a double bill with his own film *Drifters*
(1929), while Hitchcock ever afterward acknowledged the inspiration
of Lev Kuleshov and Vsevolod Pudovkin.

It is a radical misreading of Grierson to regard his conception
of documentary as a prosaically factual one. The foundational text
in which he first uses the term is a 1926 review of Robert Flaherty's
Moana, celebrating aspects of it that have a more than purely
"documentary value."[10] Paradoxically, documentary film would be
defined by him (and by colleagues) as a mode that transcends the
merely "documentary." Like others, he would try to find alternative labels to replace that word, but without success: as he wrote
in the opening sentence of a manifesto in 1932, "Documentary is a
clumsy title, but let it stand."[11] It was Grierson who articulated the
need to liven up films like *Men of the Lightship* (David Macdonald,

1940; see chapter 3): "It is the direct activist style that will create confidence and participation. . . . I don't like to call it dullness, but certainly there is a lack of narrative lift." In stepping in to sharpen up that film by re-editing, Hitchcock was in effect carrying out Grierson's own prescription—working with a third key contemporary from the film culture of the 1920s and the Film Society, Sidney Bernstein, who himself spanned the fields of feature film and documentary.[12]

In the STV program, Hitchcock links himself and Grierson in these terms: "In the early days of the cinema, men like John began to learn that the motion picture camera didn't merely have to reproduce on celluloid anything placed horizontally before it. If it was placed in certain ways, with cunning artifice, it could convey emotional aspects of whatever it was filming. Others had made the elementary discovery that it could tell stories, but John found it could observe and comment on a changing world. I myself utilized this as one of the storytellers. Others, led by John, banded together to create social documents on film."

After telling the story of the way in which government sponsorship enabled the development of an alternative system, parallel to the one within which he had built his own career, he names names: "John now gathered around him a group of brilliant young men: Robert Flaherty, Cavalcanti, Basil Wright, Paul Rotha, Humphrey Jennings, Harry Watt." Alberto Cavalcanti was producer of *Men of the Lightship;* Harry Watt was director of *Target for Tonight* (1941). Both were then in the process of moving into feature films at Ealing, using professional actors to tell topical stories. Cavalcanti and Jennings had worked together not long before, on the documentary *Spring Offensive* (1940), using another script by Hitchcock's lifelong friend Hugh Gray. Harry Watt had already worked with Hitchcock, being credited for the marine "special effects" on *Jamaica Inn* (1939); looking back, he would describe Hitchcock as "the only British feature director we respected."[13] The boundary between documentary and fiction was a fluid and shifting one, in terms both of personnel and of method. That is what made it so natural for Hitchcock to do his sympathetic re-editing work on those two early films of wartime—one of the most illuminating of all of the "lost and found" episodes that we have studied in these pages.

Grierson is, just as much as Hitchcock is himself, a "man of cinema"—the program's final celebratory words, spoken emphatically by Hitchcock to camera. It is one more instance of his status as an individual as close as anyone could be to being a universal representative of the medium: happy, late in his career, to acknowledge his respect for the documentary element in film history and film culture, as well as to acknowledge from Hollywood, in the Westcliff film, his deep roots in his native Britain, as represented even, or especially, by the drearier parts of Essex.

Epilogue
What Now?

Between the completion of this book and its publication, it is very possible that bits of new material will have come to light, at least in document form. Increasingly, early trade papers and other journals are being digitized and made more easily available in libraries and on-line, and an ever-growing number of researchers, within and beyond academia, use them to help investigate hitherto obscure corners of film history. All we can hope to have done is to have compiled a solid interim report on one important thread in this history, and to help give some extra impetus to the drive to preserve and explore the mass of film material that survives, often still unlabelled and uncared for.

The three lost films that Hitchcock directed are sure to remain major targets: the unfinished *Number Thirteen* from 1922; the complete version of *Always Tell Your Wife* from 1923; and his second feature film, *The Mountain Eagle,* from 1926. The first was held in store for a few years at least; the second may never have been publicly shown, but half of it turned up mysteriously decades later; the third was distributed in Germany and the United States as well as in Britain, and probably elsewhere. So there is a fair chance that prints of one or more will one day surface, in the wake of other previously "lost" films, such as the first film we refer to in the introduction, the

Graham Cutts and Hitchcock production *The White Shadow* from 1924, unearthed in New Zealand and shown to the world in 2011.

We have tried throughout, however, to resist treating Hitchcock in isolation, and instead to relate him to his context and contemporaries and collaborators, showing how—to adopt the verbs suggested by Jane Sloan and Ian Macdonald, respectively—he "sponged up" or "hoovered up" influences of diverse kinds, as well as responding to a variety of requests at specific historical moments.[1] Alongside those three lost Hitchcocks, there are other lost early films whose discovery would have comparable value in extending our understanding of the context, and the influences. Films such as these, completing a "top ten" of desirables:

> *Justice* (1917). Adapted from a play by John Galsworthy, a favorite Hitchcock author; directed by Maurice Elvey, for whom Alma Reville worked for several years in her formative years before meeting Hitchcock; starring Gerald du Maurier, later a good friend of Hitchcock's, and father of Daphne; and scripted by his first screenwriter, Eliot Stannard, who wrote eloquently at the time about his use, in writing this film, of associative montage, in terms that unmistakably anticipate the ideas of Vsevolod Pudovkin a decade later.

> *Dangerous Lies* (1921). The Famous Players-Lasky British film, directed by Paul Powell, whose intertitles Hitchcock referred to, in his first published film article, as an example of the use of pictorial symbolism. We have the advertisement and a newspaper account of one of his title illustrations, but no actual image.

Any of the other lost films with authentic Hitchcock titles would be a great find, but in particular:

> *Love's Boomerang* or *Spanish Jade* (both 1922). The two films directed at Islington by John S. Robertson, the

Famous Players-Lasky British director whom Hitchcock most admired. Hitchcock named two of his other silent films among his top ten at the end of the 1930s (see chapter 1). Either instance of their collaboration would be of interest on two counts: for the film itself, and for the design of the intertitles.

Paddy the Next Best Thing (1923). The successor to *Flames of Passion,* which does survive (see chapter 1), also directed by Graham Cutts and starring Mae Marsh, but this time cowritten by Stannard—the one film in advance of *The Pleasure Garden* (1926) on which his path crossed with that of Hitchcock, who was then still a junior member of the Islington staff.

Lily of the Alley (1923). Directed by Henry Edwards, who wrote so lucidly in the British trade papers about suspense versus surprise during Hitchcock's early years in the industry, in terms that he would later take over as his own (see chapter 1). *Lily of the Alley* is the film that Edwards made in 1923 without intertitles, thus anticipating F. W. Murnau's *The Last Laugh* (1924), which Hitchcock always claimed to have had no predecessors.

Woman to Woman (1923). The first film made at Islington after Michael Balcon took over and promoted Hitchcock to work for Cutts as art director and writer. If discovered, it would no doubt be hailed, like *The White Shadow,* as the discovery of a "missing Hitchcock"; it would, anyway, be an illuminating complement to that film, as one that had much greater commercial and critical success, and as Hitchcock's first big step up.

God's Clay (1928) or *Glorious Youth,* aka *Eileen of the Trees* (1929). Anny Ondra came to Britain in 1928 to make four films in quick succession, two with Hitchcock and these

two with Cutts, *God's Clay* being the first of the four.
Like *Glorious Youth* and *The Manxman* (1929), it was
an all-silent film; only *Blackmail* (1929) was reworked
with dialogue. Cutts's career, like those of Edwards and,
more dramatically, Stannard, declined after the conversion to sound; either film would allow a final sight of
him as a silent filmmaker and a comparison between the
ways he and Hitchcock worked with the glorious youth-
ful Anny.

Together with the three still-missing Hitchcocks, these seven items
thus make up a top ten wish list from among pre-1930 British titles.
One day perhaps there can be a sequel to the present *Lost and Found*
volume, with more finds to consider—both films and documents.

Other kinds of sequels could focus on other filmmakers; there
is no shortage of candidates. But no one seems a more appropriate
subject than Hitchcock for this kind of study. Could it be said so
convincingly of anyone else that—to return to Paula Marantz Cohen's
formula—"to study him is to find an economical way of studying
the entire history of cinema"? We have traced his progress, always
in the margins of the fifty-plus feature films that constitute his major
achievement, through from silent to sound, Britain to Hollywood,
obscurity to fame, from the early 1920s to the late 1960s, finding
material at every stage that anchors him in the developing technology
and history of the medium. Is there any other major director of his
time who took on, late in life, anything comparable to the range of
projects that he did in his sixties: the pair of public service appeals
(*Tactic* in 1959 and Will Rogers in 1966) combined with the two very
personal testimonies (Westcliff in 1963 and *Hitchcock on Grierson*
in 1969)? Who else had the combination of iconic status that inspired
the appeals to him and the generosity that led him to respond in the
way he did?

If this were to become a *Lost and Found* series—not for us but
for others—it is appropriate for Alfred Hitchcock to have led the way.

Acknowledgments

The starting point for this book was the research undertaken from Paris by Alain Kerzoncuf on two of the short films directed by Hitchcock in 1944: *Aventure Malgache* and *The Fighting Generation*. The results were published as articles in the Australian online journal *Senses of Cinema* in November 2006 and February 2009, respectively: "Hitchcock's *Aventure Malgache* (or the True Story of DZ 91)" and "Alfred Hitchcock and *The Fighting Generation*." The two articles created enough interest to suggest the possibility of a more extensive study of the lesser-known parts of Hitchcock's long career. To give wider international scope to the research, Charles Barr came on board as collaborator, working from England. A generous grant from the Leverhulme Foundation enabled him to spend six weeks visiting a range of American archives in late 2012, one outcome of which was an article on Hitchcock's re-editing of *Men of the Lightship*, published in the *Hitchcock Annual*, no. 18 (2013).

We thank above all the Leverhulme Foundation; also the editors of *Senses of Cinema* and of the *Hitchcock Annual* for their encouragement, and for allowing us to make use of the three published articles within chapter 4.

For a wide range of other kinds of help, we are grateful to many people in Britain, America, and elsewhere:

In Britain, to the staff of these institutions: the British Film Institute, notably Nathalie Morris and Jonny Davies of Special Collections, and Jo Botting, Bryony Dixon, Simon MacCallum, and John Oliver; the Cinema Museum in South London, notably Ronald Grant, Martin Humphrey, and Simon Audley; the University of East Anglia Library, notably Bridget Gillies; the Theatre Collection at Bristol University, notably Heather Romaine. To Karl Magee, archivist at Stirling University, and Phil Wickham, curator of the Bill Douglas Centre at Exeter University. Also, for various kinds of useful information and advice, to Mark Aldridge, Geoff Brown, Don Fairservice, Dick Fiddy, Kay Gladstone, Mark Glancy, Sheldon Hall, Janice Healey, Veronica Hitchcock, Dimitri Kennaway, Don McLean, David Meeker, Mikaela Mikalauski, Henry Miller, Lawrence Napper, David Pattern, Michelle Paull, Laraine Porter, Lucia Stuart, Cathy Surowiec, Chris Taylor, Michael Walker, Clare Watson, and Helen Wheatley.

In America, to the staff of these institutions: the Margaret Herrick Library at the Academy of Motion Picture Arts and Sciences, Beverly Hills, notably Barbara Hall (who has since moved on) and Jenny Romero; the New York State Archives at Albany, notably Bill Gorman; the Museum of Modern Art film department in New York, notably Ashley Swinnerton; the New York Public Library, notably Elena Rossi-Snook; the University of Texas at Austin, notably Janet Staiger and Christelle Le Faucheur; and the Library of Congress in Washington, notably Rosemary Hanes and George Willeman; also to Richard Allen, Janet Bergstrom, Peter Bogdanovich, George Lefferts, Bill Paul, and Philip Skerry.

Elsewhere, to Valdo Kneubühler of the BiFi Cinémathèque in Paris; to Ronny Temme and Leenke Ripmeester of the EYE Film Instituut Nederland in Amsterdam; to Terese Lundin of the Riksarkivet in Stockholm; to Elma Soiron and Henri Dominique Bonifas (son of Paul Bonifas) in France; to Russell Campbell, Sarah Davy, and Roger Horrocks in New Zealand; and to Norbert Aping in Germany, Nandor Bokor in Hungary, Rolando Caputo in Australia, Christophe Dupin in Belgium, and Erik Hedling in Sweden.

Finally, we acknowledge a special debt of thanks to Tony Fletcher, Sid Gottlieb, Janique Joelle, Patrick McGilligan, Christopher Philippo, and Charles Roche.

Notes

Introduction

1. Sloan, *Alfred Hitchcock,* 37.

2. For details of the website material on the restoration of the silent films, and on other Hitchcock-related material accessible via the British Film Institute (BFI), see the "Other Resources" section of the bibliography.

1. Before The Pleasure Garden

1. McGilligan, *Alfred Hitchcock,* 46.

2. Hitchcock interviewed by Mike Scott for the British TV company Granada, 1966. Material from this is included in, for instance, the DVD/Blu-Ray edition of *The 39 Steps* (1935) released by Criterion in 2012.

3. Taylor, *Hitch,* 40.

4. Taylor, *Hitch,* 40. For the likely influence of Fitzmaurice on Hitchcock, see Spoto, *The Life of Alfred Hitchcock,* 55–56.

5. Truffaut, *Hitchcock,* 31; Balshofer and Miller, *One Reel a Week,* 161.

6. Hitchcock interviewed by Oswell Blakeston in *Film Weekly,* 9 July 1930.

7. Truffaut, *Hitchcock,* 27.

8. Gottlieb, *Hitchcock on Hitchcock 2,* 62.

9. Before very long, Islington would lose its position as a state-of-the-art studio. The 1930s saw some ambitious studio construction by British companies—for instance, at Ealing, Denham, and Pinewood. By 1938, when Hitchcock returned there to make *The Lady Vanishes,* it was seen as being cramped and under-resourced. According

to Googie Withers, who played one of Margaret Lockwood's friends in that film, "Gainsborough's Islington studios were abominable. To get there, you had to drive through slums. When you arrived, there was this awful old building and the dressing-rooms were dreadful. The make-up room was a box and the canteen food was uneatable." Interview by Brian McFarlane in his collection *Sixty Voices*, 234.

10. Hitchcock O'Connell and Bouzereau, *Alma Hitchcock*, 33.

11. Taylor, *Hitch*, 42; McGilligan, *Alfred Hitchcock*, 55.

12. The Hitchcock chapter in Bogdanovich, *Who the Devil Made It?*, is based on the two sets of interviews conducted in 1963 and 1972 but omits Elsie Codd's name. The full interview tapes are held in the Bogdanovich collection at the Lilly Library, Indiana University, Bloomington.

13. A pioneering piece of research on Elsie Codd, by Clare Watson, includes a full list of her published articles. See the Women and Silent British Cinema website, http://womenandsilentbritishcinema .wordpress.com/?s=codd.

14. Hitchcock interviewed by Oswell Blakeston in *Film Weekly*, 9 July 1930.

15. Brunel to Balcon, 11 November 1925, box 112, Adrian Brunel papers, BFI Special Collections, London.

16. Stannard is not given an on-screen credit for the sixth of these films, *The Ring*, but all sources agree that he contributed to it; see, for instance, Taylor, *Hitch*, 89.

17. Hicks, *Hail Fellow, Well Met*, 34.

18. This cutting is pasted into the Hugh Croise scrapbook, item 155/2, John M. East papers, BFI Special Collections.

19. Hitchcock to Brunel, box 112, Adrian Brunel papers, BFI Special Collections. The full letter is reproduced in an article by Nathalie Morris on the BFI website: "Hitchcock Writes Home," updated 28 April 2014, http://www.bfi.org.uk/news/hitchcock-writes-home.

20. *Always Tell Your Wife* was filmed for the first time soon after its theatrical run, with Hicks and Terriss; a full-page advertisement for its screening in London appears in the supplement to *Kinematograph Weekly*, 2 April 1914. None of the trade press coverage of the 1923 version refers back to this earlier one.

21. O'Dell, *Representative Photoplays Analyzed*, vii, 133–37.

22. Balcon, *A Lifetime of Films*, 16.

23. The relation between the three films *The Little Minister, The White Shadow,* and *Vertigo* is discussed further in the introduction to the second (2012) edition of Barr, *Vertigo*.

24. Raymond Paton, *The Autobiography of a Blackguard* (London: Hutchinson, 1923; 2nd film edition, 1925).

25. Hitchcock was interviewed by Charles Champlin in a 1971 episode of the series *Frame of Reference* on the educational chan-

nel KCET LA, tied to a screening of *The Cabinet of Dr. Caligari* (Robert Wiene, 1920), about which he speaks with knowledgeable enthusiasm.

26. Balcon to Brunel, 17 November 1924, box 112, Adrian Brunel papers, BFI Special Collections.

27. In another version of the film, from German archives, the kiss is staged differently: she kisses him on the forehead instead.

28. Walker, *Hitchcock's Motifs*, 330.

29. The essay was first published in *Screen* magazine and has been much anthologized since—for instance, in Mulvey's own collection *Visual and Other Pleasures*.

30. For more on Stannard, see Barr, "Writing Screen Plays: Stannard and Hitchcock," and Macdonald, *Screenwriting Poetics and the Screen Idea;* also see the essay on him by Michael Eaton on the BFI's Screenonline website: http://www.screenonline.org.uk/.

31. See, for instance, the report in *Kine Weekly*, 13 August 1925: "A British Producer's Experiments: Graham Cutts and the new Theory of Continuity." It ends by quoting him on the "long-cherished dream" of a picture shot entirely without cutting. It is of course possible that he and Hitchcock had discussed this dream together, before going their separate ways.

32. McFarlane, *Encyclopedia of British Film*, 163.

2. The Early 1930s

1. The two versions of *Blackmail* were screened at the Academy of Motion Picture Arts and Sciences Sam Goldwyn Theater on 18 June 2013. Thanks to Don Fairservice for his report on the impatience of the audience.

2. See Rockett, *Irish Film Censorship*, 85. For Australia, see "The Year in Australia," in *The* [British] *Kinematograph Year Book* (1930), 33–34.

3. For fuller details of the Irish response to *Juno* and also to *Blackmail*, see Charles Barr, "The Knock of Disapproval: *Juno and the Paycock* and Its Irish Reception," *Hitchcock Annual*, no. 17 (2011).

4. Born in 1880, Thomas Bentley had been a busy director since 1912. He specialized in Dickens adaptations, first as a stage performer and then as writer and director: his first six films were based on Dickens, as well as several later ones. His sixty-ninth and final film was *Old Mother Riley's Circus* in 1941.

5. Truffaut, *Hitchcock*, 69.

6. Taylor, *Hitch*, 103; Sloan, *Alfred Hitchcock*, 94.

7. McGilligan reprints in full seven very short stories written by Hitchcock for the *Henley Telegraph* between 1919 and 1921. The fourth of these, "And There Was No Rainbow" (September 1920),

is similar to "The Wrong Flat" but with a backstory. A man advises a shy friend on how to pick up a woman, but on getting home that evening he finds that the woman the friend has picked up and is being entertained by is his own wife; McGilligan, *Alfred Hitchcock,* 38–40. "Revenge," the first story to be broadcast, in 1955, within the series *Alfred Hitchcock Presents,* has a comparable twist ending, when we learn that Vera Miles's character has identified *the wrong man* as her assailant—but her vengeful husband has already shot him dead.

8. Brunel to Carroll, 9 February 1930, box 153, Adrian Brunel papers, BFI Special Collections, London.

9. Brunel to Pommer, 28 February 1925, box 112, Adrian Brunel papers, BFI Special Collections.

10. Hitchcock to Brunel, box 112, Adrian Brunel papers, BFI Special Collections; reproduced in Nathalie Morris, "Hitchcock Writes Home," updated 28 April 2014, http://www.bfi.org.uk/news/hitchcock-writes-home.

11. All the material on the scripting of "The Wrong Flat" comes from box 54, Adrian Brunel papers, BFI Special Collections.

12. The discovery of a print of *Mary* was marked by an informative short article by Richard Combs in *Sight and Sound* (Autumn 1990), "Hitchcock's German Double": "The film only surfaced recently on East German television, and through the FIAF exchange programme the National Film Archive has acquired a print for reference purposes."

13. Only two speaking parts, both small ones, are played by the same actors in both *Murder!* and *Mary:* Druce (Miles Mander), husband of the murdered Edna, and the Prosecuting Counsel (Esme Chaplin).

14. Truffaut, *Hitchcock,* 77.

15. Leitch, *Encyclopedia of Alfred Hitchcock,* 203.

16. In his Hitchcock biography, published one year later than Leitch's book and possibly drawing on it, McGilligan makes the same error. But he does usefully quote from a forgotten memoir by the British theater man Charles Landstone, who as a German speaker was cast as a member of the jury for *Mary.* Landstone describes how he exactly copied the gestures of his opposite number from *Murder!,* Kenneth Kove, and a comparison of the two jury scenes bears this out; McGilligan, *Alfred Hitchcock,* 136–37.

17. Truffaut, *Hitchcock,* 214.

18. Hitchcock talked to Truffaut about his disappointment with John van Druten: "I was offering him a camera in the place of his typewriter." Truffaut, *Hitchcock,* 82. See also Taylor, *Hitch,* 116.

19. Eden Phillpotts was author of the play *The Farmer's Wife,* filmed by Hitchcock in 1928. *Yellow Sands* was filmed in 1938 by Herbert Brenon. There is no record of any film of *Priscilla Runs Away* by Elizabeth Armin.

20. Taylor, *Hitch*, 115; Spoto, *Life of Alfred Hitchcock*, 133.

21. McGilligan, *Alfred Hitchcock*, 682.

22. McGilligan, *Alfred Hitchcock*, 681.

23. Montagu to Balcon, 26 September 1977, box 417, Ivor Montagu papers, BFI Special Collections.

24. Email message from Roger Horrocks to Charles Barr, 30 October 2013.

25. Montagu to Balcon, 4 May 1936, box 57, Ivor Montagu papers, BFI Special Collections. Following quotations also taken from this source.

26. Žižek, *Enjoy Your Symptom!*, 232.

3. The War Years

1. McGilligan, *Alfred Hitchcock*, 281.

2. Saville to Bernstein, 17 September 1941, Bernstein papers, Imperial War Museum (IWM), London.

3. *London Can Take It* was a communal production by the same MoI-controlled film unit. Directors who worked on it included Harry Watt, Pat Jackson, and Humphrey Jennings; it was edited by Stewart McAllister, who went on to edit both *Men of the Lightship* and *Target for Tonight*. The American journalist Quentin Reynolds supplied a powerful voice-over commentary.

4. Report of March 1943, National Archives, Kew (NA): INF 1/58.

5. The brief review is not signed, but it is likely to be the work of the magazine's regular film critic, William Whitebait (pseudonym of the playwright and critic G. W. Stonier).

6. Bernstein to E. St. J. Bamford, 3 April 1941, Bernstein papers, IWM. Bamford was an MoI administrator, not himself a member of the Films Division. Following quotations also taken, unless otherwise stated, from this source.

7. Despite Patrick McGilligan's claim that "there is no evidence he was ever reimbursed," this same summarizing memo of 3 April shows that, although Hitchcock took no fee, his costs of $4,428.10 were repaid to him in full; McGilligan, *Alfred Hitchcock*, 281.

8. Arthur Jarratt was a naval officer who did varied wartime liaison work in the United States. Like Bernstein, he had extensive experience in film exhibition.

9. Vaughan, *Portrait of an Invisible Man*, 46–53. Vaughan, who died in 2011, does not mention the existence of the Hitchcock re-edit and may not have known about it.

10. Cavalcanti, a Brazilian, already had considerable experience in French cinema as writer, art director, and avant-garde director, before joining Grierson's GPO (General Post Office) Film Unit in 1933; he was based at Ealing from 1940 to 1946. David Macdon-

ald spent all of his career in the commercial industry, apart from a short wartime spell in documentary, first as director of *Men of the Lightship* and then with the Army Film Unit, notably as producer of *Desert Victory* (1943). Hugh Gray's script credits included Alexander Korda's imperial epic *The Drum* (1938). Gray (1900–1981) is now best known as the translator of two volumes of essays by the French critic André Bazin, *What Is Cinema?*, published in 1967 and 1971. He was an early film professor at the University of California, Los Angeles, closely associated with the magazine *Film Quarterly:* see "Hugh Gray: In Memoriam," on the first page of the Spring 1981 issue. Hitchcock's correspondence with, and about, Gray, and the funding of his research in the 1960s, is in the Hitchcock papers in the Margaret Herrick Library, Academy of Motion Picture Arts and Sciences (AMPAS), Beverly Hills: 112.f-1337.

11. GPO Film Unit memo of 13 July 1940, NA: INF 5/66.

12. Part of an encouraging telegram from Bernstein to Hitchcock on 24 October 1940 reads "think Sherwood Montgomery very good" (i.e., very good choices). Unlike Robert Sherwood, Robert Montgomery is not mentioned again in these records, and the idea of using him may have been shelved.

13. H. A. V. Bulleid, "Famous Library Films no. 23, *Men of the Lightship*," *Amateur Cine World* (September–November 1944): 118–21. The fact of post-synchronizing is confirmed in MoI documents: NA: INF 5/68.

14. Vaughan, *Portrait of an Invisible Man,* 48–50.

15. Cavalcanti's insistence, after seeing the initial rushes, on replacing most of the actors with nonprofessionals is expressed in a forceful telegram of 1 March 1940, in NA: INF 5/66. Leonard Sharp's busy film career lasted from 1935 to 1958; he is probably now best remembered as the pavement artist in the final scene of the Ealing comedy *The Ladykillers* (Alexander Mackendrick, 1955).

16. Royal Air Force representatives had been arguing that the film ought to show aircraft flying to the defense of the lightship and chasing off the attackers, an argument so clearly foolish that they soon came round and agreed "to arrange forthwith facilities for the proposed lightship film in the form in which it is summarised in Mr Hugh Gray's general treatment." Hugh Gray had done the treatment based on a range of visits and consultations. Dialogue is credited to David Evans, who was present for much of the shooting. For all this, see NA: INF 5/66.

17. Vaughan, *Portrait of an Invisible Man,* 50.

18. Whereas Vaughan credits this bravura passage, which he analyzes shot by shot, to the film's editor, linking it to other instances of his work, Ian Aitken prefers to credit it to the film's producer, linking it to his notable record of experimentation in France and then

England. Both authors stress the sympathy between producer and editor: whichever of them took the initiative here, the other must have approved. Vaughan, *Portrait of an Invisible Man, 50*; Aitken, *Alberto Cavalcanti, 65–67*.

19. Montagu to Balcon, 26 September 1977, box 417, Ivor Montagu papers, BFI Special Collections.

20. Reynolds, *All About Winston Churchill,* 152.

21. See Bret Wood, "Foreign Correspondence: The Rediscovered War Films of Alfred Hitchcock," *Film Comment* 29, no. 4 (1993): 54–58; Sidney Gottlieb, "Hitchcock's Wartime Work: *Bon Voyage* and *Aventure Malgache,*" *Hitchcock Annual* 3 (1994): 158–67; J. Justin Gustainis and Deborah Jay DeSilva, "Archetypes as Propaganda in Alfred Hitchcock's 'Lost' World War II Films," *Film and History* 27, no. 1 (1997): 80–87; James Vest, "Phones as Instruments of Betrayal in Alfred Hitchcock's *Bon Voyage* and *Aventure Malgache,*" *French Review* 72, no. 3 (1999): 529–42.

22. Taylor, *Hitch,* 193.

23. Unless otherwise stated, background information on the two films is drawn from the Sidney Bernstein papers at the IWM.

24. Taylor, *Hitch,* 298.

25. Manny Yospa was interviewed by Charles Drazin on 14 March 1995 for the Broadcasting Entertainment Cinematograph and Theatre Union (BECTU) Oral History project. (This and other BECTU tapes can be accessed at the library of the British Film Institute.) Yospa worked for twenty more years in the camera department and remained active in the union.

26. Belfrage, *All Is Grist,* 114. Osbiston went on to a long career in British films, mainly as editor, but with a codirector credit on Bernard Miles's film *Chance of a Lifetime* (1950).

27. See McGilligan, *Alfred Hitchcock,* 348.

28. This document also comes from the Bernstein papers at the IWM.

29. Truffaut, *Hitchcock,* 160.

30. This MoI document about the release of British films in Liberated Europe is found in NA: INF 6/2470.

31. Truffaut, *Hitchcock,* 161.

32. Bernstein papers, IWM. It is not clear whether, in the event, Dauphin contributed to either film. Arthur Calder-Marshall was an experienced writer who worked in the MoI Films Division for much of the war.

33. All the material that follows is from NA: HS 9/326/7.

34. Truffaut, *Hitchcock,* 81.

35. Elma Soiron, telephone interview with Alain Kerzoncuf, June 2006.

36. Bonifas had far more experience of British cinema of this

period than anyone else in the cast of either of these MoI shorts, not excluding John Blythe of *Bon Voyage,* who was in David Lean's film of *This Happy Breed* (1944). His wartime films included six features at Ealing and another MoI short film of 1944, *Two Fathers.* Directed by Anthony Asquith, this was written by V. S. Pritchett, who had worked on *Bon Voyage* and would later contribute to *The Birds,* and like *Malgache* it gave a role to Paulette Preney. Bonifas's busy postwar film career would include a role as the stamp dealer in Stanley Donen's *Charade* (1963).

37. David Meeker, email message to Alain Kerzoncuf, 16 May 2006.

38. Walker, "E.R. Stettinius, Jr.," 65.

39. Leigh, *Mobilizing Consent,* 124.

40. Leigh, *Mobilizing Consent,* 124.

41. Hecht, *A Child of the Century,* 583, quoted by Gottlieb in "The Unknown Hitchcock."

42. Documents on the 1964 UN project are held in the Hitchcock papers in the Margaret Herrick Library, AMPAS: 105 f.1282.

43. Taylor, *Hitch,* 194.

44. See Vaughan, *Portrait of an Invisible Man,* 153–57; McGilligan, *Alfred Hitchcock,* 372–74; Gladstone, "Separate Intentions." The title of the *Sight and Sound* article by Elizabeth Sussex is "The Fate of F3080," that being the MoI project number.

45. Robin Wood's 1965 passage linking *Psycho* to the camps is reprinted unchanged in *Hitchcock's Films Revisited* (1989), 150—and in later editions.

46. John Buchan, *Huntingtower* (London: Hodder and Stoughton, 1922). The passage quoted comes from early in chapter 9.

47. John Buchan, *Augustus* (London: Hodder and Stoughton, 1937), 345.

48. Crossman, *Palestine Mission,* 21–22.

49. The torturer is played by Martin Kosleck, referred to earlier in the context of *Watchtower over Tomorrow.*

50. Documents held in the Zuckerman collection, University of East Anglia Library.

4. After the War

1. The Allen script is held in the Hitchcock papers in the Margaret Herrick Library, Academy of Motion Picture Arts and Sciences (AMPAS), Beverly Hills; McBride's article, "Alfred Hitchcock's *Mary Rose:* An Old Master's Unheard Cri de Coeur," is in *Cineaste* (March 2001).

2. Letter from George Lefferts to Alain Kerzoncuf, 23 February 2011.

3. Negotiations in 1967–1968 over Hitchcock's introduction to

the reissue of the novel *The Lady Vanishes* are in the Hitchcock papers, Margaret Herrick Library, AMPAS: 119.f-1381.

4. Gottlieb, introduction to *Hitchcock on Hitchcock*, xiv.

5. The six-page commentary script, as sent to Hitchcock, is held in the library at Stirling University, home of the Grierson archive. A letter from Peggy Robertson to STV, accepting the commission on Hitchcock's behalf, is dated 9 December 1968.

6. Truffaut, *Hitchcock*, 240.

7. John Grierson, review in *The Clarion*, October 1930; reprinted in Hardy, *Grierson on the Movies*, 110.

8. Ryall, *Alfred Hitchcock and the British Cinema*, 177. The Lindsay Anderson quotation is taken from his article "Alfred Hitchcock," *Sequence* magazine, no. 9 (1949).

9. Durgnat, *The Strange Case of Alfred Hitchcock*, 97.

10. "Of course *Moana*, being a visual account of events in the daily life of a Polynesian youth, has documentary value. But that, I believe, is secondary." From Grierson's review of the film in the *New York Sun*, 8 February 1926; reprinted in Hardy, *Grierson on the Movies*, 23–25.

11. Grierson, "First Principles of Documentary," first section originally published in *Cinema Quarterly* (Winter 1932); reprinted in Hardy, *Grierson on Documentary*, 78–89.

12. Bernstein's major involvement with documentary came through his wartime work at the Ministry of Information, and later at Granada Television through the launch of the powerful and influential weekly series *World in Action* (1963–1998).

13. Watt, *Don't Look at the Camera*, 121.

Epilogue

1. Sloan, *Alfred Hitchcock*; Macdonald, *Screenwriting Poetics and the Screen Idea*.

Bibliography

Books

Aitken, Ian. *Alberto Cavalcanti: Realism, Surrealism and National Cinemas*. Trowbridge: Flicks Books, 2000.

Auiler, Dan. *Hitchcock Lost*. Amazon Kindle, 2013.

Auiler, Dan. *Hitchcock's Secret Notebooks*. London: Bloomsbury, 1999.

Auiler, Dan. *Vertigo: The Making of a Hitchcock Classic*. London: Titan, 1999.

Balcon, Michael. *A Lifetime of Films*. London: Hutchinson, 1969.

Balshofer, Fred, and Arthur Miller. *One Reel a Week*. Berkeley: University of California Press, 1967.

Barr, Charles. *English Hitchcock*. Moffat: Cameron and Hollis, 1999.

Barr, Charles. *Vertigo*. 2nd ed. London: BFI Film Classics, 2012.

Barr, Charles. "Writing Screen Plays: Stannard and Hitchcock." In *Young and Innocent: The Cinema in Britain 1896–1930*, ed. Andrew Higson, 227–41. Exeter: University of Exeter Press, 2002.

Belfrage, Colin, ed. *All Is Grist*. London: Parallax, 1997.

Bogdanovich, Peter. *The Cinema of Alfred Hitchcock*. New York: Museum of Modern Art Film Library, 1963.

Bogdanovich, Peter. *Who the Devil Made It?* New York: Ballantine, 1987.

Brunel, Adrian. *Nice Work: The Story of Thirty Years in British Film Production*. London: Forbes Robertson, 1949.

Chabrol, Claude, and Eric Rohmer. *Hitchcock*. Paris: Editions Universitaires, 1957.

Crossman, Richard. *The Palestine Mission: A Personal Record*. London: Hamish Hamilton, 1947.

Durgnat, Raymond. *The Strange Case of Alfred Hitchcock*. London: Faber and Faber, 1970.

Gifford, Denis. *The British Film Catalogue 1895–1970*. Newton Abbot: David and Charles, 1973.

Gladstone, Kay. "Separate Intentions." In *Holocaust and the Moving Image: Representations in Film and Television since 1933*, ed. Toby Haggith and Joanna Newman, 50–64. London: Wallflower, 2005.

Gledhill, Christine. *Reframing British Cinema 1918–1928: Between Restraint and Passion*. London: British Film Institute, 2003.

Gottlieb, Sidney, ed. *Hitchcock on Hitchcock*. London: Faber and Faber, 1995.

Gottlieb, Sidney, ed. *Hitchcock on Hitchcock 2*. Berkeley: University of California Press, 2015.

Hardy, Forsyth, ed. *Grierson on Documentary*. London: Collins, 1946.

Hardy, Forsyth, ed. *Grierson on the Movies*. London: Faber and Faber, 1981.

Hecht, Ben. *A Child of the Century*. New York: Simon and Schuster, 1954.

Hicks, Seymour. *Hail Fellow Well Met*. London: Staples, 1949.

Hitchcock O'Connell, Pat, and Laurent Bouzereau. *Alma Hitchcock: The Woman behind the Man*. New York: Berkley Books, 2003.

Horrocks, Roger. *Len Lye: A Biography*. Auckland: Auckland University Press, 2001.

Houston, Penelope. *Keepers of the Frame: The Film Archives*. London: British Film Institute, 1994.

Kapsis, Robert E. *Hitchcock: The Making of a Reputation*. Chicago: University of Chicago Press, 1992.

Leff, Leonard. *Hitchcock and Selznick: The Rich and Strange Collaboration of Alfred Hitchcock and David O. Selznick in Hollywood*. London: Weidenfeld and Nicolson, 1987.

Leigh, Michael. *Mobilizing Consent: Public Opinion and American Foreign Policy 1937–1947*. Westport, Conn.: Greenwood, 1976.

Leitch, Thomas. *Encyclopedia of Alfred Hitchcock*. New York: Checkmark Books, 2002.

Low, Rachael. *The History of the British Film 1918–1929*. London: Allen and Unwin, 1971.

Macdonald, Ian W. *Screenwriting Poetics and the Screen Idea*. London: Palgrave Macmillan, 2013.

McFarlane, Brian, ed. *The Encyclopedia of British Film*. 2nd ed. London: Methuen, 2005.

McFarlane, Brian, ed. *Sixty Voices: Celebrities Recall the Golden Age of British Cinema*. London: British Film Institute, 1992.

McGilligan, Patrick. *Alfred Hitchcock: A Life in Darkness and Light*. Chichester: John Wiley, 2003.

Moorehead, Caroline. *Sidney Bernstein*. London: Jonathan Cape, 1984.

Mulvey, Laura. *Visual and Other Pleasures*. Basingstoke: Macmillan, 1989.

O'Dell, Scott. *Representative Photoplays Analyzed*. Hollywood: Palmer Institute of Authorship, 1924.

Reynolds, Quentin. *All About Winston Churchill*. London: W. H. Allen, 1964.

Rockett, Kevin. *Irish Film Censorship*. Dublin: Four Courts, 2014.

Rotha, Paul. *The Film till Now: A Survey of World Cinema*. With an additional section by Richard Griffith. London: Vision, 1963. Orig. pub. London: Jonathan Cape, 1930.

Ryall, Tom. *Alfred Hitchcock and the British Cinema*. Chicago: University of Illinois Press, 1986.

Sloan, Jane E. *Alfred Hitchcock: A Filmography and Bibliography*. Berkeley: University of California Press, 1995.

Spoto, Donald. *The Life of Alfred Hitchcock: The Dark Side of Genius*. London: Collins, 1983.

Street, Sarah. *Transatlantic Crossings: British Feature Films in the United States*. New York: Continuum, 2002.

Taylor, John Russell. *Hitch: The Life and Work of Alfred Hitchcock*. London: Faber and Faber, 1978.

Truffaut, François. *Hitchcock*. Expanded edition. New York: Simon and Schuster, 1985.

Vaughan, Dai. *Portrait of an Invisible Man: The Working Life of Stewart McAllister, Film Editor*. London: British Film Institute, 1983.

Walker, Michael. *Hitchcock's Motifs*. Amsterdam: University of Amsterdam Press, 2005.

Walker, Richard L. "E.R. Stettinius, Jr." In *The American Secretaries of State and Their Diplomacy*. Vol. 14. New York: Cooper Square, 1965.

Watt, Harry. *Don't Look at the Camera*. London: Paul Elek, 1974.

Wood, Robin. *Hitchcock's Films Revisited*. New York: Columbia University Press, 1989.

Žižek, Slavoj. *Enjoy Your Symptom! Jacques Lacan in Hollywood and Out*. London: Routledge, 2007.

Other Resources

Since website content is so much less stable than printed material, the conventional method of providing full URLs, often extending to a full line or more, along with the precise date and time they were accessed, has limited value: the reader may struggle to transcribe these from the printed page and may then find—especially after a few years have elapsed—that the link no longer works. Search engines are generally quick to function on the basis of a few relevant words. In the week when the text of this book was being finalized, in mid-April 2014, the entire output of Pathé News was uploaded onto YouTube, including *Let's Go Bathing!*, the 1931 item said to have been directed by Hitchcock. The full URL is http://www.youtube.com/watch?v=qv9VTvwvh8Q, but in order to access it all that is needed is to type the film title into the YouTube search box, or indeed into Google's search box, and it shows up at once.

In line with this principle, we have supplied few precise URLs, in endnotes or in what follows, as opposed to broader indications of what can be searched for and where.

Film

When our research began, the main place to look for neglected films was still the film archive. Access to rare film prints was provided by, among others, the Library of Congress in Washington (*Men of Lightship "61"*); the Netherlands Film Museum, aka EYE (*The Man from Home*); and above all the British Film Institute (BFI) National Archive (all of the other pre–*Pleasure Garden* films plus the Baird Television item). Recently, many of the films we refer to have become more easily viewable, on YouTube or via the BFI's own outreach strategy.

In addition to *Let's Go Bathing!*, YouTube currently offers *Elstree Calling* (in separate sections), *Murder!* (shorter version), *Mary, Men of Lightship "61,"* and *The Will Rogers Appeal* (again, the shorter version).

The BFI's Mediatheque installations are modern versions of the Kinetoscope parlors of the 1890s that predated theatrical film exhibition; their array of machines give individual viewers free access to a wide range of films. Currently, nine are in operation, mainly in libraries: the initial one at BFI Southbank, and others in Birmingham, Bradford, Cambridge, Derby, Glasgow, Manchester, Newcastle, and Wrexham. At the time of writing, the repertoire includes all of the Graham Cutts–Hitchcock collaborations that survive in part or whole (*Flames of Passion, The White Shadow, The Passionate Adventure, The Blackguard,* and *The Prude's Fall*), plus *Elstree Calling* and the Westcliff film. An online search for "BFI Mediatheque" leads to full details of the venues and of currently available films.

Another expanding resource is the BFI's online coverage of British film history: http://www.screenonline.org.uk/. From this portal it is easy to follow links not only to Hitchcock and his films but to others such as Cutts, Adrian Brunel, and Eliot Stannard. Links are given to a wide range of archival film clips, including many that we refer to in these pages, but for copyright reasons access to these is currently restricted to "users in UK libraries, colleges and universities." This still leaves a lot of good material accessible from anywhere, essays as well as factual data.

Documents

The two foundational documents for this book were articles on *Aventure Malgache* and *The Fighting Generation* published in the Australian online journal *Senses of Cinema* in November 2006 and February 2009, respectively. At the time of writing they remain fully accessible online, either by using the full URLs (http://sensesofcinema.com/2006/feature-articles/hitchcock-aventure-malgache/ and http://sensesofcinema.com/2009/feature-articles/hitchcock-fighting-generation/) or by typing in the name of the films or of Alain Kerzoncuf. They incorporate more material on these two films than we have had space to include in the book.

In subsequent research, we have made use of six main sources of archival documents: in California, New York, and Paris, and three in London.

The Margaret Herrick Library in Beverly Hills (http://www.oscars.org/library/index.html), a division of the Academy of Motion Picture Arts and Sciences, is indispensable to researchers on Alfred Hitchcock, as on much else, since it holds a mass of his papers deposited by his family. Although these contain relatively little from his career in Britain, they have still been a major resource for us, as have others among the library's collections such as those of Famous Players-Lasky/Paramount and of Jane Novak.

The Museum of Modern Art in New York has links with Hitchcock that go back to the 1930s and a document archive that enables those links to be traced. A search for "Hitchcock" on their film website (http://www.moma.org/visit/films) leads to extensive material, including full details of the centenary exhibition mounted in 1999.

La Cinémathèque française, which likewise has long-standing links with Hitchcock, has its own strong interactive website (http://www.cinematheque.fr/), with much material on him and on his friend Henri Langlois, the archive's cofounder. Both website and library are helpful to Hitchcock research—for instance, in enabling the frequency of screenings of his films to be traced through the decades.

The National Archives (NA) at Kew in West London, formerly the Public Record Office (PRO), are the source of much material on *Men of the Lightship, Aventure Malgache,* and the concentration camps project. Their website too is highy devoped: http://www.nationalarchives.gov.uk/. As an alternative to on-site research, material can be ordered from a distance and copied and sent. Some material—though none that we have used here—is directly accessible online.

The Imperial War Museum (IWM) in South London holds the papers of Sidney Bernstein that derive from his wartime work at the Ministry of Information. These have been drawn on here for the study of his wartime collaborations with Hitchcock on *Men of the Lightship* and later *Bon Voyage* and *Aventure Malgache*. At the time of writing, the IWM website still gives no information about these papers, which await full cataloguing, but they are accessible to any researcher who books an appointment: http://www.iwm.org.uk/collections-research/ research-facilities. The website does give a link to an oral history interview with Bernstein, conducted by Kay Gladstone in 1982.

Type "BFI Special Collections" into a search engine and you are led straight into an introductory page and "gateway": http://www.bfi .org.uk/archive-collections/introduction-bfi-collections/exploring-collections/special-collections.

Facilities at the BFI Reuben Library are nothing like as spacious as at the Margaret Herrick Library, but the holdings are extensive, thoroughly catalogued, and searchable online, including the two collections of most relevance to this project, those of Adrian Brunel and Ivor Montagu.

A further BFI online resource (http://www.bfi.org.uk/news/ restoring-hitchcock-1-how-film-restoration-begins) provides an account by Bryony Dixon and Kieron Webb of the restoration work on Hitchcock's own early films as director. As in the case of Screenonline, audiovisual extracts play out in some areas, not others; but even in the absence of these, the text and the images are still informative.

Another point of entry is the account of handling the variant versions of *Champagne* from 1928: http://www.bfi.org.uk/news/ restoring-hitchcock-4-trouble-champagne.

Of the multitudinous other sources of material on Hitchcock, in print and online, one is outstandingly useful: the Hitchcock "wiki" run by Dave Pattern, http://www.hitchcockwiki.com/wiki/Main_ Page. It provides a very full assembly of information about books, chapters, articles, and reviews, always up-to-date, and gives direct access to many items.

Index

Screen Classics

Screen Classics is a series of critical biographies, film histories, and analytical studies focusing on neglected filmmakers and important screen artists and subjects, from the era of silent cinema to the golden age of Hollywood to the international generation of today. Books in the Screen Classics series are intended for scholars and general readers alike. The contributing authors are established figures in their respective fields. This series also serves the purpose of advancing scholarship on film personalities and themes with ties to Kentucky.

Series Editor

Patrick McGilligan

Books in the Series

Mae Murray: The Girl with the Bee-Stung Lips
    Michael G. Ankerich
Hedy Lamarr: The Most Beautiful Woman in Film
    Ruth Barton
Rex Ingram: Visionary Director of the Silent Screen
    Ruth Barton
Von Sternberg
    John Baxter
Hitchcock's Partner in Suspense: The Life of Screenwriter Charles Bennett
    Charles Bennett, edited by John Charles Bennett
Ziegfeld and His Follies: A Biography of Broadway's Greatest Producer
    Cynthia Brideson and Sara Brideson
The Marxist and the Movies: A Biography of Paul Jarrico
    Larry Ceplair
Dalton Trumbo: Blacklisted Hollywood Radical
    Larry Ceplair and Christopher Trumbo
Warren Oates: A Wild Life
    Susan Compo
Crane: Sex, Celebrity, and My Father's Unsolved Murder
    Robert Crane and Christopher Fryer
Jack Nicholson: The Early Years
    Robert Crane and Christopher Fryer
Being Hal Ashby: Life of a Hollywood Rebel
    Nick Dawson
Bruce Dern: A Memoir
    Bruce Dern with Christopher Fryer and Robert Crane
Intrepid Laughter: Preston Sturges and the Movies
    Andrew Dickos
John Gilbert: The Last of the Silent Film Stars
    Eve Golden
Saul Bass: Anatomy of Film Design
    Jan-Christopher Horak

CPSIA information can be obtained at www.ICGtesting.com
Printed in the USA
BVOW03*1458120415

395572BV00001B/2/P